Holy Spirit-Filled Chaplaincy

What God is Doing Beyond the Walls of the Church

Chaplain John P. Boyce

HERE I AM
PUBLISHING, LLC

HERE I AM
PUBLISHING, LLC

780 Monterrosa Drive
Myrtle Beach, SC 29572
704 604 726

Dedication

In Psalm 68:6 (NIV), we are told "God sets the lonely in families." I dedicate this book to my wife and three children. Dorothy, you showed me how to love. David, Ashlee, and Mikala, you have brought joy to my heart and flavor to my soul. Thank you, family, for making my life full!

This book is also dedicated to chaplains who work to restore hope, salvation, restoration, and healing into the lives of those whom God has called them to serve.

Acknowledgements

I am also grateful to the late Dr. John Q. Kenzy who exemplified strong leadership. He became the spiritual father to many of us students by demonstrating whole-hearted commitment and dedication to God, family, and ministry. Through strong discipleship, he helped me be the man, husband, father, and chaplain I am today.

Contents

Contents

Contents

Introduction

I was inspired to write this book after attending an Assemblies of God chaplains' conference in Springfield, Missouri. The theme of the conference was Spirit-filled Chaplaincy. The main purpose of this book is to strengthen and encourage chaplains in their calling to pastoral care ministry. It is also written for pastors, deacons, lay ministers, and church members to understand the ministry of the chaplaincy and the essential work we do. My desire is for pastors and churches to pray with us and for us and to stand with us in ministry together, "Until we all reach unity in the faith, and in the knowledge of the Son of God and become mature, attaining to the whole measure of the fullness of Christ," (Ephesians 4:13, NIV).

It is not a Bible college, seminary, or CPE instructional. Many of you reading this book are educated. For some, it may be an introduction into the chaplaincy. Others may have been in the ministry for a while, and this book will challenge you to continue to do the work God called you to do. Develop your own style of ministry and be comfortable with whom God created you to be. Spirit-filled chaplaincy is not just about God working through the chaplain's ministry but God's work in the chaplain himself/herself.

Although the title of this book is *Holy Spirit-Filled Chaplaincy*, I do not want to mislead the reader into believing it to be about miracles, signs, and wonders. There are many other books on that exciting subject. I am a hospice chaplain and help people prepare for physical death and spiritual life hereafter. I have not seen many physical healings; however, I have witnessed countless spiritual and emotional ones. Although I have experienced first-hand healings and witnessed God healing others, this book is more about God's grace in comforting His people with Spirit-filled words of hope, comfort, grace, and salvation. Jesus told the disciples not to rejoice in signs and wonders but that their names are written in heaven. We are not sure if heaven rejoices when a person is healed; probably so, but it is clear heaven does rejoice over one sinner who repents and accepts Jesus as his/her Savior.

Foreword

Welcome to the unique and often transformative journey of chaplaincy. In the pages ahead, you will discover the heart and soul of a calling lived out by a lifelong hospice chaplain, who has poured out his life in the most acute times of illness, suffering, and death. But don't think this will be a sad read—quite the contrary! You will find it insightful, rewarding, and even humorous at times.

As a chaplain, you are entrusted with the sacred task of providing spiritual care in non-religious settings where the demands are diverse. Your presence, empathy, and Spirit-empowerment will become vital tools for comforting patients, families, and fellow team members alike. Chaplain John, as I know him, writes from his own experiences. This book serves as a guiding light, offering insights, practical advice, and real-life stories to empower you in your role. Each chapter stands alone and will take you into the world of hospice chaplaincy.

Whether you are embarking on this path toward chaplaincy for the first time, looking to grow in your current chaplaincy, or seeking to understand what chaplaincy is like, I believe you will find this book invaluable in your ministry.

Rev. Allen M. Springer, MDiv
Staff Chaplain
Conway Medical Center
Conway, South Carolina

CHAPTER ONE

The Comforter Working Through Us

*And I will ask the Father, and he will give you another
Counselor to be with you forever — the Spirit of truth.*

John 14:16-17 (NIV)

As you walk with God, you will have plenty of opportunities to share a timely word using gifts of wisdom and knowledge. Proverbs 25:11 says, "A word fitly spoken is like apples of gold in pictures of silver" (KJV).

I stood with a man whose daughter was diagnosed with brain cancer. She now lays unresponsive in bed. He cried the entire visit. We stayed outside under the carport for about thirty minutes as he showed me the garage he and she had built together. "Every time I look at that, I think of her...now she is dying, and I can't do anything about it."

We went inside. The patient's four-year-old daughter greeted me and then asked, "Are you the one who came to pray with us?"

I replied, "Yes."

She addressed the rest of the family. "He's here; he's here," as if I were Santa Claus.

I went inside and talked to the mother, boyfriend of the patient, the patient's twin sister, and, of course, that little four-year-old girl. After talking to the family, we went into the patient's bedroom and prayed. The little girl lay next to her dying mom, brushing her hair and touching her. She began to cry. Walking on the bed towards me, she wrapped her little arms around me. There's something about a little girl that melts a man's heart.

"What have you been thinking about sweetheart?" I asked.

She responded, "I just want my mommy to live."

1

My heart sank. I felt sad and powerless. Here I am, a Holy Spirit-filled Pentecostal chaplain, yet all I had to offer them was comfort and prayer; it didn't seem like enough. I wanted God to heal her, raise her out of bed, so she could live a full life. But what I had to offer was enough, and I knew this is exactly what God called me to do.

Hospice ministry is offering words of comfort, faith, and hope. People die, and this was her time. As we stood around that bed, the Holy Spirit began to move. The atmosphere changed from chaos to peace as I helped this family accept the fact that God was calling her home. There were tears of grief but also hope—tears because of losing her but hope because she just gave her life to Christ and was baptized a month earlier. Even though God moved, I still left there heartbroken. When I got home, I asked my family to give me a little time to myself. I went into my bedroom and cried.

We cannot minister to others without the Holy Spirit's help, nor can we recover from the emotional strain this ministry causes without Him comforting us, as well.

Jesus said in John 14:16 (NLV) "And I will ask the Father, and he will give you another Counselor to be with you-forever-the Spirit of Truth." In John 14:26 (NLV), "But the Counselor, the Holy Spirit, whom the Father will send in my name, will teach you all things and remind you of everything I have said to you."

And in 2 Corinthians 1:3-4 (NIV), "Praise be to the God and Father of our Lord Jesus Christ, the Father of all compassion and the God of all comfort, Who comforts us in our troubles so that we can comfort those in any trouble with the comfort we ourselves have received from God."

We are Pentecostal Spirit-filled chaplains who believe in healing and miracles, yet the majority of our work is crisis counseling.

This word *trouble* is the Greek word *thlipsis'* referring to *internal pressure.* "It is a squeezing, confining restriction, and feeling of no way out of a situation" (*Strong's Concordance*). These are the people we deal with on a regular basis. However, the Holy Spirit is Counselor, Comforter, and the Greek word, *Parakletos,* "One who is called to our side," and "Encourager." He is working in us and through us to give comfort. The internal pressure we feel begins to decompress as the Holy Spirit teaches us what to say in those moments. He reminds us of appropriate scriptures to say. The healing of a person's needs is not always physical but rather emotional and spiritual. The person needs to hear a Word from God, and we are there to give it to him/her.

If you are a young chaplain and just beginning the journey, the adventure begins. You will eventually experience the highs and lows of chaplaincy work. This is a ministry of grace and compassion. You will be hurt at times because of Who you represent. People will take their anger out on you, but it cannot be taken personally. Go back to God at the end of the day in prayer and be healed. Though there are times of hurt, there are often more times of great joy. You will be a welcome sight to patients, families, other clergy, and your staff, as well. Chaplains are not here to poke, prod, or get temperature readings. We are here to be a blessing.

Is it unpredictable and emotional? You bet! Is it worth it? You bet! You must be willing to pay the price of ministry and go the distance. It will cost you, but the reward is greater than the sacrifice.

CHAPTER TWO

The Call to Ministry

"With man this is impossible, but with God all things are possible."

Matthew 19:26 (NIV)

When God called Gideon to lead Israel in the battle against the Midianites, he questioned why God would use him. He told God his clan was the weakest, and he was the least in his family. God, however, called him a "Mighty warrior, the LORD is with you." It is both scary and exciting to be called and used by God.

At first, we were nervous. We asked ourselves how and why God would choose vessels like us who are often the weakest and least in our families and communities.

First, we must remember that God sees something in us that we don't see in ourselves. God uses the foolish, the weak, and the uninfluential to confound the wise. Maybe it is because we know we cannot do it on our own strength. God likes to show that His mighty power does not rest in man's strength but in His. God always receives the glory, but He also gives us honor in the process.

"For the LORD GOD is a sun and shield; the LORD will give grace and glory; no good thing will he withheld from them that walk uprightly" (Psalms 84:11, KJV).

After Gideon doubted himself and questioned God's protection over Israel, he prayed over a fleece; his prayer was answered, his faith was ignited, and confidence was instilled. He knew then that God was getting ready to do something great in his life. Gideon's first command was to destroy the idol worship that his father oversaw. God commanded him to destroy the altar of Baal and burn down the Asherah pole (Judges

6:30, NIV). People in the community complained and wanted to kill Gideon for desecrating their gods. His father came to Gideon's rescue because he saw the hand of God on his son's life.

As Gideon became more confident that God was with him, the time came for action. When the Midianites formed an alliance with other countries and were getting ready to invade Israel, "the Spirit of the LORD clothed Gideon with power" (Judges 6:34, NIV). Others recognized God was with Gideon and joined the cause, but too many warriors showed up. Out of 22,000 who came to fight, God decreased Gideon's army to three hundred. Three hundred Israelites were going up against about 130,000 enemy-strong. For every one Midianite soldier, there were only .002307 Israelites. God doesn't even use half a man to win battles. God caused the enemy to go into a great panic, and the Midianites began cutting one another down in the confusion.

There is so much more to this story, but two things are important for us chaplains. The first one is Judges 6:14 (NIV). "The Lord turned to Gideon and said, 'Go with the strength you have, and rescue Israel from the Midianites. I am sending you!'" This was prior to the Spirit clothing him with power in verse 34. What God was saying is go in your own strength. Trust me, and the rest will come. Everything else will fall into place. When you received your call to be a chaplain, you probably asked yourself, "Why me, LORD? Send someone else; I'm not qualified." Little did you know God was seeing the potential giant inside of you to do the impossible. He wants us to do the incredible, the mystifying, the miraculous work of God. His will is to pour glory and honor all over you to make the impossible possible. We are called to walk into emotional chaos, confusion, and doubt and then to bring faith, order, and peace. God uses us to provide a calming presence in times of turmoil.

We are called to "give a fitting word like apples of gold in pictures of silver" to a lost and hurting world that is in desperate need of God's grace. If you are willing to present yourself as an offering to God and give Him all you have, then He will take you and multiply gifts to do the work of the ministry in your life.

The second important empowerment God did in Gideon's life is recorded in Judges 7:7-16. God told Gideon to go down to the Midian camp and listen to what the people were saying. Gideon and his servant sneaked down to the outskirts of the camp and overheard two men speaking. One was talking about a dream he had about a loaf of barley rolling into camp — destroying them.

As Gideon listened to this dream, he recalled when he hid grain from the Midianites who ravaged the land of all produce, wheat, and barley. Gideon realized he was the barley! The other Midianite said, "This can mean only one thing. God has given the Midianite army over to Gideon." Gideon's heart was full of confidence at this point because God confirmed yet again that He would fight this battle.

The scripture verse for chaplains is in Judges 7:11c (NLT): "...then you will be eager to attack. The meaning behind this word eager is "girded, prepared to fight. Your hands will be strengthened to fight." I like the word eager because it means one who cannot wait until the battle occurs. It is an extreme feeling of confidence, fearlessness, and courage. It's like a football player who tells the coach to put him in because he needs to get back in the game. He knows he's good, and more importantly, he knows he is a winner.

Once a chaplain steps out of his/her comfort zone, the heart becomes inflamed with the excitement to see what God is going to do through him/her. The chaplain can't wait to get into the game! Sitting on the sidelines is not where we belong. We are winners, and we are out to win for the kingdom of God.

The Bible gives a metaphor about a prophet who ate a scroll. It tasted sweet in the mouth but turned sour in the stomach. It's similar to when God gives us a wonderful word or a vision of a ministry. In the beginning, it tasted so sweet. But then the awful reality sets in when you preach it, and people don't buy into your vision. Opposition and even hostility will make your stomach churn. The good news is that He will bring the right people at the right time to help support the work.

When Dr. John Kenzy first began the ministry at Youth Challenge Bible Institute (YCIBI), many people did not want the kind of students he was bringing into the community. These students were often graduates of teen challenge programs. Many were ex-drug addicts and alcoholics whom God had redeemed and called into ministry.

Nevertheless, God's will prevailed, and these graduates went into ministry all over the world. If God wants a ministry, He will make it happen and the gates of hell will not prevail against it. God wants to do great things through us, and no man, not even the Devil, himself, will be able to stop us. People will see the hand of God working through us. Some will even be our own family members, and they will want to be involved. More importantly is that God is by our side.

In 2 Timothy 4:17 (NJKV), "But the LORD stood with me and strengthened me, so that the message might be preached fully through me, and that all Gentiles might hear. Also, I was delivered out of the mouth of lions."

Ministry is not easy. He did not call us so we would fail. God called us to succeed. He called us to a specific area to do a specific job at a specific time. He will move mountains that get in our way. Most importantly, He will empower us with the Holy Spirit to fulfill the work He has called us to do.

Chapter Three

My Conversion Experience

"Before I formed you in the womb I knew you, before you were born
I set you apart; I appointed you as a prophet to the nations."

Jeremiah 1:5 (NKJV)

Too many *McHale's Navy* episodes convinced me to join the Navy. I thought the Navy was going to be about girls and booze. I joined, not only to get away from my neighborhood and the police, but because "Sailors have more fun!" But then I got to the ship—reality struck. They handed me a paintbrush and said, "Get to work." I wondered, *Hey, what's this? Where is the party?* The first year I partied like a sailor and was good at it. We were getting ready to go overseas. This is what I joined up for. This is what I had been waiting for my whole life: finally, partying, girls, booze, and the exotic South Seas! I couldn't wait to go! And then it happened: God showed up.

A Catholic priest came onboard. I was raised in the Catholic church and attended twelve years of Catholic school. I even served as an altar boy and considered the priesthood. But I liked girls too much. When I saw the priest, I knew I had to change my life. The only way I could describe how I felt at the time was *seedy*. I was spiritually dirty, and the lifestyle I was living wasn't right. I needed to clean up my life. I started going to mass onboard the ship.

There was a Mexican sailor, Pete, who had been witnessing to me for months, but I never understood what he was saying. I assumed it was the language barrier, but it wasn't that. It was the enemy keeping me from hearing the gospel. It was "the god of this world (that) has blinded the eyes of unbelievers." "Satan, the god of this world, has blinded the minds of those who don't believe. They are unable to see the glorious light of

9

the Good News. They don't understand this message about the glory of Christ, who is the exact likeness of God" (2 Corinthians 4:4, NLT).

One Marine carried a Bible in his hand as he walked by the galley. This marine seemed to glow with a *presence* like I had never seen before. I wanted whatever it was he had. One day I was serving him lunch and said to him, "There is another guy on this ship who carries one of those." He looked excited about it and wanted to meet him, so I told him his name.

Then, my friend, Pete, invited me to their Bible study. There were six of us crammed into one little room. As I listened, my heart became responsive to what they were saying. They knew God personally, and I wanted to know Him, too. I asked Jesus to forgive me and to come into my heart. I felt a peace come into me. I woke up the next morning feeling pure; it was a feeling I had never felt before. The sinful lifestyle I had lived, which caused that deep *seedy* feeling was gone. I was forgiven.

Romans 5:1 (NLT) says, "Therefore, since we have been justified through faith, we have peace with God through our Lord Jesus Christ.... In verse 20 (NIV), it says, "But where sin increased, grace increased all the more." I finally had peace in my life for the first time, and it felt good!

That next night we met again, but I had to leave early to go on the 8:00 p.m. to 12:00 a.m. watch. As I got up to leave, one brother said, "Hold on; we want to lay hands on you and pray for you to receive the baptism of the Holy Spirit." They began to speak in tongues as they laid hands on me in prayer. I had heard them the night before praying in tongues, and although I didn't understand it, I knew it was from God. I felt power coming from their prayers.

Baptism of the Holy Spirit

As they laid their hands on me, the Holy Spirit filled me. Not only did I have peace, but now I had an empowerment. I went on watch that night and told everyone about Jesus! Some thought I had gone nuts, but others respected me. I wanted to share this experience with everyone I could, and I did with boldness, power, and without fear.

About three days later I asked God to give me the gift of tongues. I was in the prayer room alone, praying. I began allowing God to loosen my tongue so I could speak this heavenly language. As I trusted God more, I began to say one word. I remember the feeling I had when it came out. I was excited and, with more faith, asked for more words. As I poured out my heart to Him, tongues began to flow out of my mouth.

Tongues are utterances when our spirit cries out to God in an angelic language that only our spirit and God's spirit know and understand. Tongues express intercession for others, ourselves, or even praise. In the church setting, it is followed by an interpretation (2 Corinthians 14).

In Acts 2, the believers were in the upper room waiting for the gift of the Holy Spirit to be given after the resurrection of Jesus. All of a sudden, a mighty rushing wind came into the room; tongues like fire rested upon their heads, and they were all filled with the Holy Spirit. This is important to understand because of the spiritual significance of wind, fire, and tongues. Wind in the Old Testament represented the Spirit or breath of God. It is the Hebrew word *Ruach* where God's Spirit created the world. In us He re-creates us to be born-again or literally born from above. It is a new birth and a new spiritual experience with God dwelling in us. Fire represents purification. We have to be purified before we can begin sharing the gospel. Tongues of fire represent a purified heart to boldly speak the gospel. All the people in that room were changed, even Peter who was previously fearful and timid. Peter preached a powerful message in the streets of Jerusalem, and 3000 people came to believe.

God changed me the same way God changed Peter, and He can change you. He desires to give that kind of empowerment to all of us. God wants first to purify you with salvation in Christ. Secondly, He wants to empower you with His Holy Spirit so He can use your tongue to boldly preach the gospel. For chaplains reading this who are not Spirit-filled, I would encourage you to seek this Baptism. It will transform your ministry and your life.

EXCOMMUNICATED FROM THE CATHOLIC CHURCH

The priest invited me to his stateroom to give me a gift for my twenty-first birthday. He handed me a book on catechism; I groaned inwardly. I didn't want to learn about religion; I wanted to know God and the Bible.

I politely declined it. "I started attending these Bible studies with these Christians on the ship," I said.

He said, "They are a cult; you shouldn't associate with them."

That made me a little defensive. "I get more out of their Bible studies than I do out of your mass." As it came out of my mouth, I knew that was the wrong thing to say, but he pushed my buttons. Maybe it was this brave new Spirit inside of me standing up to him or maybe it was just my old stubborn nature or maybe a little of both; I don't know, but what I did know was that I experienced God, and no one could tell me otherwise!

His demeanor changed. He narrowed his eyes with near contempt and then told me in a stoic voice, "You are no longer my son; I am no longer your father. I excommunicate you from the Catholic church." He then turned his back on me. I left discouraged, but I knew I had a genuine encounter with God.

I was hurt. The Catholic church was all I knew. Two thousand years of church history, my church, my community, and my Irish Catholic culture were all gone in an instant. My family thought I went nuts and joined a cult. I lost most of my friends on the ship and at home. I felt so isolated and spiritually orphaned. Fortunately, all my new Christian friends had similar experiences and understood. God tested my commitment. I made my decision to follow God regardless of the cost. Not only did I leave the Catholic church, but I had to surrender my dream of partying. I imagined God saying, "Okay, son, you are going overseas. You joined the Navy to live like a *McHale's Navy* sailor. Now, things have changed. What are you going to choose?"

I answered, "LORD, nothing compares to You. Even if I never feel Your presence again, I will still believe." I had no desire to drink or carouse. God filled that void.

My new life in Christ was exciting. I spent the next five months in Asia. I was sober every morning, and life was adventurous! The Christians on the ship took me under their wings and discipled me daily. As we sailed to different ports, we sought out Christians in other countries. We had fellowship with the local churches and helped in prison and orphanage ministries. We went hiking and snorkeling. I was baptized by a Baptist pastor in the Philippines at his ministry where he cared for prostitutes and orphans. My new life in Christ was full of purpose and meaning. It was far more satisfying than my original plans in joining the Navy. That lifestyle left me feeling empty, but this lifestyle gave me purpose.

God redeemed me April 11, 1996, on my natural and spiritual golden birthday. Eleven years to the date of my ex-communication, I was ordained into the Assemblies of God. I had come full circle and felt like I had a spiritual heritage once again. It felt good to belong to a fellowship, such as the Assemblies of God. They adopted me, and I am grateful!

It is difficult to give up all you know. But Jesus reminds us in Matthew 19:29 (NLT), "And everyone who has given up houses or brothers or sisters or father or mother, for my sake, will receive a hundred times as much in return and will inherit eternal life."

Though I lost some friends and a spiritual heritage in the Catholic church, God has given me so much more. The gains have been more than the losses. In Philippians 3:8 (NIV), it says, "What is more, I consider everything a loss because of the surpassing worth of knowing Christ Jesus as my Lord."

CHAPTER FOUR

God's Call to Chaplaincy

...for God's gifts and His call are irrevocable.

Romans 11:29 (NIV)

I was twenty years-old when I accepted Jesus as my savior and twenty-one when I received a call to ministry, while still in the Navy. Everyone on board noticed what happened to me. Even the captain of the ship, who just one year earlier put me in the brig, was now appointing me the ship's Christian lay pastor. I went from the brig to the pulpit in one year!

During my first years in the Navy, I spent them as a deck seaman. I swabbed the deck, painted, and slushed cables. During my last year in 1986, I took a test to become a cook and made Petty Officer Third Class. Not knowing what I would do once I got out of the Navy, I decided to pray and fast, which wasn't easy as a cook. I also asked my Christian brothers to pray for God's will for me. I went to work that day and was in the back of the galley cooking french-fries by myself. The other cooks were on the other side preparing lunch. I was contemplative and in a prayerful mood. It was quiet except for the roar of the fries cooking. All of a sudden like a thunderbolt, the word *Chaplain* was spoken into my spirit. It was not audible, but it might as well have been. At first, I was shocked. I felt like Gideon. *Why me? I'm just a cook!* It was something that had never entered my mind. That's how I knew it was from God. I kept this to myself all through lunch. As I was cooking fries, I began thinking about this exciting call. I remember having mixed feelings of both joy and terror. I thought to myself, *What an awesome call! What an awesome responsibility, but am I capable?*

God answered my prayer but quite honestly, it terrified me. I was excited about my future, but my past haunted me. I was afraid of failing God. I joined the Navy because I didn't do well in college. Qualifications for chaplaincy meant I not only needed a Bachelor's degree, but a Master's degree. Nevertheless, I trusted God's call to be irrevocable even though I doubted my own capabilities. By faith I accepted the call believing Him to help me through school. I then told my Christian brothers. They were thrilled and confirmed my calling as they had seen the evidence of God in my life as the ship's pastor.

WAITING ON GOD

Soon after my honorable discharge, I applied to one of the Assemblies of God colleges but was denied. They said I wasn't ready for college and needed more time to mature. So, for the next three years, I worked as a cook in a nursing home and got involved in a local church by helping with youth and ushering.

In Proverbs 18:22, we're told, "He who finds a wife finds a good thing and obtains favor from the LORD" (ESV). After attending the church for about a year, the pastor asked me to help out with the youth group. I was working with the youth when Dorothy, the children's pastor, asked me to help with a project she was working on; she was intelligent, pretty, and I enjoyed talking to her, so I gladly agreed. We stood outside the church after the service, talking for a long time about the project. She was sweet, kind, and had a nice soft voice. I liked her right away. She liked me, too! Eventually, we decided to go out just as friends. We went to the park and then out to dinner. I was nervous and didn't want to let on that I liked her, so I made her buy her own meal. She had a look of surprise and probably a little embarrassed in front of the cashier. I saw her head shake but with a chuckle as she paid her own way. I eventually asked her out on a date and did pay that time. To this day she never lets me forget, so I have to pay from now on!

As we worked together and dated, she told me she had attended and graduated from Youth Challenge International Bible Institute in Sunbury, PA. It was a school specifically designed for graduates of Teen Challenge who felt a call to ministry. Teen Challenge is a one-year drug and alcohol program. Youth Challenge Bible Institute was a three-year Bible Institute. I wasn't crazy about going to a non-Assemblies of God school, so I kept resisting. Furthermore, I was not a former drug user, so I didn't think I would fit in.

Dorothy said she was not a drug user either, and although it is primarily for Teen Challenge graduates, the school is open to anyone who wants to study for ministry. She warned me it was hard work. I was fine with that. There were no other doors opening, so I decided to check it out. We eventually made arrangements to drive up there for the weekend. Dorothy stayed with a staff member, and I stayed in the dorm. We went during the fall semester, so I was able to speak to students about the school. We went to the Friday night church service. All new people were asked to introduce themselves. To my girlfriend's amazement and mine, I blurted out, "I'm John and this is my fiancé, Dorothy." I hadn't even asked to marry her. She said for the first time in her life she was speechless. When I sat down, she just stared at me, waiting for an explanation. I didn't have one. I was just as shocked as she was!

We went out after the service for a late-night snack. I looked at her and asked, "Well are you going to marry me or what?" How elegant I was. What a romantic marriage proposal that was. She'd probably imagined all her life from childhood up to that point that her knight in shining armor would take her out to a nice, fancy dinner, sweep her off her feet, and with a group of violinists playing, her boyfriend would ask her to marry him. Instead, this poor girl got, "Well, you gonna marry me or what?" I was still quite a mess back then, but she loved me and saw the diamond in the rough.

I looked in her eyes and told her I loved her. She said, "I love you, too, and yes, I want to marry you, too, but where's my ring?"

I had no idea I was going to ask her to marry me, so I didn't have one. I stammered, "Uh, oh…Ummm…no, I don't have a ring." Dorothy, who is the problem solver, ordered onion rings and put one on her finger. With a wide grin, she said, "Here it is!" And then we ate it.

When I saw the school and talked with the students, I felt the presence of God there. I knew right then and there this was the place for me. It was a no-frills school. The desks were wobbly, the carpet was worn, there was no air conditioning in the spring, and there was very little heat in the winter. But God was there. I wanted to begin a new chapter in my life there with Dorothy. Marrying her and studying at YCIBI were two of the best decisions I ever made. This began a new and exciting chapter in my life!

COLLEGE CAREER

I started YCIBI in the fall of 1989 and graduated spring 1992. In one of my classes, Doctor John Q. Kenzy, the President of YCIBI, said some Bible college students had a dual major. They got a secular degree, as well as a biblical one in case the ministry didn't work out. I decided right then and there it was ministry or nothing. I did not want the idea in my head that I could fall back on something else as a safety net.

YCIBI was a tough school. It was like a three-ring circus with no nets. Classes were held in the morning, work practicum was in the afternoon, ministry or study was at night, and chapel services were on Friday night. I had a hard time there because we were busy all the time. Their philosophy was "idle hands are the devil's workshop." They lived up to it! I'm a contemplative person and needed my quiet time, so it was difficult for me. But Saturday was Dorothy and our day together. If she was working, I spent a few hours watching a good movie. I needed some *me time,* as well. Also, we were not allowed to take out student loans. The Administrative policy was, "If you are going into ministry, you have to learn to live by faith." God provided every semester, and I graduated debt-free.

I spent a lot of time at the altar in prayer, wrestling with myself more than anything else. At the altar is where God did a lot of His work building my character. He was always dealing with me about something that would come up in class, and I would get convicted of yet another area in my life that needed changing. Many were small areas, but every once in a while, He would show me something big that needed to be transformed. I called them *chunks.* It hurt letting go of old patterns, behaviors, and thoughts, but He replaced them with better attributes. God not only discipled me in class, but changed my heart at the altar.

Youth Challenge International Bible Institute was where I learned what real ministry and discipleship meant. Two of the main scriptures we lived by were, "For the Son of Man came not to be served but to serve and give His life as a ransom for many" (Matthew 20:28, NLT). The second was a prophetic word by David Wilkerson, founder of the school, who prophesied, "This is the school of the unlatched shoe." The meaning is based on Jesus washing the disciples' feet at the Last Supper. YCIBI was a school of serving others with love. We served diligently and in a healthy environment where the Word of God was put into practice. I learned how to be a man, husband, and father through the "Marriage and Family" class. I learned how to be a servant through ministerial practicum, discipleship, and Bible classes. When I graduated, I left being well-balanced, highly-educated in the Bible, and with the knowledge that ministry is hard work. More importantly, I learned how to develop a relationship with God and depend on Him for everything.

Dr. John Q. Kenzy became my spiritual father. Dr. Kenzy was famous for his one-liners. One of his most renowned was, "Keep your knees down, your chin up, roll with the punches, and give God all the glory."

I'm sad to say Dr. Kenzy died June 19, 2019. A year before he died, I wrote him a poem called "The Family Tree," expressing my gratitude for his outpouring of love and encouragement into our lives. In the poem, I quoted the scripture I cited earlier from Matthew 19:29, "And everyone who has given up houses or brothers or sisters or father or mother, for my sake, will receive a hundred times as much in return and will inherit eternal life." I received so much from him as my spiritual father, but I will see him again. His family said, "He went home with the Lord singing praises and feeling God's glory." What a beautiful way to end one life and walk into the next.

YCIBI was a three-year Bible Institute where I needed to be. The Assemblies of God college that denied my application years earlier had been correct. I needed more time to grow and learn, and YCIBI gave me that strong foundation.

CHAPTER FIVE

Transformed by Illness

It was good for me to be afflicted so that I might learn your decrees.

Psalm 119:71 (NIV)

I transferred into Central Bible College (CBC), now called Evangel University in Springfield, MO, for my fourth year of college. I was in college full time, in the Navy reserves, working on staff and working as a kitchen supervisor at Maranatha Village, which is the Assemblies of God Retirement Home. I was burning the candle at both ends. God still needed to do some serious work in my life.

My work ethic was strong and sincere, but my motivation needed adjustment. I wanted to save the world through work and ministry. My prayer life dwindled. I replaced God's presence with business and work. I did it to myself. I walked myself right into a nine-month sickness. I became a workaholic.

I became frustrated and angry. Serving God was not joyful anymore. I was tired, burned out, angry, and discouraged. Instead of relying on God, I took on more responsibilities than I should have.

At CBC, I was in the chapel when the pastor preached on anger. Half of the student body went to the altar for prayer. I remember saying, "God, please deliver me from this anger." I was operating on my own strength but didn't know how to handle everything. I was on edge. I would snap at my wife and yell at people at work. Though I was saved, I still had anger issues. I prayed to God to change me.

I need your help. Everything in my life is falling apart. I don't have a safety net. I didn't get a dual major; I'm in this ministry all or nothing, so please HELP ME!

God answered that prayer in a way I didn't want but in a way that I needed. I began getting sick. I lost twenty pounds in one week. My wife took me to the hospital, but they just rehydrated me and sent me home time and again. During this time, God put me on a sleep fast. He would wake me up at 3:00 a.m. for prayer. It seemed I couldn't get enough prayer time with Him. In hindsight, it became clear that He was getting me ready for the biggest battle of my life. After about a month of misery, they finally admitted me to the hospital with colon problems. At first, they didn't know what it was. The thought of cancer came to our minds, but the LORD spoke the same scripture to Dorothy and me separately. "This is not unto death" (John 11:4, KJB). We were comforted that I was not going to die, but we still didn't know the cause. My doctor finally diagnosed it as ulcerative colitis. My colon was full of ulcers.

I lost thirty more pounds. I was fed with lipids and TPN (total parenteral nutrition) through my veins. I was not allowed to eat by mouth for three months. I was so tired and in pain every day. My days were spent watching tv and sleeping. When I was awake, I spent a lot of time fantasizing about eating something. "When I get out of here, we are going to stop at every restaurant in Springfield, and I'm going to eat this town out of food," I told my wife one night. Oh! How I missed eating!

As I lay in the hospital bed, I watched people through the window eating burgers as they walked out of a well-known fast-food restaurant. I laid in bed thinking how that big hamburger with special sauce would taste, how the juices would explode in my mouth, and how the drippings would run down my cheek. I felt like I was sinning by lusting after a burger! Then I looked at everyone coming out of there with a burger and fries and thinking, *they don't appreciate what they have.* I actually got mad at them, thinking they were taking that food for granted. Then I thought, *Never again will I take food for granted.* To this day I am sincerely grateful when I pray over a meal.

Dorothy sometimes sneaked in donuts, which skyrocketed my blood sugars. I would throw it up three hours later, but man, was it worth it! I got caught by a nurse one time.

"Why is your blood sugar so high?" The nurse had a suspicious look in her eye. "Is that powder on your lips?"

"Yep," I replied, grinning.

No apologies here! She just shook her head. I saw a smile on her face as she turned away. I wasn't the easiest patient for those poor nurses. However, my illness educated me more than any class ever could have. I was schooled on the bed of affliction. It was a time of experiencing God. YCIBI taught me a lot and changed me, but God wanted to do an even deeper work. He is really never done with us anyway. No longer was I sitting in chapel services hearing others telling me about God; I was experiencing God for myself in my hospital room. I wasn't working, nor was my day filled with ministry, study, or classes. I was alone with God. He poured His love into me for no reason at all other than because He loved me. I didn't have to earn His approval, acceptance, or love through work or actions. I only had to be His son whom He enjoyed being with. At first, I was shocked by His grace. It was an experience of God's love on a whole new level. Scripture became alive and more real than ever before. Instead of focusing on suffering, endurance, and the trials and pains of life, His Word revealed forgiveness, intimacy, and joy.

I was experiencing what the mystic Teresa of Avila called "the Gift of Tears" from a heart filled with love. I couldn't stop crying. That intimate presence of God was overwhelming, and all I knew was, "God loves me so much that I can barely contain it." I took Jesus's words literally. "Come to me all you who are weary and burdened, and I will give you rest. Take my yoke upon you and learn from me, for I am gentle and humble in heart, and you will find rest for your souls. For my yoke is easy and my burden is light" (Matthew 11:28-30, NASB). I simplified it in my own words: "Rest in the yoke of the LORD as you do His will." Ministry and work became enjoyable again. When I got better, I served God out of a heart of love rather than works.

I have learned to walk with God as I work. Where He says to go, I go. When he says to stop, I stop. My answer is "yes" to God. I put boundaries on myself. I don't allow others to put responsibilities on me that God has not. I did my work and often went the extra mile. But now it is because I work out of love and not duty.

I watched an interview with Charles Stanley. One time he asked his deacons how they felt about ministry. The number one answer was, "We serve out of duty." He was saddened by this answer and sought to change their ministry from being a burden to a joy. No one wants to serve God out of duty, obligation, or guilt. That is not joyfully serving God. "He whom the Son sets free is free indeed" (John 8:36, KJV). God wants to set us free from the pressures we put on ourselves in the ministry. He does not want us burnt out and angry.

At our graduation ceremony from the Assemblies of God Theological Seminary, Dr. George Wood shared, "Your joy will not come from ministry; it will overflow from your relationship with the LORD. From that, you will enjoy the ministry." 2 Corinthians 4:16 (NKJV) says, "...Outwardly we are perishing, but we are being renewed daily." When I was ill, my body was deteriorating, yet I never felt more alive. I carry that experience with me to this day. It has changed my entire outlook on God, people, and ministry.

One day I was talking to a patient in hospice who was sitting in her room all day. I asked her if she was okay.

She said, "Pastor John, people think I'm lonely, but I am not. I am here with my God and my memories. I think about when my husband used to serenade me and when I spent time with my children. God is with me, and I am not alone nor am I lonely."

I understood what she meant because I experienced the same thing when I was ill. I was not alone either. I believe an angel was with me in my room, so I talked to him and called him Bob. Every day he kept me company. I probably drove him crazy, but I never felt alone. There was something spiritual in that hospital room. It may sound weird, but I believed he was there with me. I had nothing to do but talk his ear off, watch TV, and when the Holy Spirit moved me, I would enter into spontaneous worship. When I was done, I would turn the TV back on or turn to poor old Bob. God's presence was there. When I see Bob someday, I'm going to thank him for being there with me and then apologize for talking to him so much.

The illness continued. I was down to 140 pounds. The doctor would pretend to look for me because I was so pale and blended in with the sheets. I was on prednisone. It made my face swell, my hair fall out, increased my appetite, elevated my blood sugars, and made me an emotional basket case. Oh, Joy!

I felt helpless and vulnerable. I was not in control anymore. I used to be strong. I lifted weights, but now I couldn't even lift myself into bed. I remember thinking that one of these skinny little nurses could come in here and snap my neck like a twig, and I wouldn't even be able to defend myself. I was broken and humbled. I asked Dorothy why she married me. She said, "Because I knew deep down you were good, but it had to reach the surface. I think it's reached the surface."

I nodded. "Yes, God has broken me, but He is rebuilding me into an even better man." I cried. I said I was sorry for being angry. We hugged each other. We knew God was working, and it was coming to an end. I felt guilty because Dorothy now had the added responsibility of the sole breadwinner, lawn care, home-keeping, plus taking care of everything else. She was awesome during this time. She still made time to come up every night to visit me. She read the Bible to me because I had blurry vision from the prednisone, and then we would pray. She took her vows seriously: "In sickness and in health...till death do us part."

I was in the hospital for the entire summer of 1993. Then that August, my insurance canceled our policy. We owed the hospital $75,000 because they said I had a pre-existing condition from when I went to the doctor in Pennsylvania for stomach pain.

My wife then found Baptist Memorial Hospital in Memphis, Tennessee, that took me on pro bono. The surgeon, Dr. Britt, operated on me for free even though it was a four-hour surgery.

The hospital only charged me $10.00 a day. Dorothy had to stay in a hotel. The church, my family, and many friends donated money, and it covered all expenses. We did, however, need to file bankruptcy for the $75,000. Nevertheless, God provided for our needs.

After the surgery, Dr. Britt said to me, "John, that was the worst colon I have ever seen. I had to take out your entire colon and rectum and give you an ileostomy."

God took out my colon, but He gave me a new heart in the process. God sometimes uses sicknesses and illness to get our attention. David said in Psalm 119:71, "It was good for me to be afflicted so that I might learn your decrees" (NIV). It was on my bed of affliction where I found my Savior in a whole new way. God draws near to the brokenhearted. Where suffering is we find God's grace to endure. I have found in ministry and in my personal life that the more we suffer, the harder the trial, the more difficult the pain, the more personal God becomes.

It took a few months to recover. I was weak, but I went back to work. I had to take off that fall semester from Central Bible College, however. I showed up for drill at the Naval reserve center to report for duty in September 1993.

The personnel man said, "Didn't anyone tell you?"

"Tell me what?" I asked.

"You were medically discharged from the Navy," he said.

I felt numb. I stood there speechless. Indeed, he was, too. He could see the look of disappointment on my face. *This can't be happening. This is a mistake*, I thought to myself. *I have a call to be a Navy chaplain.* I was confused, disillusioned, disappointed, and discouraged.

I pulled myself together and finally said to him, "I was called to be a chaplain." He said, "I'm sorry to have to be the one to tell you this, but you were medically discharged, but you can appeal it."

Deep down in my heart, I knew I couldn't serve as a chaplain with an ileostomy. The work is too demanding and dangerous. I left in tears. As I drove home, a song came on the radio called "Sail on Sailor." God spoke to me through that song to keep sailing forward, and He will eventually give me direction. I had peace even though I had tears.

After much prayer and soul-searching, I reflected on what He said when He called me into the chaplaincy. I realized that He never said military chaplain but just spoke the word "chaplain" into my heart. Since I was in the Navy, I reasoned that is what He meant. At that time, I was still a young Christian and didn't know there were other types of chaplains. I felt God's leading me to continue my education to go on to seminary and work toward possibly becoming a Veteran's Administration Chaplain.

I went back to Central Bible College with a completely new outlook. I re-evaluated my priorities. I resigned my position at the church and no longer had to serve one weekend a month in the Navy Reserves. I focused on my studies, work, and one type of ministry. I volunteered at a hospital providing pastoral care. I didn't feel burdened anymore. I was so much happier.

I got up every morning at 5:00 a.m. for devotion. I could not wait to talk to my LORD Jesus and have Him speak back to me. I prayed from 5:30 a.m. to 6:00 a.m. From 6:00 a.m. to 6:30 a.m., I read the Word. Then I rode my stationary bike while watching the news. After a shower and dressing myself, I ate breakfast and then was off to school. By that time, my body was energized by exercise, my mind was engaged with world events, and my spirit was ready for the day. I learned from my illness to take care of body, mind, and spirit.

I graduated from Central Bible College and went on to the Assemblies of God Seminary. I was there for three more years of intense study. It was hard but well worth the experience. On my first day of class, the President of the seminary, Dr. Del Tar, met with all the incoming students. He handed each of us a towel and shared a devotional on serving. If you visit the seminary building, a statue of Jesus, washing the disciples' feet is the first thing you see in the foyer.

Dr. Del Tar challenged us to use our knowledge to grow in relationship to God. He called it *knowledge on fire.* We were not there just to get head knowledge but a heart to serve people. These three schools I attended, YCIBI, CBC, and seminary were great schools that taught the same theme: "Love God and Serve Others." My illness made the education complete.

CHAPTER SIX

Liberal Theology

Don't be misled: "Bad company Corrupts Good Character."

1 Corinthians 15:33 (NIV)

I graduated seminary with a Masters of Divinity in 1997. I then accepted a two-year position as a resident Chaplain at The Williamsport Hospital in Pennsylvania. I graduated there with six units of Clinical Pastoral Education (CPE). This was challenging. I was the only evangelical student out of ten. Some were conservative, but others were very liberal. One chaplain was even an atheist.

My education there was good in some ways but not good in others. I did not feel I could relate to others with my spiritual struggles because of our theological differences; nevertheless, I did learn terrific pastoral care skills. Ministering in a pluralistic setting did not come easy. I felt alone, but God was with me.

Some of my current chaplain colleagues had great experiences with Christian Clinical Pastoral Education. If I had to do it all over again, I would have gone that route.

One chaplain I worked with during my residency told dirty jokes quite often. In our Interpersonal Relationship Group, I said that we needed to have a more respectful decorum in the office. I said if someone walked by and heard some of these conversations, they would lose respect for the sanctity of our spiritual care department. It ran rampant in our office, and the consequences finally caught up with him. That chaplain didn't listen to me and made a sexual joke in a nurses' meeting. He was fired. I knew it would catch up with him. He was not a spiritual man. Patients complained that he never prayed with them. This man was a minister, but he was not saved or emotionally mature.

The chaplaincy can be filled with carnality. "They will act religious, but they will reject the power that could make them godly. Stay away from people like that" (2 Timothy 3:5, NLT).

Carnality has infiltrated the church and affected even its ministers. There is a story about a friar named Dominic in 1221 A.D. "When he was in Rome, seeking authorization for his order from the Pope. The Pope gave him a tour of the treasures of the Vatican and remarked complacently, "Peter can no longer say, 'Silver and gold have I none'" (Acts 3:6, NIV).

Dominic turned and looked straight at the Pope and said, "No, and neither can we say, 'Rise and walk'" (*Biographical Sketches of Memorable Christians of the Past* by James E. Kiefer). Money and power can corrupt individuals and entire churches.

The Laodicean church was rich but poor spiritually. They were lukewarm and powerless. Jesus told them He would spit them out of His mouth if they did not repent. When compromise enters the church, it grieves the Holy Spirit, and miracles cease to happen. Secular religion replaces God. Jesus stood outside of the door of the Laodicean church knocking to come in. At one time, Jesus did reside there. The Apostle Paul wanted his letters read to them (Colossians 4:16, NLT). The church was probably healthy at one time and like all churches had to deal with problems. Laodicea, however, never dealt with their self-sufficient attitude by declaring, "I am rich, I have acquired wealth and don't need anything" (Rev. 3:17, NLT). They did not need God's daily bread; they made their own. Somewhere along the way, they removed God. They made a conscious decision to rely on themselves instead of living by faith. They wanted the church to run their way and not God's. Jesus asked them once again if He could come in. We know by church history the Laodicean church became religious, in name only, and lost the spiritual gifts. They paid a heavy price for the choices they made. Many churches around the world have lost the presence of God while the people inside refuse to open the door when Jesus knocks. They claim spiritual authority when in reality they have none. They have head knowledge but no heart knowledge and can no longer say, "rise up and walk."

In 2017 at the Assemblies of God Chaplains' Conference in Springfield, Missouri, Chaplain (Major General) Cecil R. Richardson shared stories about nine people he had personally ministered to in his forty-one year military career. Each of them was a senior military officer who had been convicted of fraud, domestic abuse, incest, sexual assault, production of pornography, grand theft, or rape. "The one thing they all had in common," he said, "is that they were all chaplains!" This is the way secular chaplains can act. I've seen it firsthand. We are not secular chaplains. We are to be Holy Spirit-filled chaplains called to change the world rather than being changed by the world.

Unfortunately, some work their way into the chaplaincy as if it were a job rather than a calling, thereby, making a real mess of the pastoral care department. Many have not had a conversion experience. I worked with an atheist chaplain. He was into the New Age Movement and always wore his crystal around his neck. This atheist believed truth to be relative. He said, "Truth changes according to whatever society decides at the time."

He had no absolutes, no boundaries as he built his spiritual house on sand. Thank God that we have an unchangeable truth and an unchangeable God who does not change like shifting sand. Our spiritual foundation is built upon the rock. "Jesus is the same yesterday, today, and forever" (Hebrews 13:8, NKJV). He does not change!

I hate to admit this part of my spiritual walk, but liberal theology began to affect me toward the end of my two-year residency. I realized this while officiating yet another funeral service for someone who never confessed Jesus as Savior. I told the family that their mother went to heaven. Her son, who I think was a backsliding evangelical, came up to me after the service and told me his mother wasn't saved. I told him God's grace covered her. He walked away knowing I was wrong. When it came out of my mouth, I knew I was wrong, too! I knew at that moment I needed to get out of the chaplaincy. Bad company was corrupting my good character.

Thankfully, the two-year residency was ending. God knew it was time to leave. I was so disappointed in myself that I never wanted to go back into the chaplaincy. I realized how easily influenced I can be, and it scared me to think of going back into it. I thank God He doesn't give up on us. "And I am sure of this, that he who began a good work in you will bring it to completion at the day of Jesus Christ" (Philippians 1:6, ESV).

CHAPTER SEVEN

Obey Spiritual Leadership

*Obey your spiritual leaders, and do what they say. Their
work is to watch over your souls, and they are accountable
to God. Give them reason to do this with joy and not with
sorrow. That would certainly not be for your benefit.*

Hebrews 13:17 (NLT)

After one and a half years in the chaplaincy in 1996, I went up for my Ecclesiastical Endorsement with the Assemblies of God. The Leadership Board told me I needed to do a two-year pastorate at a local church. I told them I was not called to pastor; God had called me to be a chaplain. The Director of the Chaplain Department gently encouraged me two times to take a position as a pastor because the committee wanted me to *get seasoned*. I was about to argue for the third time when the Holy Spirit spoke to me right then and there: "Obey your spiritual authority." They looked at me, hoping it resonated.

"Okay, I'll do it," I said. I didn't tell them the LORD had spoken to me.

After finishing my two-year residency at the Williamsport Hospital in 1999, I took the pastorate at a small church in Fleetwood, Pennsylvania. It was a much-needed time for spiritual healing for me after being around secular chaplains for two years. After two years of pastoring, I went back to the chaplain committee.

"The last time I was here," I told them, "I argued with you about not wanting to be a pastor, but the LORD told me to obey my spiritual authority. Because I obeyed, God has blessed us."

They laughed and remembered me giving them a hard time. They said they appreciated my honesty. I showed them pictures of the children we adopted while I pastored there. I told them that never would have happened if I hadn't obeyed their spiritual leadership. I thanked them for hearing from God for me. They were proud of me and laughed as they looked at the pictures. They said I had made a good impression and endorsed me as a chaplain. I don't know how spiritual leaders put up with us sometimes. We live in a culture where people don't respect spiritual authority. The Bible is very clear about this. "Now we ask you, brothers and sisters, to acknowledge those who work hard among you, who care for you in the Lord and who admonish you. Hold them in the highest regard and in love because of their work. Live in peace with each other" (1 Thessalonians 5:12-13, NIV).

PASTORING FIRST ASSEMBLY OF GOD IN FLEETWOOD, PENNSYLVANIA: THE JOYS AND CHALLENGES OF OBEDIENCE

"Trust in the LORD with all thine heart, and lean not on your own understanding. In all thy ways acknowledge him, and he shall direct thy paths" (Proverbs 3:5-6, KJV).

Dorothy and I adopted three children during those six years at Fleetwood. We never thought we would have a family because of three miscarriages, but God blessed us with a family. "God sets the lonely in families" (Psalm 68:6, NIV). Before we had children, Dorothy and I were happy but unfulfilled. The home was missing children in it. I remember coming home from work one day, looking at her, and asking, "Is this it?" Poor Dorothy, having to be stuck with me.

We got involved in foster care and eventually adopted all three children. Those stories in and of themselves are nothing short of miraculous. Each one was prayed for, and God answered our prayers. We were lonely; those children needed a home, so God put us all together in one happy family. Honestly, I couldn't wait to be released from the church and become a Veteran's chaplain. The church wasn't growing; I wasn't happy. But I heard nothing. *Where are You, God?* my heart cried. *We are going on three years and then four. I was only supposed to do two.*

Then I realized my heart was not in the right place. I wasn't pastoring; I was just doing my two-year obligation. I confessed to the LORD that I wasn't showing leadership or vision. I saw all the things that needed changing but never did anything about them. *Okay, LORD. If*

You are keeping me here, then I will make the necessary changes. I needed time with God.

So, I got away for a weekend for prayer. I called some friends and had them pray with me. They gave godly advice, which was confirmed in prayer. I came back from that weekend of prayer and made the necessary changes. I had to remove some from leadership. I never asked them to leave the church, but they did. Since it was a small family church, many relatives of those leaders left. We weren't growing, and those in leadership were not spirit-filled and always resisted change. It was a stoic church. I remember looking out into the congregation one Sunday morning, thinking to myself, *I wouldn't even want to come to this church!* That's pretty bad when the pastor thinks that about the church he is pastoring.

On its best day, the church had forty people, and that was with visitors. After removing leadership and families, we went down to twenty-three people. I convinced a few into becoming members, so we didn't have to become a district church. We had no worship team, so we used CDs. It was difficult at first but because of the fresh atmosphere, more and more families came. Within three months, we had a whole new worship team. We had two drummers, and one of them donated a set of drums. We had a family of four who sang, plus God raised up a piano player. The church grew from twenty-three people to fifty-five in only eight months. God was moving in miraculous ways with physical healings and manifestations of the Holy Spirit. It was something the church hadn't seen in years.

The success was short-lived. Within one month, four of the five new families told me they were relocating to other states for various reasons: family, work, and retirement. They loved us, they loved the church, and they loved what God was doing. Most were the ones who helped in worship ministry. The sting was hard felt. My heart sank. I felt like Job when one by one someone came with bad news. I honestly could not understand at that moment what God was doing. Things had been going great!

However, at the same time, there was an Assembly of God church plant struggling for a location. They were worshiping in a store-front building and praying about where to buy and settle. At the same time, I felt like God was releasing me from the church. I began to realize that God had me there to make the necessary changes for the next pastor. My ministry there was completed. They needed a building, and Fleetwood Assembly needed a new pastor and a new start. God's timing worked out perfectly.

A pastor friend of mine told me about a job opening for a local hospice chaplain where I lived. I was apprehensive because of my negative experience with the chaplaincy, but God's call as a chaplain remained in my life. I made a deal with God. I asked Him to let me work with Christian chaplains only. That was my only request. I know that sounds crazy, but He honored that request all the years of my ministry as a chaplain. I took the ministry position and was back in the chaplaincy.

I was not called to be a pastor; I was called to be a chaplain. But in obedience to the direction of my spiritual leadership, God blessed me temporarily with those pastoral gifts. God used my pastorate experience to teach me many things. The biggest was to understand the stress of pastoring. Pastors deal with a lot of pressure. When the church fell from forty to twenty-three people, it was depressing. But then I watched God build it back up again. If we do what He wants, no matter how hard it is, He will accomplish His will through us. Just be bold, courageous, obedient, and determined.

Do what God calls you to do even when it makes no sense. Do the right thing, the brave thing, even if it hurts. God will bless, strengthen, and see you through any circumstance as long as you obey His leading.

CHAPTER EIGHT

Focus on Strengths not Weaknesses

Since you are eager to have spiritual gifts, try to
excel in gifts that build up the church.

1 Corinthians 14:12 (NIV)

Y ou have God-given gifts, so does the ministry you excel in. Stay away from ministries where you are not gifted. Before I was saved, there was a philosophy in secular college to focus on building up our weak areas to become a well-rounded person. John Maxwell destroyed that philosophy in *The Leadership Handbook: 26 Critical Lessons Every Leader Needs.*

> Whenever I mentor people and help them discover their purpose, I always encourage them to start the process by discovering their strengths, not exploring their shortcomings. Why? Because people's purpose in life is always connected to their giftedness. It always works that way. You are not called to do something that you have no talent for. You will discover your purpose by finding and remaining in your strength zone.

Albert Einstein said, "Everyone is a genius. But if you judge a fish by its ability to climb a tree, it will live its whole life believing that it is stupid."

People need to find that one area they are good at and focus on that. You may try different types of chaplaincies before you find the one that is right for you and is God-appointed. There will be seasons in your life where you find yourself in a ministry position where you are not that great, but God has you there for a time and a purpose. When I went up for chaplain endorsement, I made it clear to the committee by telling them, "I am a good pastor but a great chaplain. I'll stick to the chaplaincy because that is where I was called." I'm a great chaplain, and I know it. Not because I have the natural capacity, but because I have the supernatural anointing, and this is how God created me. God equipped me when He called me. God equips each person when He calls them to a specific area of ministry; whether it is full time or lay ministry, everyone has gifts. Don't try to be a square peg in a round hole. Go with your strengths. Walk in an anointing of your calling with confidence and empowered giftings.

Chaplains are experts in crisis, grief, and bereavement ministries. We are there for people on the worst day of their lives. We do this daily. We are in the trenches where Jesus would go. This is where He called us.

When I left the pastorate and became a chaplain, some thought it was a step down from ministry. They had a look of disappointment, as if pastoring was the only worthy calling. Attending a sectional meeting, one pastor asked me what church I pastored. After I told him I was a chaplain, he didn't say anything. Instead, he turned his back and walked away. I knew who I was and more importantly Who called me. I don't need man's approval; neither do you.

To you, young chaplains, know who you are in Christ and never allow anyone to minimize your calling. There will always be a more prominent and prestigious ministry more known than yours, but God called you to where you are and where He wants you to be. Be satisfied and joyful where God has you, and do the best you can where you are. Don't let other's opinions be your identity; your identity is in Christ anyway, not in anything else. Even the Apostle Paul said he didn't care what others thought of him or his ministry. He didn't even judge himself.

> So, then, men ought to regard us as servants of Christ and as those entrusted with the secret things of God. Now it is required that those who have been given trust must prove faithful. I care very little if I am judged by you or by any human court; indeed, I don't even judge myself.... At that time each will receive his praise from God. (1 Corinthians 4:1-5, NRSV)

Be a servant where God has you. James and Jude, two half-brothers of Jesus, never identified themselves as Jesus' brothers but rather as slaves of God and of Jesus Christ. They remained humble in their ministerial positions. If they didn't exalt themselves on the coattails of Jesus, then ministers shouldn't seek recognition either. We need to take the same attitude of servanthood and minister right where God has us!

We are called but not gifted in all areas. When I received my call to ministry, the word *chaplain* was imprinted into my mind. I assumed it was military because of my station in the Navy, but I learned there were many other branches of chaplaincy. God has gifted me with *mercy* as explained in Romans 12:8 (NIV). "If you have the gift of mercy, do it with cheerfulness." My calling is to minister to the sick and dying as a hospice chaplain. The gift of mercy is one of my spiritual gifts. My heart is filled with compassion when I am involved in hospice ministry. I try to do it with cheerfulness if appropriate. No one wants a hospice chaplain coming into their home all dressed in black and acting morbid! I tell jokes and socialize for a few minutes before having a heart-to-heart conversation. Then I share a devotional.

After learning the fundamentals and mechanics of chaplaincy, each chaplain must develop his/her own style of ministry. Develop skills first, and then develop a unique style that's your own. What are your giftings? What are you best at doing? What are your abilities? Strive toward that end.

CHAPLAINS IN PRISON MINISTRY

When I was a pastor, one of the flock went astray and ended up in prison for a year. Every Thursday morning, I visited him in the prison chapel. While I was waiting for him one day, the prison chaplain asked me if I would visit other inmates in the meantime. I said, "Sure." Just as quickly as I said it, I regretted it. I sat with this prisoner whom I didn't know, as he went on and on blaming the system, his family, and everyone else for all his problems. He never accepted responsibility for his own actions. He said, "The prison psychiatrist got into my business, and I flipped the table and beat him up." Needless to say, I didn't say much!

There are two types of people in the world. Those who are apologetic and say, "At the time, I thought that was the best decision, but in hindsight, I was wrong. I'm sorry. Please forgive me." They don't try to justify or explain themselves. Usually, people are forgiving, and most people will accept a sincere apology.

The other type makes mistakes but refuses to admit them. They dig in even deeper, which only makes things worse. They blame everyone else for their problems. Their pride and arrogance make matters even more difficult.

When we are wrong, we need to own up to it and admit our mistakes. God will forgive our sin and put us on a path to a new beginning. "Though your sins were as red as scarlet, they shall be white as snow" (Isaiah 1:18, NKJV) and "where sin abounds, grace abounds even more," (Romans 5:20, NKJV). A life of love with a clean heart and forgiveness is worth it. God's grace is greater than any sin ever committed, and a clear conscience is peace of mind. Thank God there are prison chaplains called to this ministry because they are needed badly, but it wasn't for me. I dared not respond to this guy, so I sat and listened until the time was up. I later went to the chaplain and told him my experience, explaining I only wanted to visit my guy. He understood.

The gift of mercy brings a high degree of righteous indignation when it comes to justice. I often side more with the victim than I do with the convict. Some television shows or documentaries glamorize prisoners by giving them the spotlight. I believe that for every hour they spend on a prison documentary, they should spend two hours on the victims. There are one or more victims for every prisoner! Regardless, God calls us to love everyone, the victim as well as the aggressor; they both need healing in their hearts. They both need to know the love of Christ who alone can heal their deepest scars. God has unconditional love for the worst sinners, and prison chaplains have the unique opportunity to share redemption.

FROM SINNER TO SAINT

The book of Philemon shows the need for prison ministry. Philemon's slave, Onesimus, had run away. It was customary in the ancient world of Rome and other countries to own slaves. Philemon was a godly man who cared genuinely for people even though he owned slaves. Paul wrote the letter to Philemon asking him to take back his runaway slave — this time as a brother in Christ.

Paul taught that slaves should be obedient to their masters, not only when they're being watched, but when they aren't. We are all told "to work as if we are working for the LORD." He warns slave owners that they also have a Master in heaven and notes that they are slaves to God. In other books, Paul writes that we should all consider ourselves slaves to God.

As Americans, we can't fully understand how Philemon owned slaves yet was considered a righteous man. At that time, it was acceptable. Paul told slaves, "If you can gain your freedom, do so." In fact, it is quite possible Philemon freed Onesimus later and then worked alongside Paul. We are not sure, but Ignatius wrote of a man named Onesimus as being a highly-regarded Bishop of Asia. It is quite possible this was the same man. He went from prisoner to Bishop after years of serving Christ.

Before Onesimus came to Christ, it sounded as if he were a wild child. Paul called him useless just like a lot of pre-Christians used to be troublemakers. Sometimes they act out because there is a deep need in their lives, such as control or a need to exert their own will. Certainly, a slave must feel oppressed to the point that he would rather die than live under the authority of another person.

God had his plan in motion for Onesimus. He knew Onesimus's rebellious attitude, yet God had His hand on him. God's timing is always perfect. Paul was in the same prison as Onesimus. It is not a coincidence that Paul was there. It is no coincidence that chaplains are also already there waiting for the next Onesimus. Moreover, Paul led Onesimus to Christ and reconciled him back to Philemon, not as a slave to master, but brother to brother. Philemon verse 15 (NLT) says, "It seems you lost Onesimus for a little while so that you could have him back forever."

Prisoners have deep issues of anger and hurt. They did not end up in prison for being a boy scout. Something happened along the way to make them who they are. People act out in all kinds of ways due to hurts. There is a vacuum in every human heart that can only be satisfied by Jesus. Maybe they were influenced by the wrong crowd and felt they had no other choices. They need someone to help them get out of that mindset and see a better way of life. God can heal any heart and restore even the worst offenders.

Chuck Colson was a man with a deep hole in his heart. Born in Boston, Massachusetts, in 1931, his father was a failing lawyer with a spend-thrift mother nicknamed *Dizzy*. That tells us a lot about his formative years. Colson moved fifteen times in his childhood. After college, he met President Nixon, and the two hit it off. Both were corrupt, and they knew it.

Nixon said, "His instinct for the political jugular and his ability to get things done made him a lightning rod for my own frustrations. I made him my political point man for imaginative dirty tricks."

Colson even started talking about trampling on Nixon's grandmother's grave to show he was as mean as they come. "It was the *'in thing'* to swagger and threaten people." He had the authority, the spies, and the means to destroy people's lives, and he did. He hired a man to spy on Nixon's political opponents; the plot became known as WATERGATE.

It is said that Nixon won by a landslide because of the tarnished reputations of the opposite team. But instead of feeling good, Colson said, "They just got even more evil, more depraved, and drunk on power." His wife left him. He was known for being a heavy drinker, hard smoker, and an amoral man.

After leaving the White House in 1973, he feared he would go to jail. While looking for work, Colson got into his car and found himself in the grip of a spiritual crisis. It led to his conversion. "This so-called White House hatchet man, ex-marine captain, was crying too hard to get his keys into the ignition," he said. "I sat there for a long time that night deeply convicted of my own sins. I went to prison voluntarily, and I deserved it" (*New York Times*). Chuck Colson had owned up to his mistakes.

Thank God for chaplains and pastors who invest their lives in prison ministry. Chuck Colson said inmates are "filled with bitterness and revenge." Every day all they thought about was getting even! More chaplains are needed in the prison system so when inmates are released on our streets, they are not bent on revenge.

Redemption came for Mr. Colson. He knew he was wrong and accepted responsibility for his actions. He had a *born again* experience. He gave his heart to God and devoted the rest of his life to ministry. He established Prison Fellowship Ministries, which brings the gospel message to prisoners who were once lost just like him. He was a leading voice in the evangelical movement and donated much to ministries. He worked alongside Catholics, helping to fight against abortion and other religious freedoms.

In 2000, Governor Jeb Bush restored Colson's lawyer status rights to practice law, vote, and serve on a jury, all of which was lost when he went to prison. Governor Bush said, "I think it is time to move on. I know him; he's a great guy." In 2008 President George H.W. Bush awarded him the *Presidential Citizens Medal*. Colson made an enormous difference in the remaining years of his life. God restored him. He went to be with the LORD in 2012, not as a sinner, but as a redeemed child of the King.

Past mistakes should make us even more determined not to make them again. Chaplains are intercessors. We stick up for those who cannot defend themselves. We are advocates and intervene in a person's most difficult time of need. Sometimes we are the only ones to care about him/her when everyone else has abandoned him/her. Even Jesus felt the hurt of abandonment when all the apostles fled the night before His crucifixion. Peter felt it, too, as the one who abandoned Him.

Peter denied Jesus three times. After denying Christ twice, scripture says an hour went by. What was Peter thinking about during that hour? Did he feel guilty? Did he justify his actions? When he denied Jesus the third time, Peter cursed in anger. When people are afraid, they become angry. Anger is a mask for something deeper going on inside. Peter feared for his life; he saw what they were doing to Jesus, and it scared him. Fear gripped Peter, and he lashed out in anger. It was then that Jesus looked straight at Peter in the courtyard. When their eyes met, Peter wept bitterly. Peter had a lot of time to think about what he had done. He obviously repented. After Jesus resurrected and appeared on the shore, Peter dove into the water and swam to Jesus. He knew Jesus would forgive him.

Satan tried to *sift* or get Peter to turn away from God, but Jesus interceded for him. We have an intercessor. His name is Jesus. Jesus prays for us and intercedes for us when we sin. He speaks to the Father on our behalf. Where "sin abounds, grace abounds even more" (Romans 5:20, NIV).

Chaplains are God's voice to share the good news of forgiveness. I met a lady who loved the LORD. She was in hospice. As we prayed and had a devotional together, she lifted her hands in prayer and worship. Two weeks later at the next visit, we worshiped and read the scriptures.

"I spent twenty-one years in prison," she leaned over to me and whispered so her son could not hear.

My curiosity got the better of me. "What did you do?"

She said, "I killed some people. I was on drugs and really mixed up. The judge told me I was going to rot in jail for the rest of my life. But God in His mercy got a hold of my heart while I was in prison, and I gave my life to Jesus. I have been serving Him ever since."

I would have never thought this innocent little old lady would be able to do such a thing. God changed her from a murderer to a saint. He did the same with the Apostle Paul. His redemption is not beyond the reach of anyone.

Chaplains are there for people when everyone else abandons them, even when they feel like there is no redemption. We remind them of God's forgiveness and that He is always ready to give us another opportunity in life. Chaplains are God's instruments in restoring a person's soul and helping him/her reconcile himself/herself to God and others.

What a blessed opportunity it is to be the one to lead people to Christ and to know that they will experience all eternity in the presence of the LORD. Working in the chaplaincy ministry, you will experience sacred ground when people tell you their most intimate and personal experiences, challenges, and fears. It is an honor that someone trusts you enough to tell his/her deepest secrets and personal struggles, as well as past mistakes. It is all worth it when at the end of the visit, he/she tells you, "Thank you, Chaplain, for listening and praying with me. I feel so much better."

I'm not gifted in prison ministry, but I do minister in the medical field. I tell my patients and families that medicine doesn't solve every problem. Medication can't hug you or hold your hand. Some problems must be alleviated through counsel with a chaplain. Patients learn to trust you and respect your wisdom. When you have a word of knowledge from the Lord or wisdom to share, it brings hope to a broken heart. God calls us to use our gifts and talents. God has equipped us with gifts and talents and expects us to step out in faith and activate them. Chaplains have opportunities that most pastors don't. We are invited into an inner circle of people who would not normally step foot inside a church. We help them find God, meaning, and purpose. People turn their lives around when they have a reason to live. At one time, they were useless, but now in the hand of God, they make differences when they are released.

We have opportunities to help an alcoholic turn his/her life around; the plant worker struggling to find meaning for his/her life; and the prisoner who needs Christ. Chaplains minster to all people in all walks of life. If you are a pastor or lay person in your church, get involved in a ministry that suits your gifts and God-given personality to build the kingdom of God. Don't keep it to yourself. What God has done for us, He can do for anyone.

CHAPTER NINE

Heavenly Experiences

...was caught up to paradise and heard inexpressible
things, things that no one is permitted to tell.

2 Corinthians 12:4

After leaving the Navy, I became a cook in a nursing home. One co-worker asked me to visit her dying sister in the hospital. I had no idea what to say or do, but I agreed. I went in wearing my white cooking uniform and introduced myself as a friend of Darla's. Her face glowed and her eyes were warm and welcoming. I felt a heavenly presence about her. I had no idea what to do, so I gave her a Bible, talked to her for a bit, and prayed. She nodded, and with a gentle smile, thanked me for coming.

The next day, I saw my coworker who was very appreciative of my visit, who then told me she had passed away that night. Little did I know then that my calling would be to the sick and dying. That would be one of many experiences of witnessing God's glorious presence on dying people. Most encounters were very similar. There was always a loving presence or a glow, but each experience was as varied as they were individual.

While serving as a hospice chaplain in Reading, PA, I met a very poor woman living in a shelter. She told me a fascinating dream she had of going into heaven. She said she met Peter at the gate.

Peter asked me, "What would you like to have in heaven?" I thought about it for a moment and said, "I never had a lot of money either as a child or an adult, but I always wanted a nice house with a white picket fence." Peter said, "That is not a problem. We can have that for you." He went on to ask, "What was the biggest problem you struggled with in your life?" Without hesitation I said, "Jealousy. Every time another woman had on a prettier dress than mine, or when someone would get flowers from their husbands, I would get jealous." Peter said, "There is none of that here." Though Sally was poor financially she was not poor spiritually. Yes, she struggled with jealousy, but she went on to be with the LORD a few months later. She is struggling no more.

No more sin, shame, guilt, or temptation will ever bother us again. Revelation 21:3-4 says, "And I heard a loud voice from the throne, 'Now the dwelling of God is with men, and He will live with them. They will be His people, and God Himself will be with them and be their God. He will wipe away every tear from their eyes. There will be no more death or mourning or crying or pain, for the old order of things has passed away.'" What we struggle with down here will be no more up there.

Thelma was a 93-year-old Christian lady who loved the LORD. "I'm tired of living, Chaplain John," she said one day. "I've been laid up in this bed for the last ten years. Same routine every day. When I get up, others have to change me, feed me, and then I sleep most of the day. The next day, we do it all over again."

"That must be hard for you, Thelma," I replied, trying to empathize.

"It is, and that's why I just want to go home to be with Jesus."

Then one day as I was visiting with her, she suddenly lifted her hands in the air and said, "It is so beautiful."

"What do you see?" I asked.

She said, "I can't describe it; it is so wonderful."

I was preaching on the book of Revelation, so I was curious and asked if there really were streets of gold.

She said, "Oh hush...it feels so good...but I just can't reach it."

I visited her several times after that and talked and prayed with her. Thelma died three months later. I have heard countless stories of people who have experienced heaven. It increases my faith, and when I share these stories with my hospice patients, it increases their faith, too. There is a heaven, and there is nothing to fear.

One time at a conference, I heard an eighty-five year-old man testify. He told of his experience of falling and hitting his head. He was proclaimed dead for four minutes until the paramedics revived him. He said, "I went into heaven, and there were no old people there. Everyone was young, full of life and energy. No one was tired. They were laughing and full of joy."

Another hospice patient was an Episcopalian lady who lived in an assisted living facility. I visited her often. She continued to believe God was going to heal her. A call came to me reporting that she was unresponsive. Hearing is the last thing to go, so I sat quietly next to her bed and read scripture, sang some hymns, and prayed with her. I told her to greet me when it was my turn and that I would see her again in heaven. The weekend passed. I got a call Monday morning that she had rebounded on Sunday and wanted to see me. I walked into her room where she and her daughter were sitting.

"Chaplain John," she said. "Have a seat. I have something amazing to tell you."

I sat as she continued with a new radiance and excitement.

She said, "I left my body and was heading to this beautiful, loving place when I heard a voice say, 'There is still work for you to do.' I knew exactly what it meant. When God sent me back, I called my daughter. I told her to begin selling off my belongings and to put the house on the market and have an estate sale. I gave my car to my grandson and my jewelry to my granddaughter. I got to see their faces light up when I gave it to them. My daughter is relieved because she has been wanting me to sell the house, but I was resisting."

Her daughter started crying. Stella held her daughter's hand. There was much intimacy. The spiritual relief they both felt was contagious.

Stella said, "I must confess I wanted God to heal me. That is why I never sold everything. But these belongings were a burden for my daughter. She had to take care of all my bills, as well as the responsibilities she has with her own family." She continued, "The best part was that I gave these special things to my grandchildren while I am alive instead of in a will. The look on their faces was rewarding enough." She died two weeks later. Her work was finished. God gave her the ultimate healing!

Another lady told me in private she saw three-foot butterflies with indescribable colors. Whenever I share these stories with other patients, families, or at funerals, people often approach me later and quietly say,

"Let me tell you about my experience of heaven." They are often afraid to tell others lest they think they are crazy.

My mother-in-law shared her story of dying on the operating table in the 1950s. She said, "I went into heaven, and it was so lovely, so peaceful, and beautiful. It was so full of love. But I didn't dare share this back then, or they would have locked me up."

My mother-in-law died in 1996. God bless her soul. She always told me, "John, I'm not afraid to die; I've been there."

Jethro told me he was a heavy drinker and a brawler. He was a nasty drunk and loved to provoke fights. He was a skinny nasty redneck farmer who loved to fight. He told me he would sit at a bar and after getting drunk, he would pick a fight. He would intentionally make eye contact with another guy and say, "What? You want to kiss me?" Then he would beat up the guy!

He said, "Here I was drinking a case of beer every night after work while my mom was sick."

The Holy Spirit convicted him, and he repented of his sins and accepted Jesus as his Savior. He began reading his Bible and developed a deep, personal relationship with God. He became as gentle as anyone I have ever met. I did not know him when he was drinking and could hardly believe this man of God was at one time a nasty drunk. He shared his heavenly experience of what he called a *God dream.*

"I went into heaven in my dream. Everyone was so full of life and fun. I was walking down a road with a group of people, and all of us were laughing and having a great time. We were all full of love and joy. Then I woke up. I didn't know where I was for almost half an hour. My mom thought I had a stroke, but when I took that first sip of coffee, I came out of it and realized it was a dream, and I had been in heaven." That dream made him even more determined to live for the LORD.

After hearing many of these testimonies, I became jealous. I asked God to share heaven with me. Not that I wanted to die, but I wanted to experience what all these people were talking about. God answered my prayers with an astonishing dream one night. It was so real that it was beyond a dream; I was there. It was almost comparable to Paul going into the third heaven. I was in a country like Sweden and didn't speak their language. There were two other Americans with me, and because we didn't speak their language, they gave us the simple job of power washing a cathedral. (Now we know in heaven there will be no temple for the LORD will be the temple, but that morning I was talking to someone about power washing my house, so it slipped into the dream). As I was power washing the cathedral, an older distinguished-looking, white-haired gentleman walked by me. He wore an 18th century black overcoat and a white shirt buttoned to the top. Neither of us spoke. We nodded "Hello" with affectionate smiles as we passed. The love I had for this man and the love he had for me was unconditional. There was no pretentiousness or the emotional distance felt when you said hi to a stranger down here. Everyone loved one another. God was in everyone. All of a sudden, I heard these captivating voices. I did not see angels, but it was music I had never heard before. It was glorious! These angelic voices began to sing "The LORD'S Prayer" over the entire city. I began to weep with joy. I couldn't distinguish the tears from the power wash because I was drenched in water. I was overwhelmed!

Then the unthinkable happened; the alarm went off, and I woke up! I never felt so loved in all my life. The first thing I did was check my eyes to see if I had been crying in my sleep. There were no tears, and I wasn't soaked, but I was emotionally full. I laid in bed worshiping and talking to the LORD for I don't know how long, but it was beautiful! I felt the same way my mother-in-law did. "I'm no longer afraid to die." In fact, if God would have taken me right then, I would have gone without hesitation. I guess God is not done with me yet. He is not done with you either.

Someday it will be our time to go. The Apostle Paul had heavenly experiences. His faith was so strong about heaven that he said in Philippians 1:23 (NKJ), "For I am hard-pressed between the two, having a desire to depart and be with Christ, which is far better. Nevertheless, to remain in the flesh is more needful for you."

We long to be with God, which is better by far; however, God still needs you, Chaplain, to lead, pray, encourage, and fulfill every detail He has called you to do. He will call you home and say as he did to the faithful servant in Matthew 25:23, "Well done, good and faithful servant."

Before Dr. John Q. Kenzy died, I heard him preach one last time. He shared an experience as a little boy when his family was at a lake. His parents told him not to go in the water because he could not swim. He saw everyone else in the water safely standing and playing, but he didn't know there was a drop-off ledge.

He said, "I went into the water but not in the shallow part. I sank right down into the depths of the water. I was not afraid. I saw beautiful, angelic animals swimming in the water all around me. Suddenly, I felt a hand come up from underneath and catapulted me out of the water."

God had a plan for his life to be the president of YCIBI and to be an instrument in transforming broken lives. Satan tried to destroy the work God wanted to do in his life. He will try the same with you, but "If God is for us, who can be against us?" (Romans 8:31). If it is not your time to die, then nothing can stop the will of God for your life or the lives you will touch in the future. God still has many people for you to minister to through you. God spoke to Paul in Acts 18:10, and He speaks the same to us. "For I am with you, and no one is going to attack and harm you because I have many people in this city."

HELL EXPERIENCE

Not everyone had good experiences. I met a man who came into hospice with a lot of health conditions due to his rough lifestyle. He was raised in the church. His father was a Baptist minister. However, he did not follow in his father's footsteps. He got involved in a gang. I cannot say which one, but it is well-known throughout the United States and abroad.

Jerry told me, "I did every drug imaginable. I rose up in the ranks and became the Master of Arms. (The Master of Arms has to be tough because he keeps all the other gang members in line.) He began to tell me he kept having the same dream over and over again. He said, "I keep having this dream of a man hanging on a rope from a tree, but to my recollection, I don't remember ever hanging anyone. I never killed anyone, but I have dumped bodies in the river."

"I'm not a Catholic priest, so you don't have to confess to me." Jokingly I said, "Maybe we need to call the police about some of this stuff."

He said, "No. I'm forgiven. I just keep having these dreams." He told me the story of how he came back to the LORD.

"I was brought to the hospital about ten years ago with a heart attack. I died on the table. I went into hell, John. It was so hot there you didn't even want to move. When I moved it made it hard to breathe; it was stifling. I just stood there. I called out to God, and in His mercy, He brought me back to life. The doctors used the paddles and brought me back.

"After I settled into a hospital room, they asked me if I wanted anything. I said I wanted to talk to a chaplain. The chaplain who visited me was an ex-member of a rival gang. 'We shouldn't even be talking to each other,' I told him, and we both laughed. I told him what happened and that I wanted to rededicate myself to the LORD. 'I was raised in a Christian home, and I know the truth, but the lure of sex, money, and drugs pulled me away from God. I want to come back to God.' The chaplain led me to the LORD. That was ten years ago."

We never did figure out why he kept dreaming about seeing someone hanging on a tree. Perhaps PTSD (post traumatic stress disorder) from his violent lifestyle. Perhaps it is similar to the Apostle Paul remembering all the bad stuff he had done, yet he accepted God's forgiveness. There are some things we cannot undo. We are forgiven but the memories remain.

Hell is just as real as heaven. Chaplains and pastors need to preach the whole counsel of God, not just the pleasantries. There will be A Great White Throne judgment for the unbelievers, and the Judgment Seat of Christ for the believers. We will be judged for every word spoken and every act done. Fortunately, we who are saved will find mercy and innocence on that day, but for the unbeliever, only "blackest darkness is reserved for them" (II Peter 2:17).

I met Stephen a few weeks ago, who told me of his experience. "I went to heaven, and my family sat in judgment." They were going to judge him for everything he had ever done—both publicly and in secret. Then God said, "I'm not ready for you yet. But I tell you that everyone will have to give account on the day of judgment for every empty word they have spoken. For by your words, you will be acquitted, and by your words, you will be condemned" (Matthew 12:36-37).

I shared the gospel with Stephen and offered to pray, but he declined. I pray he did accept Christ before he died so that he stands before Christ with mercy rather than judgment.

"For all who call on the name of the LORD shall be saved" (Romans 10:13). And in Matthew 10:32-33, we are told "Whoever acknowledges me before others, I will acknowledge him before my Father in heaven. But whoever disowns me before others, I will disown before my Father in heaven."

What Sally, Jerry, Jethro, or even we have struggled with on this side of heaven will be no more when we enter into His presence and live with God for all eternity.

CHAPTER TEN

God's Provisions and God's Blessings

Teach those who are rich in this world not to be proud and not to trust in their money, which is so unreliable. Their trust should be in God, who richly gives us all we need for our enjoyment. Tell them to use their money to do good. They should be rich in good works and generous to those in need, always ready to share with others. By doing this, they will be storing up their treasure as a good foundation for the future so that they may experience true life.

1 Timothy 6:17-19 (NLT)

Those verses apply to the chaplain because we often struggle financially. As in any ministry, the chaplain is no exception. We live by faith and store up treasures in heaven, not here on earth. First, God will always supply your needs. Dr. John Q. Kenzy used to say, "If you take care of God's business, God will take care of your business." I learned to live by faith at YCIBI. God supplied every semester. He used those who gave through Alumni scholarships; others helped us at various times, and I worked hard in the summers. Ultimately, God is the One who provided. I remember one time we couldn't even afford milk. I was getting ready to eat cereal and noticed we were out of milk. That day my neighbor and dear friend Anthony Jones came over and said, "Hey John, we have an extra gallon of milk. Can you use it?" It was perfect timing!

God repeatedly provided, when I was in school and after. Whether big or small, He continues to care for us. One time we were blessed with a trip to Florida. Dr. John Q. Kenzy and his wife, Carol, gave us a week timeshare at a resort near Disney. A friend of ours who lived there was able to get all five of us into Disney World for free for a day.

I was praying about our finances, and the LORD put it into my heart to save $1,500 for the trip. *Wow! That's a lot to save on my salary,* I thought. By taking the dog for a walk, I found $35 on the side of the road. I put it into an envelope for the Disney fund. Two days later, it helped pay for the dog's rabies shot because we didn't have any money.

At church that Sunday, a good friend of mine, Tommy, came to me with an envelope in his hand. He said, "Me and Kara give this to someone different every year, and after prayer, my wife and I felt like God was telling us to give this to you."

I put it in my jacket, not thinking too much about it. Leaving it on the seat, I went to the altar to pray for people. After the church service, we got into the car, and I told my wife what happened, handing her the envelope as I began to drive. She opened it, and one-hundred-dollar bills began to empty out.

"Hold on! If it comes out to $1,500, I know exactly what it will be used for." She didn't know what God had spoken to me the night before. She counted it out on her lap; it came to $1,500. Talk about relief and a miracle. After recounting the bills, it turned out to be $1,600. So, I told Dorothy she could have the extra $100. (I'm such a good guy!) That was one of the best vacations we ever had. Someone gave us their timeshare, another gave us $1600, and still another blessed us with Disney Park tickets. Before we left, I had each of my children hold out their hands. I felt so blessed to give each one $100 each for spending money. What a wonderful God we serve!

As I reflect upon our lives, I think of all the people who blessed us so much with fellowship dinners, church services, and loving friendships. When our children were little, and we survived on meager means, we often stayed with family and friends. When we traveled to a conference and seminars, Christian friends let us stay with them with all five of us crammed into their guestrooms. The quarters were cramped but the fellowship was sweet. Thankfully the Assemblies of God conferences pay for all chaplains and their families to stay at a nice hotel during the conference. What a treat that always is!

My friend Anthony Jones used to say, "I may not know whose hand provided, but I know whose heart did." So many people blessed us along the way. My sister Dee and her husband Pete were so kind to us. They gave us a free week at their condo at the beach every year. She would say, "John, we weren't able to rent the condo out for this week. Do you want it?" It was always right in mid-summer. Dorothy and I knew they could have rented it, but they saved it just for us.

My brother-in-law Bryan blessed us with vacation trips to Alaska and cruises to the Bahamas, while other friends and family blessed us with expenses to Florida, Disney, and so many other places. We didn't have the resources, but God blessed us with favor from loved ones. God used their compassion to bless us abundantly.

I am glad for the journey God has on our lives as chaplains. Even when it hurts, even when it doesn't make sense, God is leading us. Through our mistakes, as well as our victories, God was, is, and always will be faithful to you.

I have received more than a hundred-fold in this life now, and I look forward to receiving eternal life when I die. God has blessed us with Christian brothers and sisters all over the country and world. God will take care of your needs, too. He touches the hearts of those who give cheerfully with a sacrificial heart. Please always thank people for giving to you. Some ministers we met expected that just because they were in the ministry, they were deserving of others and had an entitlement to gifts.

Keep in mind that other people owe you nothing! We are never deserving. God knows about our needs, and He will take care of them through others. They give because they love God and are ultimately giving to Him. When they see your walk with God, they want to bless you in the process. God knows your needs and desires and will abundantly bless you.

We once attended a church who never asked for money or tithes. Their philosophy of giving was, "God knows the needs of this church, and He will speak to their hearts to give." It was a thriving church, too. We must be generous givers. Brother Correa, Vice president of YCIBI, would say, "You can never out-give God." It was at YCIBI that we learned about faith pledges.

A faith pledge is being open to God with a financial amount to give even if you don't have it yet. A missionary came to the school and preached. I prayed about it, and God put $200 on my heart to give. I told my wife about it, and she wasn't too happy. We owed three months' back rent and had credit card debt. The next morning, she came to chapel and sat next to me with a grin on her face. A check came in the mail that morning, and she just had to show me! My eyes popped as I opened the check and saw $1000! It took care of three months' rent, our credit card for that month, with $20 left to celebrate at the local steakhouse chain!

Now in my older years, I can look back at how faithful God has been through both the lean years and years of plenty. I remember sitting in my backyard in Fleetwood, PA, thanking God for all that He had done in my life and the marvelous work over the years.

As I looked at the house God blessed us with, the trampoline in the backyard, and the kids' toys on the ground, my heart became so full of gratitude for all that He has provided. A scripture came to mind: Psalm 16:6 which says, "LORD, you alone are my portion and my cup. You make my lot secure. The boundary lines have fallen for me in pleasant places; surely, I have a delightful inheritance." Our pleasant places to live are not just the physical but the emotional cup that overflows from within for just how God has cared for us.

God is our inheritance. "The priests, the Levites, and all the tribe of Levi, shall have no part nor inheritance with Israel: they shall eat the offerings of the LORD made by fire, and his inheritance. Therefore, shall they have no inheritance among their brethren; *the LORD is their inheritance,* as he hath said unto them" (Deuteronomy 18:1-2, KJV).

SACRIFICIAL MINISTRY

Sometimes, you will be treated unfairly in the ministry. Jesus responded by saying, "Father, forgive them for they know not what they do." As a chaplain, minister, or a pastor, people will not appreciate nor understand your sacrifices. I don't think the average church-goer fully understands nor appreciates the sacrifices you and your family make. You may be the most educated in your church but the least paid. You may have to shop at Goodwill while others in your church shop at high-end retail stores. Your kids wear second-hand clothes on Easter Sunday, while other kids wear brand new clothes. You drive a beat-up old jalopy while the blue-collar worker drives up in a new pick-up truck, and the list goes on.

You must guard against getting jealous or bitter. If you are where God wants you, and you are doing His will, then He will provide. After all, you are *working for the LORD not man*. Your fulfillment should come from the joy of the LORD, not possessions in this world. Your joy comes from watching lives restored, marriages healed, and families reconciled.

Long-lasting friendships are developed over the years with congregants and Christian brothers and sisters met along the way. The blessings are endless. We may not be priests and Levites, but the principle is still the same. God is our inheritance. The same God Who created the world and all that is in it is the same God who will "provide for all our needs according to His riches and glory." In reflection, I must admit — it's all been worth it! There is no greater boss to work for than our Heavenly Father.

A funeral director once said, "I never worked a day of my life since I bought my own funeral home. I work every day and put in sixty hours a week sometimes, but I love what I do." I fully appreciate what he said. There are days it doesn't feel like work, but then there are most days when it does, and it should. Otherwise, God would not have promised rest from our labors. The ministry is hard, but rewarding!

Called by God to be a chaplain, I love what I do. I am good at it, I am educated in it, and I am anointed to do the work. It is what I was made to do. Therefore, to keep our priorities in order as chaplains and pastors, we must stay grateful, worship the LORD every day, and maintain a joyful heart. Luke 4:18 says, "For the Spirit of the LORD is on me because He has anointed me to proclaim good news to the poor. He has sent me to proclaim freedom for the prisoners and recovery of sight for the blind, to set the captives free." Our inheritance is not about money, power, or prestige; it is about sharing the Good News with the lost and those who feel hopeless. We cannot afford to lose sight of our calling. If we apply these principles, we will have a successful, long, and fulfilling ministry.

God will exceed your expectations in every area of your life. He took you from the smelting furnace of your past without God and brought you into a land flowing with milk and honey. He will take heartbreaks and turn them into blessings. When you think you're going in one direction and He leads in another way, it is always for a higher purpose of blessing. Even in the desert, flowers bloom. Wherever He leads—follow. He is increasing your boundaries and expanding your horizons with unexpected desires when you delight yourselves in Him.

Delight in God. Keep your priority about the kingdom and not this world. Ask for wisdom and understanding to be a better chaplain. Keep your eyes on Him and pray daily for the anointing to do this awesome work He has called us to do. He will more than fill your expectations. He will bless you in ways you never imagined. Let the joy of the LORD be your strength and find yourselves in pleasant places.

That day when I sat in my backyard was eye-opening for me. I realized just how blessed I truly am. I am positive that everyone reading this has experienced that feeling at one time or another.

"A cheerful heart has a continual feast" (Proverbs 15:15). Keep feasting; keep rejoicing; and keep a thankful heart because ultimately, it is not the blessings that make us happy. It is having a relationship with our Father that gives us joy.

This world is not our home. Enjoy this life because it goes by fast. Never forget that our primary goal is heaven—our final destination.

No matter where we find ourselves in ministry, God promises to care for you. "I have never seen the righteous forsaken or their children begging for bread" (Psalm 37:25). "Give me my daily bread; don't let me be so rich that I forget you and so poor I must steal and be dishonored but give me my daily bread" (Proverbs 30:8).

Accept your lot in life where God has chosen to place you. Ecclesiastes 6:10 says, "Everything has already been decided. It was known a long time ago what each person would be, so there is no use arguing about your destiny."

Ecclesiastes 6:9 says, "Enjoy what you have rather than desiring what you don't have. Dreaming about nice things is meaningless, like chasing after the wind."

Billy Graham wanted to give a young pastor everything he needed: a house, car, clothing, etc. But God intervened and told him no. God related that the young pastor would never learn to trust Him for all of his needs if he was given everything at once. You, young chaplain, will have to learn to rely on God. You will have to depend upon Him in times of great stress and discouragement. If someone were to supply all your needs, you would never learn to trust in God and see how He generously cares for you.

He loves you and your family and promises to care for all your needs.

CHAPTER ELEVEN

The Chaplain's Unique Temptations

No temptation has overtaken you except what is common to
mankind. And God is faithful; he will not let you be tempted
beyond what you can bear. But when you are tempted, he
will also provide a way out so that you can endure it.

1 Corinthians 10:13

Proverbs 10:6 says, "The godly are showered with blessings." The keyword in this verse is *godly*. God will not bless an unrighteous walk. You will miss blessings and opportunities when living with hidden sin. Sin causes fear and insecurity, whereas holiness creates boldness and power. Every chaplain will be faced with temptations. The good news is found in 1 Corinthians 10:13, "No temptation has overtaken you except such as is common to man, but God is faithful, who will not suffer you to be tempted above that ye are able, but with the temptation also make a way to escape, that ye may be able to bear it." Temptations are common to all of us, but because of our calling, we have specific temptations unique only to us.

Healthcare chaplains have their unique temptations. As a hospice or hospital chaplain, nurses can flirt or make overt passes at you. Dr. Kenzy's wise words come to mind. "It is not you they want; it is God in you they admire. They want that holiness for themselves; the only way they think they can have it is to have intimacy with you. When given in to this temptation, they despise you afterward for being godless." "A prudent man sees danger and takes refuge, but the simple keep going and suffer for it" (Proverbs 22:3).

I had an experience with a patient's daughter who came to the door in a robe with half her chest hanging out. I said, "Hi, where's your mother so I can talk to her, sing some hymns, and pray with her." I made it clear I was not there for her intentions. The next time I went out, she was appropriately dressed. I had another chaplain friend who said the same thing. A woman kept coming over to him dressed seductively, but he made it clear he was not there for that purpose, and she finally left him alone. We work in the field and are often alone. Keep your focus on God and see through Satan's schemes for what they are!

Rodeo and racetrack chaplains are in an environment of high energy, high excitement, and often euphoric situations. The environment can be seductive, and the temptation to join in can be enticing. The champagne flows freely and hormones rage. There is gambling, drinking, drugs, and sex all around. We hear cursing and swearing. Environments can be hostile, volatile, and violent. It can get very confusing. If you find yourself involved in any of these temptations or sins and they have taken hold of you, it is past time to get help. It's time to get out! Be in a ministry that uplifts you and challenges you spiritually—not one that drags you down. Our best intentions to help those we minister to can be the very ones that cause our downfall. In Galatians 6:1, we read, "Brothers and sisters, if someone is caught in a sin, you who live by the Spirit should restore the person gently. But watch yourselves, or you also may be tempted."

Chaplains work around a great deal of stress and trauma. After long, exhausting days, it is hard to quiet our soul. The adrenalin needs to be counteracted, so you may find yourself tempted with a drink or drugs. We say to ourselves, "I need this just one time," but then it becomes a habit, and now you rely on the drug to calm you down rather than God's presence. The temptation to self-medicate applies to every chaplain involved in intense critical care ministry. I believe this is rare, but I can see how it can happen.

Put up safeguards and accountability. As pastors, chaplains, missionaries, counselors, and anyone in ministry, one has to know when to stay and when it is time to leave. I had to leave the chaplaincy for a while only to come back more determined and stronger than ever. It is imperative, however, that wherever or whatever ministry God is calling us to that we surround ourselves with people who will bring out the best in us.

BECOMING COMPLACENT

Isaiah wrote this to the Jews leaving Babylon. After seventy years of captivity, some had gotten comfortable in Babylon. Some rose to positions of power and prominence and did not want to give up their positions of authority to start all over again in Jerusalem. Most people by this time were born and raised in Babylon. They buried family members there and felt that it was their home (Albert Barnes notes).

There are times we find ourselves outside of God's will, either intentionally or unintentionally. Instead of influencing those around us, we are influenced by them and are dragged down spiritually and have become comfortable without realizing how detrimental it has become. Some of those influencers may even be other chaplains.

I have seen too many chaplains fall into the allures of this world. They compromised their affections and stopped taking every thought captive. They began running wild in their minds with, *What if? I would be better off if.... I would be happier if....* And they walked away from ministry. They lost honor in the community; their reputation was tarnished, their credentials were taken, and Satan left them broken. This is the penalty of a prideful heart.

The world is always there, ready to embrace you, and then it rips you to shreds. That is just like the devil tempting us with the greener grass, but when we get there, it is artificial turf. It's not real, not comfortable, and leaves us wanting what we had in the first place. We end up crucifying the Son of God all over again by our sins. A once-faithful witness spirals down to destruction with the decay of the soul.

When Chaplains fall, it is because they kept their sin hidden until it took over and destroyed them. It is never worth losing the intimacy with the LORD over temporary sin. I have witnessed some of the godliest men and women walk away from God and lose it all. They stumbled over lies the devil put in their minds—that they would be happier and more fulfilled over the *what if's*. It's a pitiful sight to see them later absolutely in the flesh with no spiritual maturity where once there was a deep passion and love for God. Now there's cursing, anger, and hostility. The chaplain has not only damaged himself and his family, but the collateral damage affects the church and community.

"Take captive of every thought..." II Corinthians 10:5. When you have thoughts of, *If only...* or *I should have...* or *I would be happier if....* *If only I would have stayed in Babylon....* God delivered us from there and is moving us forward. Don't look back like Lot's wife and turn into a pillar of salt. Take those thoughts captive. Capture those rogue thoughts and put them in perspective. Reality is so much better than regret. Engage in reality and the blessings of all the gifts that God has given you. A thankful, grateful heart will win and replace a miserable, self-loathing attitude every time. To combat this is to be appreciative and thankful.

Paul sums up all truth in Philippians 4:8. "Finally, brothers, whatever is true, whatever is noble, whatever is right, whatever is pure, whatever is lovely, whatever is admirable — if anything is excellent or praiseworthy — think about such things." The Bible scholar must measure the world's truths by these words. Is it true? If it is not true then it does not conform to the gospel that brings glory to God. Is it noble, right, pure, lovely etc.? Then it is negative and brings destruction. We can use these measures in our personal lives when the enemy beats us up with condemnation, guilt, and shame. Is it true? Is it pure? Is it lovely? If not, they are negative voices that need to be replaced by how God truly sees us. In order to see clearly, we have to take the plank out of our own eyes to see clearly, to see with purity, to see truthfully. If we are healthy emotionally and spiritually, we can help patients know the truth with confidence.

When you begin to feel weighed down by all the suffering in this world, it burdens you. By working with the victims and offenders, you hear unspeakable stories. These thoughts pile upon your mind until you feel as if you are drowning in a sea of despair. Or when we have been hurt one too many times, we can comfort ourselves with thoughts in unhealthy ways.

Trials are meant to produce trust in God. God told the Israelites to praise and worship with trumpets before, during, and after battles (Numbers 10:8-10). When we are going through battles, it is imperative we look at the obstacle before us and begin to praise in faith that God will see you through.

Caleb said in Joshua 14 that he was eighty-five years-old and just as strong as "I was in my youth." He faced the giant Anakites and said, "But the LORD is helping me, I will drive them out." The key emphasis is God with him. We cannot face temptations alone; we need God and others by our side. It is important to have accountability partners.

NEED FOR ACCOUNTABILITY PARTNERS

Everyone needs accountability, whether serving in the ministry or not. Accountability partners help and encourage. Some churches I have attended did not have a men's group to provide that accountability, so I had to find an accountability partner elsewhere. God always raised up a man I could trust to share my struggles. Sharing our personal battles with others keeps us from handling them alone. Sharing sheds light on trials and temptations and brings healing. Not only do we have a confidante and friend, but there's now a prayer partner to pray for and with us when hurting, discouraged, or perplexed.

I John 1:9 (NIV) states, "If we confess our sins, He is faithful and just to forgive us our sins and purify us from all unrighteousness." God forgives us, but we still need healing. James 5:16 continues, "Therefore confess your sins to each other and pray for each other so that you may be healed." Healing comes when we have an accountability partner who we can trust with our innermost selves.

Over the years, my accountability partners have been there for me in my darkest days. Their prayers were felt, and my spirit was strengthened by their counsel. Since chaplains are often "Lone Rangers," we are more vulnerable than other ministers. The lion often attacks the weakest. The tribe isolates its prey and goes in for the kill. When we have a friend to share it with, we don't go into battle alone. We have a spiritual warrior by our side. When we pray, we cease being prey.

One of my first accountability partners was Chris. He had been hired as a chaplain, against my wishes. My boss hired him anyway. During the interview, I thought he was lazy and did not make a good impression on me. After I got to know him, I realized he was just a laid-back kind of guy. I'm glad I was wrong. Chris turned out to be one of my closest friends. We eventually built a close relationship. He trusted me and began to share his struggles, which made me feel comfortable in sharing mine. Chris was down-to-earth, non-judgmental, and kind.

My family had been in a car accident, and I was traumatized for weeks. Finally, I shared with Chris that I felt the accident was my fault. "If only I had not turned a certain way." "If I had done this instead of that, I wouldn't have caused such pain in my family's lives." On and on, I blamed myself. Chris sat there listening to me with compassion. When I finished, he just grabbed my hands and said, "Let's pray." This man's prayer was filled with power and empathy. God lifted a huge weight of grief and guilt off of me. The Holy Spirit fell on us, and I felt better.

Chris became a dear friend. He came to my children's birthday parties, and I bought cosmetics from his daughter. We supported one another's kids. Chris showed me what a true friend and a trusted accountability partner was. We worked together for five years, and I am proud to have known him. When Chris died from a heart attack, I lost a great chaplain and friend.

We need close friends in ministry with whom we can share life with. Life is filled with joys and sorrows, ups and downs, defeats and victories, and it is empowering and encouraging to have a friend. I had prayed for another friend to help me be accountable and looked for someone to replace Chris, but a friend like Chris could not be replaced. God raised up another friend, and although he wasn't the same as Chris, he was just as good—just different. God answered my prayer, and I met Jay.

Jay was a greeter at church and made us feel welcome as we had just moved to the area. We hit it off right away. We began to walk together and share our experiences. It was almost a year before I opened up to him about some personal struggles. I trusted this man and allowed myself to become vulnerable. It takes time to build trust—especially with men. We are not the touchy-feely type. It often takes a lot for a guy to be open about our feelings. When I shared with Jay, he opened up and shared some of his struggles.

I have always asked God to place a close friend in my life so I can have a trustworthy person to talk to. He has always been and always will be faithful to do so. He knows we need others for encouragement and to remain effective and moving forward. If you need a friend in your life to share struggles with, then pray and ask God to bring into your life the right person who is a good fit for both of you. I never went looking for one; I simply asked God, and He answered my prayers. He will do the same for you. He knows we need one another. Moses had Aaron, Paul had Silas, and God has a friend for you, too!

SMALL GROUP MINISTRY

Not only do we need accountability partners, but we need other men in our lives as well. Jay and I started a small group for men. We all vary in age, occupation, and race, but we are all brothers in Christ. We meet every Thursday night at a well-known fast-food restaurant. Jay reads a scripture verse; then each of us share how the verse applies to our lives. Afterward, we pray with each other. There is a beautiful presence of God with a heavy anointing. When we open our eyes after prayer, we all comment, "Wow, that felt good. I needed that!"

I am the only one in full-time ministry, but these men are serious about their walk with God. God spoke to us about being *transparent* with each other. Some of our discussions might make a sailor blush, but we are honest to admit our personal battles.

We each arrive with problems; we find solutions together, and we leave with burdens lifted! These are the types of men with whom you surround yourself. When there's a band of brothers supporting us, we fight to win. We don't let each other down. We lift one another up and give God the glory in our victories together.

TRIALS ARE TEMPORARY

Trials don't last forever; the blessing is just around the corner if we don't give up. God is not pleased when we lack faith. Hebrews 11:6 says, "But without faith it is impossible to please him; for he that cometh to God must believe that he is, and that he is a rewarder of them that diligently seek him." Diligently seek him before despair, complaining, and rebellion sets in. God rebuked the Israelites for their lack of faith when they grumbled in the desert. In Numbers 14:11, we read, "How long will these people treat me with contempt? How long will they refuse to believe in me, in spite of all the miraculous signs I have performed among them." As God provided and cared for us in the past, He will continue to do so no matter what we are facing. Trials build faith and spiritual muscles.

Arnold Schwarzenegger didn't get all those muscles by eating twinkies and sitting on his recliner watching cartoons! He went to the gym daily. His lifestyle consisted of five to six feedings a day. He ate 5000 calories per day compared to most normal people eating between 1500 and 1800 calories per day. On day one, he worked on his chest and back muscles. Day two, he worked on his shoulders and arms. Day three, he worked on his legs and lower back. Day four, he worked on his chest and back. Day five, he worked on his shoulders and arms again. Day six, he worked on his legs and lower back. Finally, on day seven, he rested from his labors. That meant dedication, commitment, and hard work to accomplish and win the title of Mr. Olympia seven times (Arnold Schwarznegger Volume Workout Routines, by Steve Shaw).

There are times we need to work on some areas more than others to be spiritually fit. Focus on those areas that need special attention and extra work. Everyone has weaknesses, so those areas need special attention. When an area was conquered by the Romans, they set up a garrison. A garrison was a small group of well-trained soldiers who kept the city orderly. We need to set up a spiritual garrison in certain areas of weakness. We don't need the whole army, just a small force to keep it under control. That could be extra prayer and fasting in that area, an accountability partner, or any other thing you need to do to maintain order in that conquered land.

The first few minutes of the day determine the course of our day. Waking up with a desire to talk to the LORD the first thing sets the tone. Choosing those first few minutes determines our attitude and goals and objectives. God called us chaplains for a purpose: to serve Him wholeheartedly and to point others to Christ. We are called to win, not lose. We are called to conquer our spiritual land before we can conquer the kingdom of darkness. We are called to come alongside others and help them out of the pit because we remember what it was like ourselves.

We are in life's battle to win, not lose. We win by holding onto our faith, knowing that God has my back and is with me in my situation.

We win when we step out in faith and share the gospel. We win when we take bold steps to come out of our comfort zones and receive new ministry ideas from the Holy Spirit. We win when we refuse to give up even when we are tired. We win on that day God gives us the crown of life. On that day, we are rewarded when God shows us all the people we touched in our ministries over a lifetime of service.

PASTORAL ARROGANCE

The LORD gave me an allegorical story about pride. There was a population of polar bears on the preservation (salvation). Everything was fine. There was plenty of food, water, family, friendship, and community. One polar bear wanted more and walked away from all the others onto a large patch of ice. All the other bears warned him to jump off and swim back to them where it was safe, but he refused to listen. He wanted more out of what the preservation had. He thought it was better somewhere else. He wasn't grateful or satisfied living on the preservation. He wanted to go his own way and do things on his own with no help from anyone else. He said to himself, *I'll show them...they are all wrong, and I am the only one who is right.*

As time went on, he found himself farther away until he could not see the preservation anymore. The nights were long and lonely, and there was no food on the patch of ice, which grew smaller and smaller by the day. He began to question his decision, but in his pride, he refused to admit he was wrong. The small patch of ice finally disappeared, leaving him in the icy water. Still, he refused to admit he was wrong, and he died a cold, broken, and pitiful death. It was a sad ending to a promising start.

When we refuse to repent, pride replaces humility, anger replaces grace, and finally, bitterness fills the vacant hole where love once lived.

Chaplains must be on guard against spiritual pride and arrogance. We are a big fish in a small fishbowl, and power can go rushing to our heads. We can forget that we are called to serve. We must continually give ourselves completely to Christ and not hold anything back.

Jonah, too, had self-righteous spiritual pride with hate in his heart towards the Ninevites. He wanted God's vengeance on these people, not

God's mercy. God had called Jonah to go to Nineveh and tell them He would destroy the city in forty days if they did not repent. The Ninevites were bitter enemies of Israel, and Jonah wanted them punished. He knew God would forgive them if they repented, and he did not want that to happen, so he ran from his responsibility. He got into a boat and sailed in the opposite direction.

There was a storm out at sea and being typical superstitious sailors, they cast lots to find out the guilty party. Jonah told them to throw him overboard; so they did. A giant fish swallowed him alive. For three days, he sat in the belly of this giant fish. Seaweed and whatever other gross things wrapped around his head. He felt like he was in Sheol (the place of the dead). Jonah cried out to God with sincere repentance. He finally surrendered to God, and the fish threw him up on the beaches of Nineveh. It's crazy what God has to do to some of us to make us do what we don't want to do.

Imagine sitting on the beach with your family. You're sitting under your umbrella with some cool tunes and your favorite beverage. The kids are boogie boarding and everyone is relaxed and having a good time. Out of nowhere, a giant fish beaches itself and vomits a man out. I don't care who you are, you are going to want to hear this man's story! God certainly got their attention. The word spread in Nineveh, and everyone repented from the least to the greatest. The king made everyone fast and wear sackcloth showing an outward sign of an inward repentance. God saw their sorrow and relented.

Jonah's heart still wasn't right. He got mad that God forgave them. But God tried to give Jonah compassion for them by saying, "These people don't even know their right hand from their left." Jonah didn't care. He sulked in the heat of the sun, watching from a distance as people repented. God comforted Jonah by growing a plant to cover Jonah's head from the sun. But Jonah's bitterness caused a worm to eat the plant. Jonah complained about that, too, and wanted to die because of all his misery.

The term worm here in Hebrew represents bitterness or poison. Jonah had deep-seated poison in his heart, and the very shade meant to bring him comfort was destroyed by his unforgiveness. God used the worm as a sign to Jonah of the worm of poison growing inside of him. Blessings and comfort are often lost because of a bitter spirit. Bitterness steals our blessings. It robs us of comfort. We can go no further until bitterness is dealt with. Jonah's story ends there.

There is a huge difference between pastoral authority and pastoral arrogance. Pastoral authority seeks to restore people with grace, humility, and love. On the other hand, pastoral arrogance seeks to bitterly judge others in anger. It seeks its own desire and not God's. It is caused by an unresolved issue with its root cause in unforgiveness and anger. Pastoral arrogance is abusive and authoritative. Power can go to anyone's head. God's ministers must deal with it quickly before we alienate people and turn them away from God. We are God's representatives to preach in love. If we don't, God will humble us one way or another.

Look to Jesus' example for pastoral leadership. He was always able to keep things in perspective. People honored him, but it never went to His head. In fact, Mary poured perfume on him as an act of honor preparing for His burial. Jesus accepted it graciously. He commended the woman when everyone else blamed her for the waste. On Palm Sunday, Jesus was worshiped as they laid palms at His feet and blessed His name. He remained humble.

People will want to honor you, and that is okay. Some may take it a step further and begin to elevate you to positions of power. If they tried to do that to Jesus, they can do the same to us. We have to come back to reality and remember that the only good in us is because of what Jesus has done. Without Him, our righteousness is as filthy rags.

Chaplains must stop imposed prestige upon them. When a Roman commander won battles, he was honored in a parade. Those he conquered were also in the parade, but as slaves. But the one thing that kept his head from becoming egotistical was his servant whispering repeatedly in his ear, "Thou art mortal." In other words, don't get too conceited; it can all be taken away from you just as quickly as you gained it; and you can be the slave in the parade instead of the honored guest.

Chaplains must give God the glory and take none for themselves!

REDEMPTION AND RECONCILIATION:
A CHAPLAIN'S FALL FROM GRACE AND HIS VALIANT RETURN
This is the obituary of a restored man of God named Evangelist Bob
Harrington (*Baptist Standard*—July 6, 2017).

> NEW ORLEANS (BP)—Famed New Orleans evangelist Bob
> Harrington, known by many as "the Chaplain of Bourbon Street,"
> died of kidney failure July 4 in Stigler, Oklahoma, where he had
> lived the last seven years with family. He was 89.
> Harrington became a well-known evangelist during the 1960s
> and 1970s following his conversion to Christianity at age 30 in his
> hometown of Sweet Water, Alabama. He was a popular guest on
> national television shows, including *Phil Donahue, Merv Griffin*,
> and *The Tonight Show* due to his one-liners and unconventional
> religious wit. In the 1970s, Harrington met atheist Madalyn
> Murray O'Hair, and the unlikely duo toured thirty-eight cities
> debating the existence of God.
> "Yes, many may say Madalyn knows the Scriptures better than
> I do, but I know the Author," he said.
>
> **Missionary to 'the Nearest Pocket of Sin'**
> Harrington's eight-day crusades, first held in tents and later high
> school stadiums and convention centers, produced thousands of
> converts. In 1960, after only a few years of preaching throughout
> the South on flatbed trailers and in tents, Harrington moved to
> New Orleans Baptist Theological Seminary with his wife Joyce
> and daughters, Rhonda and Mitzi.
> During his time in seminary, Harrington served as assistant pastor of
> First Baptist Church of New Orleans with J.D. Grey, and continued
> his ministry as an itinerant evangelist. In a seminary chapel service,
> President Leo Edleman said, "Wherever there is a pocket of sin, there
> is a mission field, and the nearest Christian to it is a missionary.
> "The nearest pocket of sin was Bourbon Street," said Harrington,
> who immediately began a street ministry armed with a micro-
> phone and a Bible.

Preaching in Bars and Strip Clubs

Several months later, deacons at First Baptist Church in New Orleans loaned him enough money for a few months' rent to open a chapel on Bourbon Street in the heart of the French Quarter. Harrington began witnessing and preaching in the bars and strip clubs of Bourbon Street. In 1962, Mayor Victor Schiro proclaimed him "The Chaplain of Bourbon Street."

Harrington's street ministry message was bold and simple: "God loves you just as you are. He knows you are a sinner and wants to save you. Don't figure it out. Faith it out!"

In 1968, he held a revival at Castle Hills First Baptist Church in San Antonio. During the revival, the owners of a burlesque club attended an evening service and became Christians. Guy and Evelyn Linton immediately closed the club and posted a sign: "Closed forever. See you in church."

National Fame Followed

Doubleday Printing published his story, *The Chaplain of Bourbon Street*, written by Harrington with Walter Wagner in 1969. Harrington went on to publish seven more books and released more than thirty record albums. The sermon album *Laughter, Truth, and Music* was released in 1965, and it became a gold album with more than $1 million in sales worldwide. Later, Harrington earned a second gold album for *The Chaplain of Bourbon Street*, a recording of his first television show. His legacy includes invigorating the Christian community with his signature slogan, "It's fun being saved."

Derailed by Personal Issues

But in time, personal issues led to Harrington's departure from ministry for a time. The "devil threw me a pass, and I caught it and ran for defeat," he said regarding his years out of the ministry.

In the 2000 November issue of *SBC LIFE*, Harrington talked about his past struggles in the article entitled, "Chastened Chaplain: A forthright account of failure and renewal." In the article, he referred to the "pass" Satan threw the evangelist during the height of his success as "pride, arrogance, self-centeredness, and stubbornness."

His first marriage ended, along with his ministry on Bourbon Street in 1977. He married again and moved to Florida but later divorced. During the 1980s and 1990s, Harrington was a popular motivational speaker, primarily with car dealerships and real estate companies. One evening in 1995 in his hotel room, he was robbed and nearly beaten to death.

Harrington had said at that time, "The phone rang, and it was Rex Humbard, my old friend (long-time pastor of the Cathedral of Tomorrow in Akron, Ohio, where Harrington had preached many times). He said it was time for me to come back to the Lord, and I did."

After divorce and bankruptcy, Harrington recalled being at the bottom, which he said, "Is right where God can use you!" Harrington began a restoration period and moved back to New Orleans. In 1998, he married Rebecca Harris Birdwell and moved to Mansfield, where he continued preaching. His wife died of a heart attack in 2010. That same year he moved to be near his younger daughter, Mitzi Woodson, and her husband, Steve, in Stigler, Oklahoma, where he regularly attended First Baptist Church in Stigler.

Harrington said many times, "I want my tombstone to read: 'Born the first time — September 2, 1927, in Cox Heath, Alabama. Born again — April 15, 1958. Died — He didn't. Transferred to Heaven.'"

Harrington is survived by two daughters: Rhonda Harrington Kelley (Chuck) of New Orleans and Mitzi Harrington Ramsey Woodson (Steve) of Stigler, Oklahoma; four grandsons; and two great-grandchildren. He was preceded in death by his wife, Rebecca Harris Harrington; one brother, Jerry Hill Harrington of Thomasville, Alabama, and one son, Robert Grey Harrington.

Though Chaplain Bob Harrington made mistakes, God's hand was upon him the whole time. He finally surrendered and once again was restored to pulpit ministry. He ended his life as a fully committed man of God. In an article, his daughter said he had gotten dementia and never remembered being backslidden. She said it was like God took all the bad memories away in forgiveness. God forgives!

We run the race. Along the way, we make huge blunders or small ones. As long as we cross the finish line with full forgiveness and a heart at peace with God, then we finish well. People may give up on us, but God never does. We may not have always run well, but God never quits on us.

It is unfortunate when a minister falls. We all feel the shock and pain, but there is still hope. I am so glad the Assemblies of God does not give up on its ministers. They recognize that sometimes pastors make mistakes. If the person recognizes his/her sin and is repentant, there's a redemptive process for morale failure in place for reconciliation and restoration.

As I read the Bible and look at the people God used, it amazes me how he uses imperfect people to accomplish His will. The twelve patriarchs of Israel were no saints, yet God used them to establish the twelve tribes of Israel. God even redeemed Aaron, Moses's brother, from idolatry.

When Moses went up to the mountain and spent forty days alone with God, the Israelites fell into idol worship. Even Aaron went astray as he helped the people make a golden calf. The people said, "This is the god who led us out of Egypt." Then Moses came down and rebuked the community. He crushed the golden calf into dust, sprinkled it in the water, and made them drink it (Exodus 32:21-24).

Yet, later in Leviticus, God chooses Aaron to be the high priest of Israel. They made beautifully-adorned priestly garments for him and placed a turban on his head saying, "Holy unto the LORD."

"Then Moses and Aaron went into the Tabernacle, and when they came back out, they blessed the people again, and the glory of the LORD appeared to the whole community. Fire blazed forth from the LORD'S presence, consuming the burnt offering and the fat on the altar. When the people saw this, they shouted with joy and fell face down on the ground" (Leviticus 9:23-24).

If God can forgive, redeem, and restore a man like Aaron, who created an idol and worshiped it, then God can redeem and restore anyone. If you are reading these words and have fallen into sin, go to your elders, confess your sin, and get back on the road to redemption. God can and will restore you. He will again use you and give you hope and a future. All is not lost. Take a step back from ministry, and get your house in order. As I Peter 5:6 (KJV) says, "Humble yourselves therefore under the mighty hand of God, so that He may exalt you in due time." Eventually, you will be able to bless God's people and experience the glory of God in your ministry once again. There is restoration.

CHAPTER TWELVE

A Chaplain's Compassion

*But love your enemies, do good to them, and lend to them
without expecting to get anything back. Then your reward
will be great, and you will be children of the Most High,
because he is kind to the ungrateful and wicked.*

Luke 6:35 (NIV)

Jesus said, "We are in the world but not of the world." You may walk
into homes where the smell of marijuana is strong, the drug paraphernalia and booze are in plain sight, but you go into that home
with a heart of love and compassion. You are there to be a light in this
dark place and pour out love when you know there is not much there.

Imagine if we would love the way Jesus loves. Imagine ministering
to the sick, the dying, the destitute and to those who cannot give back.
Love with the same attitude of Christ. The book called *The Risen* has
this message: When Peter was asked why he followed Jesus, he said, "I
saw Him hug a leper. The leper said he hadn't been hugged in a long
time....Jesus then kissed his hands. As the man walked away, he became
healed....That is why I follow Jesus" (*The Risen* Pg 271, 272. By Angela
Hunt. Bethany House Publishing, MN 2015)

We are to go after all people. We are to help them in their spiritual
poverty and fill them with the joy of the LORD. That is the Great
Commission. Too often, we don't want to be bothered by those kinds
of people because they take too much effort and time. They are the very
ones Jesus loves. He turns a Saul into a Paul and the sons of thunder
(James and John) into compassionate and loving men of God.

Reverend Curtis Dias, spends most of his time in court because he
ministers in the inner city of Massachusetts. What a testimony of hard

work and perseverance. He is changing his city one person at a time. I have ministered to bikers, convicts, drug addicts, alcoholics, and the like. We are called to love the unlovable and give grace to everyone because it is "God's kindness that leads one to repentance." When we show love to the homeless or to a tough cowboy with a bad reputation or to a race-car driver who has been divorced fifty times, their hearts melt. They drop their guard and allow us into their hurt and pain. Just maybe for the first time ever, they can express their deepest feelings because they feel safe and allow themselves to be vulnerable. That is what Jesus did. He loved the sinners. He ate with tax collectors and violent mercenaries like Judas the Zealot. When everyone else forsakes the lost and gives up on them, chaplains are there for them. They may not become a Christian, and you may not even share Christ verbally with them, but you planted that seed of compassion, and they will remember you when everyone else quits on them.

During my college days at Central Bible College, I worked at Maranatha Nursing Home where I supervised Larry, a fellow student. On Sundays, this man worked with children in his local church. He was caught sexually abusing a child in one of the local churches. The church was devastated, confused, and angry. He and his wife were told to leave the church. However, not one person from the church or elsewhere reached out to them.

God put it on my heart to visit him and his wife. They were both broken as I sat with them in their living room. The wife was humiliated, and he was overwhelmed with grief over the pain he had caused. He told me he had struggled with this sin of pedophilia for twenty years. I could only imagine how many children whose lives were destroyed by this man's sin.

It was hard to take in, but I listened to Larry tell his story with tears in his eyes. He hated what he had become. The hurt intensified because everyone had abandoned them. An anointing of love for both of them came over me, and we talked and prayed. They were so grateful that someone came to comfort them, as well. I was the only one who reached out, loved them, and prayed with them. He was repentant, but he also knew he was going to prison. That was the last I saw or heard of him.

I can visualize Jesus loving families, but I can also imagine Him going to Larry's home and gently trying to restore him. It is terrible to hear about someone hurting innocent children, but even these sinners need healing. God is here for everyone — the criminal and the victim. No one is beyond His grasp. Each one of us needs repentance and salvation, and we need to forgive lest bitterness continues to fester.

I could have responded like Jonah and said, "I don't want you to forgive that person. That pedophile (you fill in the blank), that murderer, that run-away slave, that alcoholic, that liar, that person who hurt me doesn't deserve my forgiveness. The truth is that none of us deserves God's forgiveness. We are all sinners in need of His grace.

Who are we not to forgive if God does? The Bible tells us that if we don't forgive, God will not forgive us. "But if you do not forgive others their sins, your Father will not forgive your sins" (Matthew 6:15). Jesus was beaten, scarred, nailed to a cross, and stripped naked in humiliation and pain. He said, "Father, forgive them for they know not what they do." Jesus forgave every sin imaginable on His cross. If He was able to forgive those who murdered Him, then who are we not to forgive others? We are in sin if we do not forgive.

There is no one beyond God's reach for forgiveness and redemption. Paul was a murderer who was killing Christians in the name of God. He eventually became a Christian himself who God used to write much of the New Testament. Charles Colson was a liar, slanderer, and a sleazy lawyer who God used to change the prison system. Onesimus, a once run-away slave, was transformed into a beloved Bishop of Asia. We all have a past as well as a need for continual forgiveness.

We can try to forgive and love the sinner in our own strength, but our love isn't good enough. We need God's help to do this work. We must love the sinner with God's love, a supernatural love that only comes from His anointing. His love goes beyond ours when we reach out to the outcasts of society. Others will even get angry at you for doing this. "How dare you forgive that degenerate? How dare you tell him he can be forgiven." Their venom of hate is just as ugly as what the person has done. Plato said, "No one is more hated than he who speaks the truth." The truth is Jesus loves them and He takes no pleasure in the death of the wicked. God does not want anyone to perish but all to have eternal life.

We are to love the one who is disturbed and the one who has a hole deep in his/her heart that only God can touch and fill. Will you be the one to love those that everyone else abandons? Will you be the one who sticks his neck out when others bury theirs in the sand? I hope you are brave enough to say yes and join in the ministry of reconciliation. You can't do this in your own strength, but God will give you His anointing.

Reconciling people to God is what we do. Most of the people we deal with simply need to be reminded that God has not abandoned them. They know they are separated from God and just need someone to tell them God's hands are reaching out to them through you. It is rewarding when God speaks through you with words of wisdom or a word of knowledge to break a heavy yoke of discouragement or condemnation on someone's life. People come to us after beating themselves up for what they've done or said. As you speak to them, you see the tears flow. You watch their hands lift and receive forgiveness, reconciliation, and a restored relationship with God. You see God restoring faith to believe. Chaplains are shepherds who preach against sin but also preach grace. They care for all of God's people with a pastor's heart.

The people we minister to need compassion, and they deserve our best. We need to be reminded that this is someone's parent, child, and loved one. This is God's child, and we need to overlook the physical and see the spiritual. If Jesus smelled bad odors and saw horrific sights and sounds, we would, too. Jesus overlooked those things and loved them dearly, and so must we.

STIR UP THE GIFT

At the 2020 Chaplains Seminar, David Arroyo asked, "Did God change His mind about your calling?" God does not change His mind. However, because of difficulties, we often talk ourselves out of our callings! The initial excitement of ministry and adventure has been burned out by hurt, frustration, disgrace, confusion, and doubt. We continually go out into this hurting world only for our hearts to break all over again.

When going through difficulties at work, I have often wondered whether God was moving me on or if I were just having a hard time. I prayed and asked God to show me. It seems that every time, the problem was ministerial burnout. God had to restore my burden for ministry. If you have been in the ministry for a long time, you understand those low times. You feel like running, quitting, and moving elsewhere.

God has to throw us back into fundamental situations to remind us of why we serve. It can be easy to get bored with hospice. It is the same old stories, just different people. It's the same grief, suffering, and losses. But then I look into the eyes of the crying patient or a scared family member, God reminds me that even if this is the third death of the week for you to deal with, it is this family's first. God stirs the compassion in my heart again as He continues to re-engage me in meeting people's needs. My heart swells with His love again. As God knows how to deal with me, He knows how to stir your calling and compassion again. He has to do this from time to time to keep us from being cold and indifferent.

Paul had to tell Timothy to "stir up" the gift that is within him. Timothy was a timid young man and probably felt intimidated as a young pastor. Paul told him to rekindle the flame. Let fresh oxygen into the waning fire. Remember the anointing, and be bold in it. There are times we have to "stir up" within us. We can become callous and uncaring or indifferent. We have to snap out of it quickly and remind ourselves of our special and unique calling God has privileged us with.

STAY INVOLVED

Staying in ministry is continually going out where people are. If we stay in our own heads or in our offices, we can forget what it is like in the world. We push away what people deal with and lose compassion. It's easier just to stay in our own little worlds and comfort zones. But when we incarnate ourselves into broken people, broken marriages, divorce care, grief share, and death ministry, we stay involved.

Jesus stayed involved. He took time for Himself by going to the Mount of Olives for prayer but then immersed Himself in the center of the people. He saw, smelled, and heard the needs of people He could help.

I teach about compassion fatigue and have told nurses, "If you want to stay in the ministry, you must take care of yourself." Jesus even stayed involved when he was tired. When his cousin, John the Baptist, was beheaded, Jesus went away to grieve. When he looked up and saw all the people, He began to minister out of his own grief and need. He put Himself aside and accomplished His calling to preach, heal and comfort (Matthew 14:1-14).

There are times we need to put aside our needs and meet the needs of the people. I empathize with caregivers who have to change their loved one six times a day. They are up all hours of the night. They are tired, stressed, and fatigued. But I tell them, "You can't say to your mom, 'I'll change you later; I'm tired.' Or 'I don't feel like feeding you today. I'll be back tomorrow.' No, you minister to them out of your own fatigue, your own grief, and you do what needs to be done." There are times we must put aside our own needs and minister to others even when we are tired or grieving ourselves. It is important to stay connected to the needs of the people.

At one chaplain's conference, we were challenged to get involved in the community. Some pastors got involved and loved it. They came out of their churches and offices and did ride-along sessions with police officers. Some got involved with civic activities and the local fire departments. Whether you're a pastor or a chaplain, your ministry is to the community. Keep your compassion, and go with courage wherever God leads you.

Get out of the four walls of the church and get your hands dirty. Your heart will melt once again for meeting the needs of hurting people you ride along with and encounter as you meet people you normally would not. Stir that gift back up and re-engage in people's lives. Balance your life with self-care and pastoral care in both church work and civic ministry.

CHAPTER THIRTEEN

Beware of the Wolves

...your rod and your staff, they comfort me.

Psalms 23:4

P eter's second letter to the church in Asia Minor, modern-day Turkey, was written to show them how to grow spiritually and be aware of wolves in sheep's clothing. Even Jesus warned, "Beware of false prophets, which come to you in sheep's clothing, but inwardly they are ravening wolves" (Matthew 7:15). A wolf's nature cannot be changed. Wolves are predators by nature. They are natural-born killers. They hunt primarily at night and in packs. There is nothing merciful about them when it comes to their prey. A wolf hiding in sheep's clothing will never be a sheep. Eventually, their true nature will be revealed.

Wolves infiltrate churches. They put on a good show. They tell people what they want to hear rather than what they need to hear. There are many so-called pastors preaching what is contrary to God's Word. So inclusive in their preaching, they often appear to be more gracious than Jesus Himself! People will gravitate to that type of church because that is what they want to hear. The wolf is so charismatic in his preaching that he convinces the church that there is no other truth. They are first mesmerized and then controlled.

Some will even preach there is no such thing as sin. Sin is relative. This is heresy! When we recognize our sins and repent from them, that is the first step in spiritual healing. We must recognize that we are broken people in need of grace. If there is no sin, then there is no need for God. That kind of preaching keeps people bound in sin and shame. They are being told a lie. Outwardly, they may be accepted by society, but inwardly, they are still full of turmoil.

The church needs to be Biblically literate. The Bereans were noble because they questioned Paul. They didn't just take his word for it, they studied the scriptures for themselves. Paul called them noble. Those we disciple need to be noble and ask questions so they can understand for themselves.

Revelation chapter two speaks of the church in Ephesus who "left" their first love. They replaced their relationship with God with formality, orthodoxy, and religion. Outwardly it appears righteous, but they are like Pharisees who are clean on the outside but on the inside full of filth and sin. God warns them to repent, or He will come and remove His lampstand (presence) completely.

Wolves weave their way into healthy churches. Then they get angry when questioned. They don't like it when people think for themselves. They need their people to be controlled. They are highly authoritarian and crafty and can slowly turn a thriving church into a selfish, bitter church that only cares about itself. Wolves destroy the goodness in people. They remove the love and create an atmosphere of animosity. Goodness is replaced with hostility. Unwitting people become entangled again in those things from which they were delivered.

There are people in churches who just want to stir up trouble. They are control freaks who want to change the order of everything and disrupt harmony. It takes strong spiritual leaders who have discernment to see through their duplicity.

I MET THE WOLF

When I first returned to the states from overseas, I told my family I'd be home for Christmas. I was on fire for God and wanted to share Christ with them. While being stationed in Long Beach, CA, I attended a small Assembly of God church that preached the Word and helped me grow spiritually. I met nice people—average people like waitresses and mechanics—and they all loved the LORD. They were healthy Christians. Sometimes, I spent the entire Sunday afternoon lying on the church floor by the altar reading the Bible until Sunday evening service.

Then I met the WOLF. He looked like a sheep, acted like a sheep, and said all the right things. I trusted him. Then he began gossiping about the people in the church, saying such things as, "They aren't interested in spiritual things. All they talk about is their boats, cars, and trips."

There's nothing wrong with having boats and cars and going on trips. It's all right for Christians to have fun when they put God first—it's called being a normal Christian. This man made them sound self-righteous and carnal, and I fell for it! I believed what he said, and it sidetracked me into leaving the church. He made me think I was better off following him. I left the church and followed him. I met with this guy for three months. He dragged me so far away from God. The joy I once had was replaced by confusion and anger. I thought I was following a man of God, but I had returned back to the things that God had delivered me from. I secretly drank and smoked. My heart was cold and unloving because I had been out of church for so long.

Before I met this man, I was telling my family about all that God had done in my life. I couldn't wait to come home and tell my family in person all that God had done for me and that He could do it for them, as well. But when Christmas came, I had nothing to say. I was spiritually empty. All the good that God had done was gone. It was replaced by darkness and defeat. I spent my last night of leave in front of the Christmas tree alone with a bottle of whiskey in my hand, wondering what had happened? How did I get so far away from God in just three short months? I missed the opportunity of telling my family about Jesus. My testimony was gone, and I felt ashamed. Oh, how I wish the pastor of that church came after me, sought after me, corrected, or even rebuked me, but he never did.

When I returned from vacation, the wolf picked me up at the airport. He asked me how my visit went. I told him how horrible it was. He acted like it was no big deal. That was the last time I ever saw him. It seemed as if Satan sent him on a mission to destroy my testimony. He succeeded, temporarily. In my disillusionment, I realized he was a wolf in sheep's clothing. When I came back to the fullness of Christ, I was determined to live by two rules. First, never be fooled again, and second, always help those who go astray.

The Apostle Paul dealt sternly with false prophets. Paul was fearless in protecting the sanctity of the gospel, as well as the sheep from predators. False prophets do not like being around Spirit-filled leaders. They know we see right through their egoistical deception and call them on it. The Spirit in us is greater than the spirit in them, and they know it. Confront these men and drive them out of the church if they are creating controversy. Psalm 23 speaks of a rod and a staff. The staff guided the sheep and sometimes pulled them back into the fold, while the rod beat off the wolves. They are spiritual tools that are imperative to have. We need to carry both!

One of my favorite lines in the movie *The Patriot*, was when their pastor left his congregation and joined forces with the militia. He said, "Sometimes a shepherd must tend to his sheep; other times, he must fight off the wolves."

Not only the pastor but the whole church needs to stand together in unity to defend the sanctity of the church. The pastor needs the church's support, as much as the church needs pastoral leadership during times of dissention.

Need for Pastoral Care

When sheep wander off, it's our mission to help them get back on track. Wandering takes them farther and farther away from God. It leads them into the darkness where the predators are. Wolves lie and wait to separate us and rip us to pieces. That is a time when they need pastoral care the most. They need pastoral visits with prayer and counsel to remain faithful through trials.

Do not neglect your flock! Pastoral care is essential as one of the pastoral ministries in the church. It is where the pastor meets his people where they are and in their time of need. It is a time to enter into the congregants' world and get to know them personally.

As a hospice chaplain, I have ministered to many church leaders who became ill. Their chronic illness became terminal. Time went by, maybe even years, and they were forgotten about. These shut-ins were left behind to fend for themselves against the wolves. This time the wolves represent loneliness, isolation, and discouragement. These dear people need pastoral visits now more than when they were healthy church attenders. Hospice chaplains have opportunities to restore them back to faith. We help them get that spark back that they haven't felt in years. Because of hospice ministry, they have peace with God and can die with a smile on their faces. Those are the few we reach, but what about those we don't reach—the faithful neglected? This shouldn't happen, and it breaks the chaplain's heart when we come across this all too often. There is a solution.

HIRE A PASTORAL CARE PASTOR OR CHAPLAIN FOR YOUR CHURCH

Many senior pastors are very busy and either don't have the time to visit or simply don't like doing it. They are not wired that way, and that is fine. If you are not good at pastoral care, find people in the church who are, or hire a pastoral care pastor! Pastoral care is a specialized ministry for those who are gifted in the area of mercy, compassion, and love. We are passionate about what we do, just like senior pastors are passionate about what they do. Don't hire one as a tag-a-long ministry to also be the youth or worship pastor. The pastoral care pastor will have plenty to do if he/she does it right. We are wired to connect people first to God and then to one another. We are trained in grief counseling, crisis counseling, and many other pastoral skills the average pastor is not equipped to handle. Hire a skilled pastor or train a gifted one by sending him/her to a Clinical Pastoral Education Program (CPE). Either way make sure you get them trained. Don't just throw them into the ministry as hand-holders. There is much more to it than that. Pastoral care pastors shepherd the church by visiting the sick, leading hospitality ministries, and officiating weddings and funerals. They benefit the church in countless ways. Pastoral care pastors make sure people are not neglected or forgotten about. They are worth the investment.

If we hire worship leaders and youth pastors, then why not pastoral care pastors? Some churches want to reach out more in the community and even hire chaplains to work at local prisons, homeless shelters, hospitals, and other ministry-related areas to evangelize their community. Most chaplains have the gift of evangelism. We are called to chaplaincy work because we love being out in community ministry. Consider hiring a chaplain to your ministry staff.

If you are a solo-pastor, make sure you provide pastoral care. "If I don't see you for two consecutive weeks, you're getting a phone call," I told my congregation that I pastored. "I'm not judging you for missing, but I want to make sure you're okay." Under my watch, I was not going to allow any of the sheep God put in my care to stray. No one came after me when I strayed, but under my leadership, I was going after them harder than the devil was, and with God's help, none would be lost. The people thanked me for calling them when they missed church because they knew I loved them.

That is one of the reasons why I love pastoral care. The other reason is that when I sit with people in their homes and listen to their stories, I get to know them personally. It helped me to see them as real people with real problems, not simply church people, tithers, or troublemakers. If we never get to know them or spend time with them, then how are we supposed to have meaningful relationships with them? It is easy for pastors to get caught up in the ministry of church business and neglect forming relationships. Relationships are what the church is all about.

Pastoring must be balanced with personal relationships. By preaching strong Biblical messages relevant to your congregation along with quality pastoral care, churches will be healthy and effective. Shepherds can never lose sight of either.

HANDLING HURT

When we experience hurt or difficulties ourselves, it makes us better chaplains and pastors. It makes us more sensitive to our people's needs. Those hard times help us relate to our people. We know how to help them through their trials.

People experience extreme forms of suffering, and it is our duty to help them navigate through their trials. As chaplains, we have to remember that God is already working before we arrive on the scene. Through events and circumstances, people end up on our spiritual doorstep. That is why it is important to ask the question, "What is God doing in your life that leads you here?" Are they Jonah running from God? Is this cancer causing you to think about the meaning of life?" We go into their holy of holies and ask personal questions to dig out their thoughts, feelings, and emotions. God brought them into our lives for a reason; it is our ministry to help them find purpose.

Sometimes people get sidetracked because of anger or rebellion. They deliberately walk away from God like the prodigal son. Hard as it is, it's often necessary to let them feed off the pig's trough and let them suffer. Putting them in God's hands, we can trust He will bring them to the point of such disgrace that they'll come back humbled. We must have faith that they'll be more determined than ever to live for God because they experienced the pain the world inflicted. They finally have realized how much better they had it under God the Father's love and protection. Most importantly, never forget them, and always be available for them if they deliberately walk away. They will know you care.

Being hurt in the church by other Christians can cause people to feel unwanted. These are the people who gently need reassurance and restoration. They may have been hurt by someone they trusted. They take it to heart, mulling over every word. The seed of hurt grows into a root of bitterness, turning bitterness into anger. Hurt and anger go hand-in-hand. First, they are hurt, and after dwelling on it, they may become angry.

Congregants get hurt by other people's intentional rude and selfish comments. Sometimes, not always, the other person hadn't meant to be cruel, not realizing their words were taken wrongly. But the offended person took it to heart.

In situations like these, we need to help keep their eyes on Jesus and to remind them to take up their cross and follow Him with a mature attitude. It is one thing to take up our cross, it's another to "follow Him" while carrying it. We can still carry the cross but have a bad attitude. We can carry our crosses with bitterness and anger, while holding onto hurts and disappointments. It is how we carry our crosses that make all the difference; and we need to teach that to our congregants. Secondly, remind them that even Jesus needed help carrying his cross. Simon of Cyrene was forced to help Jesus with His cross. We shepherds are not forced to help others carry their crosses; we willingly help our hurting people carry their burdens. They do not have to carry their issues alone; we are there for them. We live in an imperfect world, in an imperfect church. Christians need to grow spiritually and learn to go through difficulties and disagreements without quitting.

Our ministry is to help others carry their burdens. We are in a supportive role. We are responsible to people, not for them. They have to learn what God is teaching them for themselves. We cannot and should not take that away from them. We can, however, help them understand God is with them in their time of need.

Pastor Joy Ortega preached about this in a service one time that just made so much sense. She said, "When we feel like we are holding the world on our shoulders, the world of hurt, responsibilities, finances, stress, and pressures of life, we don't have to carry them alone. That is when Jesus comes alongside us and helps us carry the weight of the world on both shoulders. He doesn't take it all from you but helps you to be able to bear it with His help." We are not meant to carry the weight of our worlds or anyone else's world on our shoulders; that is God's job! He tells us to "cast all of our cares upon Him for He cares for us," (1 Peter 5:7).

Jesus said, "In this world, you will have trouble but take heart I have overcome the world" (John 16:33). There are a lot of difficulties in this world, but there are also a lot of joyful times, as well. There is so much to be thankful for and so many blessings and memories to remind us that life is good. Life does not end when we go through painful trials. In fact, there are often new beginnings. Trials make us stronger when we hold onto hope and trust God through life's challenges because God still has a plan for us. In Jeremiah 29:11-12, we are told, "'For I know the plans I have for you' says the Lord 'plans to prosper you and not to harm you, to give you hope and a future. Then you will call upon me and pray to me and I will hear you.'"

We don't always understand what God does, but as Isaiah 55:9 says, "His ways are higher than our ways and his thoughts greater than ours." If we try to figure it out, we will go crazy. We have to trust God even when it hurts and put our future in His hands.

The older I get the less I understand what God is doing or not doing in my life and in the lives of others. I see people suffer and go through difficulties. Yet, I know God can heal them instantly. I see good people go through hard times and bad people prosper. It can be frustrating and futile. King Solomon faced the same dilemma. He wrote about it in Ecclesiastes 7:15. "I have seen everything in this meaningless life, including the death of good young people and the long life of wicked people." "In this life, good people are often treated as though they were wicked, while wicked people are often treated as they were good" (v.14). "No one really knows what is going to happen; no one can predict the future" (Ecclesiastes 10:14). "Just as you cannot understand the paths of the wind or the mystery of a tiny baby growing in its mother's womb, so you cannot understand the activity of God, who does all things" (Ecclesiastes 11:5).

King Solomon also went on to explain some answers. "Enjoy prosperity when you can, but when hard times come, realize that both come from God. Therefore no one can discover anything about their future (Ecclesiastes 7:14). "Enjoy life. Accept your lot" (Ecclesiastes 5:18-20).

What is a lot? How many of us started out in life thinking life was going to be one way, and it turned out completely different? "Use the common blessings which God bestows with thankfulness and contentment. When people live to be very old, let them rejoice in every day of life…honor him in your youth before you grow old and say, 'Life is not pleasant anymore'" (Ecclesiastes 5:18-20).

The advantage of walking with the LORD for a long time is that we don't have to understand everything. We have learned to trust Him no matter what. We have experienced the joys and sorrows of life. As I look back at my life, I regret worrying over things that never happened. I spent too much time worrying over things that God promised He would provide. He always did, always will, and He never fails us. In my youth, I thought I had it all figured out. I thought I knew what God would do even before He did it! In fact, I jokingly said God would ask for my advice.

Now I find myself just listening to patients. I find myself, more often than not, saying, "I don't know, but God does…let's pray." I used to be certain about things. Now, I'm not certain about anything. But the only thing I am certain of is that God is on the throne, and I am not. What we can't handle, He can!

CHAPTER FOURTEEN

Hophni and Phinehas or Samuel: A Ritualistic Chaplain or a Chaplain Shepherd?

"If someone sins against another person, God can mediate for the guilty party. But if someone sins against the LORD, who can intercede?" But Eli's sons wouldn't listen to their father, for the LORD was already planning to put them to death. Meanwhile, the boy Samuel grew taller and grew in favor with the LORD and with people.

I Samuel 2:25-26

God was raising up an obedient priest; not one who only performed rituals but who walked with God. Chaplains are called to be more than a religious symbol. We are called to be a living example of God's love. Do you want to be an Hophni and Phinehas or a Samuel?

Are you a religious symbol or a shepherd? Chaplaincy ministry has the potential to be ritualistic and impersonal. We can walk into a room full of people and pronounce a ritualistic prayer and then leave. On the other hand, we can be personal. We can take the time to get to know everyone and be a positive influence as a servant of God.

The prophet Eli seems to have been a good priest himself, but his sons seem to have been a different story. His sons took the best portions of meat for themselves, but even worse, they slept with women at the altar of sacrifice (1 Samuel 2). Eli did not discipline his sons who treated God with contempt. He warned them but never removed them from spiritual leadership. It appears he was more concerned about his own family's position of power than he was about God's honor. In judgment for this, God removed his entire lineage from the priesthood. We must honor God rather than worry about offending people. The call to ministry is a holy mandate and is not always comfortable.

We are the moral voice of the corporation, military, rodeo, racetrack, hospice, hospital, or other ministries. Administrators carry a great amount of stress. They carry the weight of the organization upon their shoulders and care deeply for their employees.

Therefore, chaplains need to be emotionally involved in their place of employment. Chaplains must be present for and pray for their institutions, administrators, wardens, and leaders who are in leadership over them. Pray that they are blessed and make the right decisions to have righteous and successful organizations. Be there for them to talk to you and counsel with. If you do that, your leadership will appreciate you even more because they will see your concern for them and the institution. They know we are for them and not against them, and we are there to help them in any way we can.

There is a lot of pressure on our administrators. When the LORD puts my administrator on my heart, I pray for her and then send her an encouraging text with words of affirmation. She always appreciates my prayers. Be a blessing!

If we have shown ourselves to be trustworthy, our leaders will value our input even when we respectfully disagree with them. Chaplains work in a secular environment. If you discover something that bothers you and the Holy Spirit prompts you to speak out against it, then obey God. Trust God to give you the insight to deliver the right words in the right way.

For example, When Reiki was new and at its height, one of our staff members wanted to practice this in our healthcare institution, especially to unresponsive patients. I was not comfortable with this. My spirit was unsettled, so I prayed and did research. I discovered that Reiki has its roots in Hinduism. Approaching the administrator, I told her this discipline should fall under the Spiritual Care department or alternative therapies. Furthermore, the patient needs to be informed of its spiritual effects. People have a right to know the meaning behind unfamiliar spiritual rituals. She agreed, and the discipline was tabled.

The chaplain might be the right voice at the right time to help your company navigate through difficult decisions. You may change the course of your company by speaking up. Speak up when your opinion has significance. If the chaplain is only a silent symbol, then he/she has lost influence.

It is not always easy to obey when God speaks. God gave the young boy, Samuel, a difficult task for his first assignment. He was told to give Eli the harsh message about his sons', Hophni and Phinehas, behavior. It was a tough message to tell his mentor impending judgment was coming upon his house. Samuel told him even though he was afraid. Eli accepted the rebuke. He also understood that God was raising Samuel to be a prophet and would replace his two sons. I can only imagine Samuel's nervousness about what it was going to be like to follow God wholeheartedly. He knew it was going to take courage to oppose leaders, but knowing he was led by God gave him the confidence he needed.

Samuel walked with God his entire life. When he was older and walked into a town, the townspeople would ask if he came in peace. There was a fear of God about this man. He was highly respected by man; more importantly, he was trusted by the LORD. From childhood to death, Samuel remained obedient.

HOLY SPIRIT-FILLED CHAPLAINS ARE OBEDIENT TO GOD

It is a scary thing to hear from God. The Bible says, "Eat it; it will be as sweet as honey but will turn sour in your stomach." This scripture means when we hear from God, it is both exciting and fearful. Hearing from God is exciting but also scary. After we hear it, we have to preach it, never knowing how people will react. When preparing to preach a difficult Word, God can cause your stomach to turn, but when that anointing hits the preacher in the pulpit, there is no more fear! God's Word falls on the hearts of the congregation, and there is always a response, usually to the altar!

A chaplain hears from God and does what God asks him to do no matter how difficult the mission is. Yes, we wrestle, justify, ask God to send someone else, but that tug of the Holy Spirit in our hearts doesn't go away until we finally surrender.

Perhaps you can remember when God called you to do something you didn't want to do. Eventually, you mustered up the courage and obeyed and were glad you did. You did not get this far in ministry by neglecting God's promptings. No, you took that scary step of faith, and with an obedient attitude, you did it and continue to do so!

Ritualistic chaplains don't want to hear from God because they are afraid of Him. He might make them do something they don't want to do. They would rather go about as unnoticed figures but still get paid. These types of chaplains never benefit the company. Spirit-filled chaplains, on the other hand, receive inspiration from the Holy Spirit to do something new and out of the ordinary. Healings are done when the chaplain walks under the authority and anointing of God. Miracles occur when a chaplain is willing to step out of his natural tendencies and his "own understanding" and believe God for the impossible. This is how institutions are created or transformed.

Ministries start with a vision from God. Before Dr. John Q. Kenzy started YCIBI, he heard of a site to plant a Bible Institute. When he got to the old abandoned Odd Fellows Home in Sunbury, PA, he walked into the biggest building. It was cluttered with old furniture and trash. God gave him a vision of that room being the campus chapel. He saw students worshiping with hands lifted high. He rolled up his sleeves, and his wife and he got to work turning it into a beautiful chapel. He knew this was the place God was going to use to educate and train students to minister in Teen Challenge centers.

It was a unique Bible Institute specifically geared to train pastors to minister to those who society had given up on. Some in the community did not want it there so they opposed it.

There is always opposition to new work. Revelation 12 tells the story of a woman in labor. She had a crown of twelve stars on her head. She was pregnant and cried out in pain because she was about to give birth. But a dragon (Satan) stood in front of the woman wanting to devour the baby as soon as it was born. She gave birth to a baby boy who would rule the world with an iron scepter. The child was snatched away by God and caught up to the throne of God.

Whenever God births a new ministry, Satan is right there wanting to devour it. The ministry is a threat to him. When Dr. Kenzy began the ministry of Youth Challenge International Bible Institute, he had many townspeople oppose this ministry. Many students, ex-convicts, and drug offenders were saved through Teen Challenge, called into the ministry, and more were enrolled in the school. Many in the community did not want those kinds of people in their town.

Dr. Kenzy let God fight his battle. He told us that those who violently opposed the ministry were severely dealt with by God, and the work continued. Others recognized God's hand in this ministry and wanted to be involved in what God was doing. They gave gold and silver jewelry, diamonds, watches, and cash as the offering plates came around. The ministry became a great success.

DON'T WORRY, WONDER

Holy Spirit-filled chaplains let God be in charge. God will move in ways we least expect. Be willing to let God change your mind.

We are not called to worry but to trust and see what God does. Not only involve yourself with ministry that will challenge you and make you better, but be open to whomever God sends your way. I once preached a message called, *Don't Worry, Wonder*. Wonder how God will meet your needs. We were in the process of hiring a chaplain. We deliberated over several resumes, one of which was an exceptional young man. I met him a few months prior and told him about the position. Acknowledging the call to be a chaplain, he applied for the position at my request. He was very impressive but did not yet have the experience. I really wanted to hire and mentor this young man, but there was another more experienced candidate I felt to be God's choice for the position, so we hired him. He turned out to be the right person for the position. The one I initially wanted to hire took a position in another state in a CPE program. God knew what was best for all three of us. Listening to God and obeying Him is important for spiritual leaders.

If we are open to whom God wants in a ministry position rather than what we want, God will bless everyone involved. We need to put aside our choices, desires, and wants and pick the person God wants, even if it means bypassing a friend. We are called to make tough choices, and when we do, God will bless us even more when we make the right ones.

GET TO KNOW THEM

A shepherd loves his sheep. He lays down his life for them. He sacrifices everything. He doesn't treat them with indifference and doesn't use his people to get what he wants and leave them with nothing. He doesn't hold people or God in contempt like Eli's sons did. A shepherd confronts when necessary and has courage when it is time to take a stand. He preaches against sin and turns to God. Spirit-filled chaplains are warriors who run to the battle not away from it. A shepherd gives himself first to God then to people. A chaplain is there for his people in good times and bad.

Continue to tune your ear to hear from God. Don't just DO the duties of ministry but BE the ministry! Be personal, approachable, and compassionate with a heart of empathy for those under your care. If God gives you a word of knowledge for someone, be ready to share it with them as an answer to their prayers. Give godly wisdom, and instill confidence; hear from God, and share it with those who desperately need hope.

God gives us wisdom and insight in situations. He gives words to calm storms in people's lives; He restores hope and creates hope again. Most of a chaplain's work is with words, not in signs and wonders. We simply speak the Word of God without judging and leave the rest up to God. Jesus did not perform a miracle in front of the Samaritan woman. He used persuasive words with spiritual discernment. Proverbs 18:20 says this: "Wise words satisfy like a good meal; the right words bring satisfaction." Speaking a good word not only brings satisfaction to the speaker, but to the person who has lost hope. You may be his/her last source of hope for salvation.

The chaplain must speak to many issues within the lives of patients and their families. This may include issues regarding stress, boundaries, a patient's lack of independence, a desire to feel useful, caregiver burnout, and sleep deprivation. Sometimes, even marriage counseling is needed. Unforgiveness or chaos arises in the caregiver's home, creating conflict. The chaplain will search for the underlying issue. Something may be going on beneath the surface. Put aside the triviality of the woman at the well carrying the water. It's not about the chore of carrying the water. It's not about the chore of changing adult briefs. It's about what everyone is feeling and thinking that needs discussing. We help uncover spiritual needs, such as forgiveness and reconciliation, and help them listen to the other's point of view. The Holy Spirit will bring to mind your clinical counseling skills, education, and an anointing for that moment. The chaplain is not there to talk about the weather but rather the elephant in the room. Sweeping issues under the carpet only creates greater frustration. We are there to address issues and resolve conflicts. We are being paid as professionals by professionals, and we need to deliver and do what is expected of us.

We have a saying in hospice when a ton of information is vomited at the patient and family before even asking them what their needs are. We call it *The Hospice Hurl*. Too often as evangelicals, we do the equivalent of an *Evangelism Hurl* all over a person without listening or getting to know him/her. To build a relationship with someone, you must get to know the person personally, taking the time to learn who he/she is. Make an effort to understand the person's thoughts, feelings, and understanding of God. To listen means to know. After building a personal relationship and learning about that person, you can comfort him/her with wisdom from God and even have opportunities to lead him/her to Christ.

People make mistakes. As difficult as it is, we must learn to be gracious with them the same way God is gracious with our mistakes.

For example, before I became a Christian, I was prejudiced toward Germans even though my heritage is a little part German. I never liked that I was German and would conveniently leave that out, saying I was Scotch-Irish. I lumped all German people together with Hitler. Growing up, our neighbors were Jewish, and they were the nicest people. In fact Mr. Holt fought in World War II and lost his toe to frostbite while he was fighting the Nazi regime. It made me angry because of what Hitler did to the Jews. So, in my childhood foolishness, I perceived all Germans to be bad people.

SHEPHERDS LOVE ALL PEOPLE

Now that I have been saved for over thirty-five years, God has taken that prejudice for Germans out of my heart. I can genuinely say I have a love for everyone. Ironically, God called me to pastor the Pennsylvania Dutch who are German. God removes hate and replaces it with love.

I have met both Germans and English survivors from World War II and heard all kinds of stories from both sides. An English lady explained her fear as a child hiding in the cellars during air raid bombings over England. As I listened to her stories, I kept thinking how awful it must have been for her at ten years of age. She recalled the sights, sounds, smells, and fears from eighty-six years ago. It never left her mind, all because men wanted to dominate and control other men! What a depraved world we live in! Wars affect all families. On the other side of the war was Henri.

Henri was a wonderful German man. He was in hospice services with heart failure. As we talked one day, he told me this story. "I had a little brother named Georgi. He was sick with a respiratory infection when my family fled into Poland." Henri's eyes began to brim. "The town we fled to with my mother, father, and six brothers and sisters didn't want to help us. They called us Nazis because we came from Germany."

Leaning in to listen close, Henri told me his story of being in Hitler's Youth.

"They forced me to be a part of Hitler's Youth. I didn't want to. I was only ten-years-old. My parents objected, but the German guard made me go with them. Then, they brainwashed me."

Stunned at his admission, I encouraged him to go on. "What happened to Georgi and your family?"

"We thought he was getting better. No doctor in the town would come because everyone there hated Germans." Henri's voice cracked as a tear slipped down his cheek. "Georgi died a day later. He was only two-years-old." Henri wiped his eyes with the back of his hand. I comforted Henri the best way I could, telling him he would soon see Georgi, and he began sharing his own glimpses of heaven.

"I already did," he exclaimed. A weak smile of confidence graced his face.

"Tell me," I encouraged.

"Well, I love flowers," he said. "I died and went to heaven. There are beautiful trees and acres and acres of flowers. Flowers that I have never seen before. It was beautiful! My parents and Georgi were there, too. But they waved at me and told me it's not my time to come yet."

A deep love in my heart grew as I prayed with this couple because I took the time to get to know them. The wife became tearful during the prayer. Henri passed away several weeks later. How far God has brought me from my old sinful, selfish, hostile nature to where I am today. If I weren't a Christian, I would never have given them the time of day. I thought to myself as I left how much God had changed me. It's easy to hate when we don't to get know others. It's also easy to offer a prayer and leave just as fast. But getting to know the people we pastor gives us a greater understanding of who they are and a deeper appreciation for what they have been through. Everyone has a story; all it takes to find out is a pastor's heart and a willingness to listen.

God wants us to work together in unity. Hate divides, but love unifies. The world always gets it wrong by dividing people by race, color, and ethnicity. The church is different. Galatians 3:28 reads, "There is neither Jew nor Greek, there is neither bond nor free, there is neither male nor female, for ye are all one in Christ Jesus" (KJV).

Individual people choose to be good or bad. They choose whether to follow God or not. To be selfish or caring all comes down to a personal choice. God's grace, mercy, and kindness change us from what we were to who we are now. We cannot credit it to good works on our own. It is His Spirit changing and challenging us to do the good things He had planned for us. Even before we were born, God had a plan for you and me. He knew a long time ago when we were acting stupid and being selfish that someday we would get our acts together. He is patient with us, and when we finally surrender, He uses us as instruments of peace.

Put Love into Action

Jesus, the Prince of Peace, delivered us from hostility. He broke the barriers of prejudice of all kinds by breaking the barrier of hostility. God replaced it with peace and love toward each other. Christ's death on the cross reconciled humans to God and all nationalities to each other in the body of Christ. We live in a sarcastic world where some people insult and hurt others. How about we start to honor and give compliments to one another rather than tear each other down?

It seems we have lost common courtesy in our society. Scriptures even teach common courtesy. "Rise in the presence of the aged." "Treat younger women as sisters and older women as mothers." When my doctor walks into the room where I am waiting, I stand to shake his hand. He tells me not to, but I do because it shows respect. I pray for common decency to return to society. We all know how good it feels when someone does something nice for us. It touches the soul and warms the heart especially when not expected. I heard a story of a lady standing in line with her child at the grocery store; the child began to ask for candy.

The Mom said, "We can't afford it. Daddy is out of work."

The man behind her overheard the conversation and handed her a $50 bill saying, "Ma'am, you must have dropped this."

The woman welled up with tears and quietly said, "Thank you."

Generous people are delightful to be around. They don't hold onto their money tightly. When they see a need, they give, and God blesses them for it. Jesus talked about using money to be a blessing to others and gain a good reputation (Luke 16:9).

There are so many random acts of kindness that we can do in Jesus' name. Ideas include leaving an encouraging note and greeting and making a new person feel welcome at church. Bring toys to a homeless shelter. Leave flowers at the front desk of a nursing home, asking staff to give it to someone who needs encouragement that day. Leave a note on someone's car. Send a care package to a soldier and so many more (bucketlistjourney.net).

I challenge myself to do this on a regular basis. At the Goodwill store one day, I overheard a lady telling her three children she could not afford something they wanted. I handed the lady a ten-dollar bill. A little later when I saw her again, she pointed to me and said to her three daughters, "That's the man who gave it to us." I noticed a few toys in her cart for the girls. Love connects us to one another, and it doesn't take much effort. We may never know the impact of a simple, kind gesture or a word of encouragement. Winston Churchill said, "We make a living by what we get; we make a life by what we give."

Why do we put our faith into practice? Because God planned for us to do good works a long time ago (Ephesians 2:10). He wants us to continue to be used and to be a blessing. It is easy to tear down, but it takes effort, work, dedication, and commitment to build up. It is even easy for chaplains to look a blind eye. Let's go the extra mile and hear from God and do more than our title says to do. Let's do what God tells us to do as we are led by the Holy Spirit. As we are changed by love, the world is changed, too.

"What the World Needs Now Is Love" is a 1965 popular song with lyrics by Hal David and music composed by Burt Bacharach. It was first recorded and made famous by Jackie DeShannon.

Chapter Fifteen

Societal Sins and Accountability

*He appointed judges in the land, in each of the fortified cities
of Judah. He told them, "Consider carefully what you do,
because you are not judging for man but for the LORD who
is with you wherever you give a verdict. Now let the fear of
the LORD be upon you. Judge carefully, for with the LORD
our God there is no injustice or partiality, or bribery."*

2 Chronicles 19:5-7 (NIV)

A country without mercy is cruel, and a country without justice
is just as cruel. It seems like today, right is wrong, and wrong
is right and sin is celebrated. There needs to be a balance of
justice and mercy.

Judges 19-20 talks about the town of Gibeah. The tribe of Benjamin
did an unspeakable sin to a Levite and his family. In their perversion,
the townspeople wanted to rape and kill this man of God and his
family. This Levite sacrificed his concubine to these men, and they
abused her all night until she died. The Levite then cut her body into
twelve parts and sent them throughout all of Israel to show what the
town of Gibeah had done to them. This enraged the entire nation of
Israel to fight, defeat, and punish the tribe of Benjamin in order to
restore justice to society. Israel recognized corporate responsibility
and acted righteously.

The leading citizens of Gibeah were guilty (Judges 20:5, NLT),
and all Gibeah became an accessory to their crimes by failing to
discipline them. The tribe of Benjamin, in turn, had a responsibility to bring Gibeah to justice; failing to do that, they would

all share in the guilt. Had Israel not done something about Benjamin's sin, the guilt would have extended to the entire nation' (*NLT Commentary and* Judges 20:12-13, NLT).

Israel was a theocratic nation. When one tribe acted foolishly, it was up to the other tribes to hold them accountable in the eyes of God. America is not a theocratic nation; however, our laws and morality are based upon Judeo-Christian values. Everyone is accountable to God, but the frustration for Christians is that we are seeing our Judeo-Christian values replaced by secular humanism. The further we get away from God, the further our principles do, as well. We are a light in our country and try to share God's standards of justice and righteousness, but many are no longer listening. We should never acquiesce. We have had it good for a long time and transitioning from a Christian society to a secular one is difficult for us. God's word is true regardless of the direction society goes. We are corporately responsible as well as individually. Our words ought to be "we have sinned" (Daniel 9:5). Daniel included himself in his prayer. Israel was judged for their sins; America should expect no less. We need to hold our nation accountable because if we don't, our whole nation will be judged. Nations can only stand strong if there is justice.

"Herodotus was a Greek writer credited with being the first historian." It is said that he published *The Histories* around 425 B.C. and focused on the Greco-Persian Wars (https://www.britannica.com). Nations can only stand strong if there is justice. In Herodotus's writings, there is a story about Sisamnes, a corrupt Persian judge. He was active in the Persian empire during the reign of Cambyses 2 of Persia. When Cambyses discovered a bribe to influence Sisamnes's verdict, he had him flayed alive and his skin was cut into leather strips. The successor was Otanes, Sisamnes's son. Cambyses wanted to ensure Otanes feared what would be done to corrupt judges by having the leather strips of his father draped over Otanes's chair.

This action was a symbolic reminder that injustice would not be tolerated, nor could justice be bought. Modern day judges, lawyers, and politicians should take note! Corruption affects all of society. Isolated instances add up! Christians have a higher calling, not just to civil laws but holiness before God. Hopefully, we are influencing society.

POLITICS AND THEOLOGY

Justice and mercy are a huge part of any society. Proverbs 28:4 (NIV) is paraphrased and says to reject the law is to praise the wicked; to obey the law is to fight for them. Evil people don't understand justice, but those who follow the Lord understand completely. And in Proverbs 28:28 (NIV), it says, "When the wicked rise to power, people go into hiding; but when the wicked perish, the righteous thrive."

Israel was judged severely because the upper, political, religious, and economic classes oppressed the lower class. These leaders committed acts of violence, treachery, and lies. They had become morally bankrupt from the top down, and God would stand for it no longer. "For my people's wound is too deep to heal" (Micah 1:9, NLT) In Micah 2:1 (NLT), "What sorrow awaits you who lie awake at night thinking up evil plans? You rise at dawn and hurry to carry them out simply because you have the power to do so." Political leaders can become drunk with power. They have to remember that God placed them in power to serve, and if they do not, God will remove them, as well.

Political leaders reading this book need to be mindful they are ultimately answerable to God.

> The prophet Micah declared, "I said, 'Listen, you leaders of Israel! You are supposed to know right from wrong, but you are the very ones who hate good and love evil. You skin my people alive and tear the flesh from their bones. Yes, you eat my people's flesh, strip off their skin, and break their bones. You chop them up like meat for the cooking pot. Then you beg the LORD for help in times of trouble! Do you really expect him to answer? After all the evil you have done, I won't even look at you!' This is what the LORD says: 'You false prophets are leading my people astray! You promise peace for those who give you food, but you declare war on those who refuse to feed you. Now the night will close around you, cutting off all your visions. Darkness will cover

you, putting an end to your predictions. The sun will set for you prophets, and your day will come to an end. Then you seers will be put to shame, and you fortune-tellers will be disgraced. And you will cover your faces because there is no answer from God. But as for me, I am filled with power—with the Spirit of the LORD. I am filled with justice and strength to boldly declare Israel's sin and rebellion'" (Micah 3:1-7, NLT).

In the Old Testament, spiritual leaders held kings accountable. Healthy accountability between kings and priests balanced society especially when there was mutual respect for one another. The Prophet Nathan rebuked King David about his sin with Bathsheba (2 Samuel 12). Daniel corrected Nebuchadnezzar, (Daniel 2); and advised Darius the Mede (Daniel 6). Nehemiah rebuked the rich oppressors and corrected political leaders (Nehemiah 6). A man of God told King Amaziah of Judah not to make an unholy alliance with Israel. The King listened to this "Unknown" man of God and was blessed for doing so (2 Chronicles 25). There are many unknown ministers who hear from God. Listen to them! Prophets and priests alike have confronted kings and rebuked leaders. We are no different. Pastors need to hold governmental leaders accountable.

When politics oversteps its boundaries into theology, ministers must hold it accountable. It seems that politics has infiltrated every area of society, including theology, science, and sociology. Most issues are not political but spiritual anyway. We chaplains must make our voices heard in ethics boards and must act as a moral compass when it affects our institutions, as well as society in general.

Mother Teresa was furious that corrupt soldiers in India were taking the food for the poor and keeping it for themselves. She held leaders accountable and demanded they give the food to the people where it was intended. When she stood with boldness and fearlessness the soldiers backed down. Jesus often shamed the spiritual leaders for their hypocrisy, and they didn't say another word because they knew they were wrong. There is still such a thing as wrong and right!

SHOULD CHRISTIANS INVOLVE THEMSELVES IN POLITICS?

Some Christians are called to politics while others are not. We must do our civic duty by voting and being active, but we also must be careful not to involve ourselves "in civilian affairs" if that is not our calling. II Timothy 2:4 (NIV) admonishes, "No one serving as a soldier gets entangled in civilian affairs, but rather tries to please his commanding officer." This verse does not mean we should not get involved in politics, but rather that pastors need to be careful politics doesn't replace ministry. This applies to anything else that takes a pastor away from his primary responsibility as a pastor. Some commentaries I have read have included this to mean pastors should not work secular jobs. This is not true because we know from the scriptures that the Apostle Paul worked as a tentmaker; while Paul worked on tents he prayed and carried around with him such an anointing, "so that even handkerchiefs and aprons that had touched him were taken to the sick, and their illnesses were cured and the evil spirits left them (Acts 12:19, NIV). Our lives are our ministry, and we minister wherever we are. However, if God leads you personally to quit your secular job and focus all your attention on ministry, then take that step of faith believing for God to provide.

It is our duty to stand up against societal sins because Jesus said in John 16:8 "The Holy Spirit...convicts the world of sin" (NKJV). The Holy Spirit dwells in us; therefore, the world is convicted of its sin when Christians rise up and say something is wrong! Over the centuries, Christians have always voiced their opposition to societal sins, and we will not stop now! Christians have an obligation to be involved in politics to influence godly practices so our nation and our people will be blessed.

William Temple wrote,

> The method of the church's impact upon society at large should be twofold. First, the church must announce Christian principles and point out where the existing social order is in conflict with them. Second, it must then pass on to Christian citizens, acting in their civic capacities, the task of reshaping the existing order in closer conformity to the principles. (Devotional Classics).

He goes on to say,

> If you are not doing all that you can to find the remedy, you are guilty before God. The church is likely to be attacked from both sides if it does its duty. It will be told that it has become political when, in fact, it has merely stated its principles and pointed out when they have been breached. The church will be told by advocates of particular policies that it is futile because it does not support theirs. If the church is faithful to its Commission, it will ignore both sets of complaints and continue as far as it can to influence all citizens and permeate all parties (Pg 252).

In Romans 13:1, the Bible says, "Let everyone be subject to the governing authorities, for there is no authority except that which God has established. The authorities that exist have been established by God" (NIV). Political leaders can trust Christians to obey righteous laws, but when laws are written that oppose God's word, don't expect Christians to follow them. We will not follow anything that contradicts God's laws. Man's laws are fallible, but God's are infallible. Regardless of what is going on in our world, we have to keep our eyes on Jesus individually and as a church. Roman emperors, such as Caesar, Caligula, Nero, Domitian, and other corrupt emperors, were never mentioned by New Testament writers. Instead, Paul, Timothy, John, Peter, and all the other epistles focused on remaining faithful during persecution, not blaming whoever was in power at the time.

Our society is becoming more corrupt with each generation. Spiritual leaders used to be honored. Pastors started universities and hospitals. They were once held in high esteem. Then they became tolerated and now even hated. In just one generation, we see the decline in America. In one generation, we also see the decline of Israel in the Old Testament.

Israel was prosperous when they situated themselves in the promised land of milk and honey. They grew in power, influence, and dominance. King David and King Solomon were wealthy. Israel prospered under their leadership. Kings and queens from other nations brought them gifts of gold and silver and precious jewels. Israel became wealthy, prosperous, and gluttonous drifting farther and farther from God. Then they began worshiping other gods. God sent them prophets to warn them to repent, but they didn't listen and suffered the consequences for their actions. In just 100 years from 800 B.C. to 700 B.C., they lost their power (Books of *Amos, Joel* and *Hosea*). They were corrupted internally. The Assyrians invaded, then Babylon, then the Medes and Persians. After those nations stripped them of all their wealth, they enslaved them, and they were handed over to the Greeks, then Romans. Famine, pain, and suffering were their recompense rather than peace and blessings.

I see the same demise in America. The people are voting for corruption. Each generation is getting further away from God. As a response, we, as the church, need to be getting closer to God. The time will come when nominal Christianity will no longer be accepted in the church. We must get ourselves spiritually prepared for more hostility and persecution from secular society.

In 1 Timothy 1:8-12 (NIV), "We know that the law is good if one uses it properly. We also know that the law is made not for the righteous but for the lawbreakers and rebels, the ungodly and sinful, the unholy and irreligious; for those who kill their fathers or mothers, for murderers, for adulterers and perverts, for slave traders and liars and perjurers — and for whatever else is contrary to the sound doctrine that conforms to the glorious gospel of the blessed God, which he entrusted to me."

The word "properly" means "lawfully" and "one who competes according to the rules." When our laws are upheld, there is justice in our nation, but when they are misused, overlooked, abused, or ignored, there is chaos, dishonesty, and violence.

Rebelliousness means "insubordinate"; those who do not obey the laws. We need more subordination in our society. We need obedience to godly authority and righteous laws. When I was in the Navy and a sailor got out of hand by disobeying a superior, there were consequences. I was on watch on the Bridge when an enlisted man refused an order and began giving the officer of the deck attitude. I was shocked! I had never seen such disrespect. The officer was visibly angered, and within seconds, that enlisted man was physically removed by the master of arms, thrown in the brig, and eventually dishonorably discharged. Subordination is a good thing. It shows respect for authority, order, and the rule of law.

Paul goes on to address adulterers and perverts, literally sexually, immoral, and homosexuals (*Bible Hub*). And he goes on to say, "Whatever else that is contrary to the sound doctrine that conforms to the glorious gospel." Sound hear means "without error or perversion." It is the purest form of truth there is. If anything opposes it, it is wrong. Behavior must conform to the gospel. Truth cannot be renamed or reimagined regardless of how many in society want it to be so. Every "New Truth" must be measured by the gospel.

CHAPTER SIXTEEN

Market Place Ministry

*Woe to those who call evil good and good evil, who
put darkness for light and light for darkness, who
put bitter for sweet and sweet for bitter.*

Isaiah 5:20 (NIV)

Charles C. Ryrie writes, "The church is rebuked for permitting the false teaching of a prophetess who openly advocated apostasy. Her actual name may or may not have been Jezebel, but she was a true Jezebel in her actions (1 Kings 16; 2 Kings 9). She promoted immorality and idolatry (vs.20) in a doctrinal context that is described as the "deep things of Satan"—his attempt to make wrong seem right (vs.24) (Ryrie 31).

It is difficult to know what to do sometimes. As Christians, do we stand up and condemn sin in society? Or, do we do as the Apostle Paul says, "Judge those inside the church; God will judge those outside." I am afraid that the church has become so accustomed to being accepted by society that we are afraid to offend people. The gospel message is not only love and gentleness but warning and conviction. The Holy Spirit convicts the world of sin in regards to righteousness, and He uses our voices to do it. Jesus said, "Where do well dressed people live but in palaces, but John the Baptist came in camel's hair, a leather belt and eating locusts and wild honey" (Matthew 3:4, NIV).

Our pastor forefathers were kicked out of the very places some of our churches are acting like today. We need to exchange our suits for some street clothes and do some market place preaching. We need to warn, admonish, and make people feel ashamed of their sinful behavior instead of proud of it. We need to do so with a spirit of love and not condemnation or judgment. We cannot be rude as Christians or come across as self-righteous, angry, or prideful. Paul exhorts us in 1 Corinthians 13:4-7 (NIV),

> Love is patient, love is kind, it does not envy, it does not boast, it is not proud. It is not rude, it is not self-seeking, it is not easily angered, it keeps no record of wrongs. Love does not delight in evil but rejoices with the truth. It always protects, always trusts, always hopes, always perseveres.

Jesus was brutally honest in his market place preaching. In John chapter 9 we see Jesus is not alone. The Father is with Him. Chaplains who are called to street preaching and market place ministry should never go alone. Yes, you have the anointing and the power of the Holy Spirit within you, but you need support because of the persecution, insults, and hatred that will be spewed upon you.

Jesus challenged the establishment. In John chapter 8, we see how He dealt with those who were self-righteous and in sin. Verse 19 says, "You do not know me or my Father." In verse 21, He says, "You will die in your sin. Where I go, you cannot come." This angered them. In verse 26, He said, "I have much to say in judgment of you," and in verse 36, He says, "As He continues to preach to them, He tells them in verse 37, "You have no room for my word." In verse 43, He tells them they are unable to hear what God has to say. He then tells them their father is the devil and not God. Then He told them He is the "I am" in verse 58. This made them furious to the point they picked up stones to murder him, but Jesus slipped away.

Jesus gives us the perfect example of confronting society with its sin. He had a righteous anger about what He saw His Jewish society had become. He preached the truth with love. We know this because some became believers. In verse 30, "Even as he spoke, many put their faith in him." When we preach in hostile situations, we had better be spiritually prepared. Pray and fast before entering confrontational ministry.

I would encourage all Christians not to disparage street evangelists by thinking they are bringing reproach to the gospel message because they are preaching to people who may never hear the message otherwise. They will bear fruit because some will put their faith in what they are saying. Instead of being embarrassed by them, walk up to them and encourage them. Stand next to them in solidarity and prayer.

I have a friend who is a singer in a band. He is a Christian and plays in night clubs. He said he saw a street preacher outside of the club where he was playing that night. The preacher was being cursed at and ridiculed. He said he felt bad for the guy, but he was too embarrassed to stand by his side. God began dealing with him about getting out of that scene and singing Christian music. Perhaps this is a clear example of my friend getting too involved in *civilian affairs*. When it comes to obedience, one must be willing to put it all on the line, even if it is a career.

Jesus was not afraid to offend them; He blatantly told them they were "not going to go to heaven, they were children of the devil, and they want to carry out the devil's desires." Jesus cared about his community, so He boldly spoke out against it; so should we. We love the people in America so much that we want to warn them about the evils of sin. One of the things I have noticed about my generation as opposed to my grand-parents' generation is regarding worship ministry. Much of the worship is about how God has changed *my life*. How much God has done *for me*. Whereas, our grandparents were about what God *can do for others*. How God can be "Bringing in the Sheaves." There needs to be a better balance of both, but we cannot just focus on ourselves but have a burden to save the lost. We need a burden for lost souls once again. Street preachers have caught this vision. Catch it with them. Jesus was the ultimate street preacher and discipleship pastor. Jesus was well-rounded in ministry. He built His ministry, one upon another to three diverse audiences.

The first audience was in the market place where He confronted societal sins but also reminded them of God's love for them. This is where He got their attention. He intrigued them here. The second audience if they wanted to hear more, He preached in the countryside where He taught them further with parables and sermons. As He taught truth and freedom, many put their faith in Him. Those who came to hear Him teach about God were seeking something more. People were weary of religion and wanted meaning in their lives. People are still the same today. They long for truth. Jesus began satisfying their souls. The third audience was when He preached privately to His disciples. This is where He explained the parables and invested more heavily into the lives of believers.

We are called to all three as ministers of the gospel. We are called to town halls, community centers, and schools to oppose destructive societal sins. We are also called to answer those who are curious and want to hear more about having a personal relationship with God and living right in society. Lastly, we are called to "make disciples of all nations" (Matthew 28:19-20, the Great Commission). He demonstrated the best model for building a church. He showed us how to do it. It sounds easy, but it's not. Nevertheless, if we really want to impact our communities, then this is the risk we must take.

The Bible tells us we will be hated and persecuted for preaching truth. It's time we not only begin making our voices heard once again in society, but be willing to suffer the consequences. Peter and other Apostles experienced persecution in Acts 5:41-42 (NIV). "The Apostles left the Sanhedrin, rejoicing because they had been counted worthy of suffering disgrace for the Name. Day after day, in the temple courts from house to house, they never stopped teaching and proclaiming the good news that Jesus is the Christ."

In Acts 5:12-14 (NIV), "The Apostles performed many miraculous signs and wonders among the people. And all the believers used to meet together in Solomon's colonnade. No one else dared join them, even though they were highly regarded by the people. Nevertheless, more and more men and women believed in the LORD and were added to their number."

There is a sacred, secret feeling of God's presence in times of persecution. You feel closer to the LORD than ever before, as if He's standing right beside you. Persecution sets our priorities in order. The things of this world are not important anymore. The only thing that matters is the truth and publicly proclaiming it. When Christians step into the realm of risk-taking evangelism, they become emboldened and preach with more and more courage regardless of the opposition. I would encourage every Christian to get involved with your church in reaching out into your community. It has so many benefits. First, it will bring you closer to God. Second, you will unify the church and each other. Lastly, get beyond your needs and see the needs of others. God wants to use you to be a blessing to others.

Paul wrote the letter to the Philippians from prison. He talked about his own persecution for preaching the gospel. People tried to stop Paul's preaching, but it had the reverse effect—the gospel spread. Paul's cultural problem was the Judaizers. Evangelists will always face a cultural problem when preaching Christ.

Our culture wants to water down the gospel message. "If you preach that hard, you will turn people away." "Be more inclusive." "Don't say it's wrong to do such and such." Well, such and such isn't working and is destroying people's lives. I would rather preach the gospel and have people's lives transformed, marriages saved, and families restored than preach a watered-down message that leaves people enslaved to sin.

People Need Truth

The church is seeing an increase of false pastors and prophets rise to power. They are preaching what itching ears want to hear. Micah 2:11 (NIV) says, "If a liar and deceiver comes and says, 'I will prophesy for you plenty of wine and beer' that would be just the prophet for this people!"

Beware! The dividing line is coming! Right and wrong are becoming blatantly obvious. Over the years, we have heard of prophets prophesying when Jesus will return, only for the prophet to then turn around and blame the church for not praying hard enough. We are in a fight between good and evil. Christians will be forced to make bold decisions to follow Christ regardless of the direction our culture is heading. Thank God, most people still love the truth; they see through deception and cleverly-instigated lies. No matter how the lie is spun, discerning people see through duplicity and still long for truth.

Bank tellers can spot a phony bill immediately because they know what a real bill is. When Christians study the Word and have an intimate prayer life, they see the lie because they are so accustomed to the truth. Conversely, when people are constantly lied to, one of two things happens. One, they are skeptical of the Bible because it is so antithetical to what they have been taught. Or two, that when the truth is told to them it makes perfect sense. They may have always known they were lies intuitively, but now they have a reason to believe otherwise. When they hear the truth for the first time, it is liberating and *sets them free.* This is the risk in market place ministry.

We need hard preaching where the Holy Spirit can speak through calloused hearts and break down walls and barriers. The gospel message still works. It penetrates the heart, causing a godly sorrow with repentance and a changed life.

People are hardened these days. We face a culture of skepticism, sarcasm, intolerance of the gospel message, and even hostility toward God's Word and His people. Titus 1:12-13 (NIV) states, "The Cretan's own prophets have said, 'Cretans are always liars, evil brutes, lazy gluttons.' The saying is true. Therefore, rebuke them sharply to be sound in the faith." Americans are cynical, sarcastic, hardened, and even hostile to the gospel; therefore, rebuke them sharply, so they can be sound in the faith, too!

God is still moving, speaking, and reaching deep into a person's soul with a message of hope, healing, and a life filled with purpose and meaning. The Apostle Paul said, "Preach the Word. Be prepared in season and out of season" (II Timothy 4:2, NIV). The New Living Translation uses the word favorable. There are times when we preach in favorable situations and other times unfavorable ones. There are times when people are receptive to the gospel message, and there are times when they are not. It can be discouraging when we preach but do not see any results; nevertheless, God's Word does not return void. Seeds are planted.

I preach at two independent living centers on Sunday mornings. One is established and has mature Christians. The other one is a new work. Most of the people coming to the new work were nominal Christians with no convictions; some were even Buddhists. It was hard at first because I got those blank stares. Then God began to move as I continued to preach. The church began to grow as they listened and responded to the Word.

I pray God raises up more chaplain street preachers who preach with love, conviction, and accompanying signs and wonders. When you see a street preacher, and he is preaching the truth in love, stand beside him, encourage him. When you see a pastor standing up for just causes, make it a point to be there to support him and show solidarity. Too often we stand alone on an issue. When the church begins to mobilize itself, the world had better watch out because change is coming. Stand beside these men and women of God. Although God is by their sides, they will be encouraged when you stand with them, as well.

TAKE A STAND

God calls us to speak the truth in love. There is a time and a place for righteous crusaders, men like Martin Luther King, who spoke those words, "I have a dream."

Or the words of the philosopher John Stuart Mill, who said, "Bad men need nothing more to compass their ends, than that good men should look on and do nothing." They dared to take a stand, and others were emboldened to stand with them. There were times in church history when preachers, pastors, and spiritual leaders had to rise and take a stand against the destructive consequences of sin and put everything on the line for justice.

Saint Telemachus, a fourth-century monk, was so appalled by the gladiator fighting that he ran out into the colosseum and tried to stop the two men from killing one another. The crowd was so angry at the monk, they stoned him to death. The Christian emperor Honorius was so moved by the monk's martyrdom that he issued a ban on gladiator fighting (*The Voice of the Martyrs*). The gladiator games ended that day because of one man's zeal for God. This is the power of love. Jesus showed us a new law: The Law of Love. We see here the power love commands. Just by being Christians, we change the world.

Are you a Martin Luther King who works within the church yet calls for transformation from both within and without the church? Martin Luther King had his spiritual boundaries in order. He prayed, heard from God, and spoke what God wanted him to say to both the church and society.

We are called to be a light in this world. We live in a politically-correct world where people are afraid to speak the truth. We are fighting a zeitgeist (spirit of the times). We have to remember that even though we do not agree with someone's morality, he/she is not the enemy. The enemy is principalities and demonic powers in high places, influencing those whose minds are not redeemed, as per Ephesians 6:12. Satan and his emissaries are working overtime in America and across the world to wreak havoc and destruction. The human mind cannot conjugate depravity, such as we have seen. They are so evil they have to be demonic, but people open themselves up to Satan and allow him to use them in such a perverse way. In recent developments, we see the direct impact of such sinister behavior in our country and abroad that can only be conjured up in the mind of a demonic figure transferred into the mind of man. The depravity then becomes normalized.

We are slowly losing godly morality and need to fight back with prayerful spiritual warfare, while voicing our concerns. I believe if we do not change direction, the church will be persecuted in America.

Jeremiah 8:21-22 (NLT) says, "I hurt with the hurt of my people. I mourn and am overcome with grief. Is there no medicine in Gilead? Is there no physician there? Why is there no healing for the wounds of my people?" The prophet tells the reason why in Lamentations 2:14b: "They (the prophets) did not save you from exile by pointing out your sins." Sins of the people must be pointed out!

"'What sorrow awaits the leaders of my people—the shepherds of my sheep—for they have destroyed and scattered the very ones they were expected to care for,' says the LORD..." (Jeremiah 23:1, NLT). "Then I will appoint responsible shepherds who will care for them, and they will never be afraid again. Not a single one will be lost or missing. I the LORD have spoken" (verse 4, NLT).

In 2 Corinthians 5, "We demolish arguments and every pretension that sets itself up against the knowledge of God." Satan likes to *pretend* to have truth. His truth is sinister, but Christians have discernment to see through.

We must pray for boldness and take a stand. We must have spiritual courage even if it means persecution. The dividing line is coming! Right and wrong are becoming blatantly obvious. We have to take a united stand against the evils in the world. If we don't stand together, we will be divided. The time is coming when Christians will no longer be able to remain silent but will be forced to make a decision to either stand with the world or with Christ. It is not too late, but we all have to make a decision as to which side of the line we stand on.

CHAPTER SEVENTEEN

The Chaplain's Marriage

Husbands, love your wives, just as Christ loved the church and gave himself up for it...and the wife must respect her husband.

Ephesians 5:25; 33 (KJV)

FOREVER FAITHFUL

The marines use the phrase "Semper Fi," which means "Forever Faithful." When we took our vows on our wedding day, we vowed to care for each other in sickness and in health, for richer or poorer, till death do us part. For us, it has been mostly for sicker and poorer! We have been married for thirty-five years, and it took some doing. We both had our hang-ups and difficulties trying to become one flesh. Sometimes, marriage is easy, but other times, it takes work.

Stress from the ministry affects our marriage and family. Ministry creates every kind of emotion possible. Pastoring was the most bipolar job I ever had. You may officiate a wedding in the morning and a funeral in the afternoon. We carry people's burdens because we care deeply for the people we serve. I've striven to always put my family first with few exceptions.

One time, David and Ashlee were in the car, ready to go to the zoo for the day. The diaper bag was packed, juices, snacks, strollers, and the kitchen sink were all loaded when I got the call. There was a tragedy with a family in the church that needed immediate attention. The call was on speakerphone. I looked at my wife with a shrug of my shoulders and an "I'm sorry" look. We both knew I had to go.

Stress also affects caregiver marriages. As a hospice chaplain, I met a couple who were fighting as they were caring for a family member on hospice. I asked, "How did you two get along before?"

They gave me a quizzical look. "Before?"

"Before becoming a caretaker for your relative on hospice."

"Great." They agreed. "We did a lot together and never fought."

"You know, when you suddenly become a caregiver, it can take a toll on your marriage. Caregiving creates a unique kind of stress, anger, bitterness, and a list of other emotions that can affect even the healthiest relationships." I pointed out a few areas they could work on, both individually and as a couple. They weren't able to see why they were fighting because they were so busy living chaotic lifestyles. Sometimes people just need a gentle push in the right direction with a professional helping them identify the root cause. After they realized how they were living and made the necessary changes, their lives were much more peaceful.

Husbands and wives deal with the demands of work, family, ministry, and marriage. Marriage takes work. One of my favorite sayings is by Clint Eastwood, "Marriage is made in heaven—but so is thunder and lightning!" Thunder and lightning are powerful forces but so is marriage! If these powers are harnessed correctly, the marriage can be passionate. When we keep the design God aligned for the marriage, everything else builds perfectly into place. Christ is the head, husbands lead, wives support, and children follow. This structure for the family is as old as time began with Adam and Eve. It worked then, and it works now, regardless of trends and fads. Even when this is followed, marriage has its difficulties.

Ministry can create conflicts in the marriage. Long hours or lengthy times away on ministry trips cause temptations and frustrations, even among the most spiritual. Long hours away from home can create conflict and bitterness. The wife may feel she is all alone raising the kids, while the husband feels he is on the road providing for his family. Times like these may be necessary, but over the long haul, it can be very detrimental. A pastor colleague of mine, Reverend Bryan Koch, was involved in an extensive building project at his church. He was spending long hours at the office. His wife had enough of it and called the church office asking for a pastoral visit from him. I think she got her point across! It's a funny story, but it speaks volumes! God does not cause, nor want division in your home over ministry. He created us to be with one another, not separated from each other. If ministry is causing your marriage to fall apart, then it is time to re-evaluate your calling or use of time. Don't be another statistic. Take immediate action before it is too late.

I have come across too many divorced chaplains. Chaplains need to guard their own emotional weaknesses, temptations, and vulnerabilities. We often work with the opposite sex. We work with nurses, doctors, and office staff. It is easy to find a person who will say, "You deserve better. You deserve to be happy. She's not respecting you, or he is not loving you the way you deserve to be loved." Run like Joseph if you hear these words! Keep people out of your marital business. Others don't need to listen to your woes about your spouse. If they aren't helping, then they are hurting. Find a trusted friend or fellow minister to talk about your problems. All relationships go through difficult times. That's why we need people to lift us up. This fidelity of commitment goes both ways. The same warning goes for the chaplain's wife. My wife worked as a manager at Walmart and would often get hit on by other guys. She always declined their offers because we have put God first and our marriage second.

The movie *Fireproof* gives a great example of God's unconditional love. In the movie, the man gives this explanation. "When one of the marriage partners loses their love for the other, it is the obligation and duty of the other to save it by pouring love into the other—even if it is not reciprocated." That is a hard thing to do.

If you have been married for a while, you've probably had an argument. Perhaps you think it's beyond fixing. However, it is "not our will, but God's will be done." There are times when we need to put our interests aside and hear the voice of God to "love your wife and kids and spend time with them." Dr. and Sister Kenzy always said, "L-O-V-E is spelled T-I-M-E." Time allows room to reconnect and remember why you fell in love with this wonderful person in the first place. Time together builds stronger marriages and healthier families. Spend time together without the children. Hire a babysitter and take that special lady out on a date and spoil her! Time away from ministry will renew how much you love and appreciate each other. Neither partner will ever tire of hearing those cherished words, "I love you," and when those words are spoken, even daily, it strengthens the bond of marriage.

Church members who are reading this, help your pastor or chaplain and his wife if they cannot afford a baby sitter on their salary. Pastors often leave their extended family and minister in a new area. Please offer to watch their children. If the church cannot afford a better salary, there are other ways to take care of them. Slip them a Pentecostal handshake with a $100 for a night out. Buy groceries and leave them on the doorstep. Pastors sacrifice so much for the ministry; the last thing to sacrifice should not be their marriage. They are taking care of you spiritually; take care of them physically. When you invest in your pastor's marriage, you are ministering to them and showing how much you love them.

SEXUAL INTIMACY

Spend time in sexual intimacy. Sexual intimacy is deeper than the physical. It brings us closer together and creates a stronger bond emotionally and spiritually.

Tim and Kathy Keller write in their book, *The Meaning of Marriage*, "Indeed sex is perhaps the most powerful God-created way to help you give your entire self to another human being. Sex is God's appointed way for two people to reciprocally say to one another, 'I belong completely, permanently, and exclusively to you.'"

"Sex...is your covenant renewal service" (Tacoma Christian Counselor).

Proverbs 5:18 (NIV) says, "May your fountain be blessed, and may you rejoice in the wife of your youth."

The older we get the more in love we become. I have always been comfortable with Dorothy and she with me. Our attraction was not only physical, we enjoyed each other's company, and we still do. Therefore, in lean times and times of plenty make a conscious effort to do things together.

The Apostle Paul said, "The two become one flesh" in Ephesians 5:31. The two becoming one flesh is deeper than sex; it's about an emotional unity. When we marry, we have to prune parts of ourselves in order to get along well together. One flesh means to be in unity.

When two single people date, they learn to compromise. They cannot go in opposite directions as they did when they were single. Now, they have to think about the other person's needs, desires, and wants. There is accountability. Out of respect, you let the other know where you are going and when you will be returning.

You decide together who can pick up the kids on Wednesday afternoon. Who will drive your daughter to band practice and your son to football? Married couples work together. You can't always have it your way anymore. Selfishness has no part in the marriage. There is a pruning that takes place. When that happens, new growth comes forth. You have to lose parts of your independence in order to be inter-dependent. By striving toward that goal both individually and as a couple, you will discover there are more gains than there are losses. The two become one in direction, goals, values, and worship. Then, coming together sexually enhances the relationship more and deepens the bonds of love. One cannot be more open, available, and vulnerable than when we are naked physically, emotionally, and spiritually with our spouse. When Adam and Eve were naked in the garden of Eden, there was no shame, no concealment, no hidden secrets, and no falsehood between them. They were open and honest with each other. They literally *knew each other* inside and out. Sexual and emotional intimacy is designed to be pure. We are not to cover ourselves with fig-leaves, but to be fully transparent with one another. This is marriage in its purest and most intimate form.

AVOID A CRITICAL SPIRIT

It is easy to fall into the trap of becoming critical. Make sure nothing comes between you and your spouse. I don't care if it's in-laws, out-laws, friends, family, church people, or even your own children—nothing comes between you and your spouse—ever! Ephesians 4:29 (NIV) says, "Do not let any unwholesome talk come out of your mouths but only what is helpful for building others up according to their needs so that it may benefit those who listen."

Chaplains are often around non-Christians who do not support our worldview. Critical people can influence you into being critical in your marriage. They may say things like, "You deserve better," or "You shouldn't have to put up with that." Those who don't know the LORD operate with fly-by-night feelings rather than a vow of "til death do us part." This attitude can affect your attitude toward your spouse. Be very careful that no one puts a negative attitude into your spirit about your spouse. If words do not build up, then they are tearing down.

Men thrive on respect. Women, respect and appreciate your husband for working hard to provide a roof over the family's head and food on the table.

When I officiate a wedding ceremony, I often quote Ephesians 5:33 (NLT). "So again, I say, each man must love his wife as he loves himself, and the wife must respect her husband." A man who is constantly belittled, degraded, and/or disrespected by his wife will walk around with his head hanging, feeling disgraced and humiliated.

A woman who is as Proverbs 27:15 (NLT) says, "A quarrelsome wife is as annoying as a constant dripping on a rainy day;" She will kill a man's spirit. We must constantly remind ourselves that words and actions penetrate deep into one's spirit and affects him/her critically and deeply. No one can hurt us as deeply as the one we vowed to love. No one likes to see a man emotionally beat up by his wife and vice versa. It is uncomfortable and unnatural to observe—an embarrassment to witness.

When King David brought back the ark after his conquest, his wife, Michal, despised him in her heart. She scorned him for dancing like a commoner in front of the slave girls. Her critical spirit was the end of that relationship! It wasn't long afterward that David committed adultery and murder to get what he should have received from his wife: respect and affection. Instead of being in the arms of his wife, he was in bed with Bathsheba.

When husbands and wives do not give each other the needed affections, one or the other will be tempted to seek love elsewhere. 1 Corinthians 7:5 (NIV) says, "Do not deprive each other except for mutual consent and for a time, so that you may devote yourselves to prayer. They come together again so that Satan will not tempt you because of your lack of self-control." Guard your marriage; guard your soul. "Guard your heart above all else, for it determines the course of your life" (Proverbs 4:23, NLT). God calls us to love our spouses unconditionally.

Most of the men I meet are hard workers. We sometimes work two jobs and as much overtime we can get so we have extras for the family. That is how we show our love. Men are different; we express our love differently. We don't think of the details as Mom does, but we love our family just as much; we show it differently. Different does not mean less than. We may not always be carrying our emotions on our sleeves, but we love just as much, care just as much, and want to help just as much. Sometimes, we just don't know how. Women are more natural at emotional things than men, but we do care. Men have to work at being more affectionate. We have to intentionally think about giving, serving, and loving where these attributes come naturally for women. I've worked with men over the years in men's groups, counseling, etc. and found us to be the same when it comes to showing appreciation, affection, and serving. We have to be told to do these things; it doesn't come naturally for us. Some men are great examples, and I have learned to be better by their example.

While I was in Bible college, I worked with a lady at Maranatha nursing home whose husband died several years earlier. During a lunch break one time, she talked about him. She loved him, and he adored her. He came home early from work every Friday at noon and did all the housework, so they could spend Saturdays together instead of doing chores. She said, "I loved him so much; he was a great man, and he loved me and the kids." Stories like hers motivate me to be better. I remembered that story when I pastored years later. I copied his example. I came home early on Fridays to cook and clean, so we could spend time together as a family. I never would have thought of doing something like that on my own. We, men, need to stretch ourselves by reading marriage and family books. As new ideas are presented, allow the Holy Spirit to change us into better husbands and fathers.

As a chaplain, I was asked to officiate vow renewals for seven couples at a local Assisted Living Facility. One older gentleman who had been married for sixty-five years, said in front of his wife, "I'm not renewing my vows; I'm keeping the one I made sixty years ago." He took his vow seriously. I'm sure even for him marriage took effort.

Marriage is loving that person even when you don't feel like it. Marriage is caring for that person when he/she is old and feeble. Marriage is a vow to God and our spouse that we are committed no matter what.

Malachi 2:16 says God hates divorce. Divorce is cruel because it affects everyone in the immediate and extended family, as well as society. I saw the direct results divorce had on our neighborhood children. My kids often brought over friends from the neighborhood. We would sit by the campfire, and they would tell me their stories. Some told me their parents had rented out their rooms, and they were "sleeping in the closet"; or "we don't have dinner times; these marsh-mellows are my dinner." "Dad is in jail, and Mom has a new boyfriend."

Nothing surprises me anymore. The real casualties are the children who feel betrayed and abandoned, and they often blame themselves. Their minds are not equipped to handle divorce. They see their parents fighting all the time and don't know what a happy marriage is. They are not taught life skills or the proper way of handling conflicts. Their trust is broken, and the odds of them having a healthy family themselves are low. The hurt extends to grandparents, aunts, uncles, and the children who are caught in the middle of custody battles. God says he hates divorce because of the destructive path it leaves in its wake.

Most divorced people agree that one or both had visions of grandeur that the grass was greener. If you want a Spirit-filled marriage, do some pruning and get the marriage healthy again. Too many people lose what God gave them simply because they haven't maintained what they already have.

Divorce is based on selfishness. In Proverbs, Solomon reminds his son to keep on guard. Pour energy into the marriage. Divorce happens when one or both parties stop trying and succumb to selfish interests. Divorced couples often admit it was the most painful experience they ever had.

However, God is also the God of second chances. If you are divorced and on your second marriage, don't carry around the guilt, weight, and mistrust from the previous marriage. A friend of mine went through "Divorce Care." It is a thirteen-week course that mends the wounds and hurts of divorce. I would recommend it for anyone who has gone through the pain of divorce. No matter which marriage it is, do all you can to ensure it is your last marriage. Guard it, protect it, pray over each other, and work hard at keeping it Spirit-filled!

Chaplains, keep your head on straight. Don't allow anything to destroy the good person God brought into your life. Marriage and family are worth fighting for, living for, and dying for. Surround yourself with like-minded friends who want the best for both of you.

SHOW APPRECIATION

God created us uniquely male and female to glorify God, but we each have different ways to express love. Love is serving the other and doing special things for one another. Doing these practices will always work. The first is to appreciate her. Show appreciation for all your wife does. Be thankful for the daily chores she does, such as cooking, cleaning, and laundry. Appreciate her running the children around to doctors' appointments, errands for grocery shopping, clothes shopping for the kids, and so much more. Appreciate her love for the entire family.

Another practice is to only see the good in the other and not the bad. Don't be on the giving or receiving end of criticism. The world is full of negativity, but the home is our sanctuary. It is a place where we can come home to a family that loves us when we had a bad day. It is a place where the children can relax and be their crazy selves. It is a place where Mom's heart is full of people who love and honor her. Create an atmosphere of love where affirmation is high. Having an affirming, positive attitude creates an atmosphere of fun and security for the whole family. Think before pointing out the negatives. Replace it with something positive. Marriages represent the relationship between Christ and His church. It is a love relationship.

As my son and his girlfriend, Hamilton, put an oak stain on a table he built, I walked up behind her. "Hamilton," I said, "You know a guy needs his ego stroked often."

She grinned with a twinkle in her eye. "Oh, I know. I told him how proud I was of him."

"David, a woman needs a lot of love," I said to my son and nodded toward his girlfriend with a wink.

He said sarcastically, "Oh, boy! Do I know."

I thought she was going to smack him, but he was joking. He gives her a lot of attention and affection, so I'm proud of him. I reminded them both to look for and find the good in each other.

God created us uniquely different to complement each other. One person said, "Our generation is so busy trying to prove that women can do anything men can do, women are losing the unique qualities that set us apart—the God-given femininity and unique way our Creator designed us. Women weren't created to do everything a man can do... women were created to do everything a man can't do" (anonymous).

When gas was $4 a gallon, my wife drove thirty miles out of her way to a store. We were spending the day together, and I said to her, "Why are we going way out here when we could have gone to Walmart just down the road?" Little did I know of her intentions. She shopped and shopped not only at that store but others up that way. She didn't buy anything for herself. She had this all planned out to buy clothes for the kids and me. It hit me that driving thirty miles out of the way was not out of the way for her. I was thinking of the gas money, while she was thinking of the family. I realized that I will never understand what my wife is thinking, but I know one thing: She takes care of us! I value the difference in her and appreciate her because she is nothing like me! This world has certainly done a number trying to conform and confuse sexual identities. As women show their love for the family by buying things for us; men show love by providing for their families.

As much as a man needs respect, a woman needs love. She doesn't want love; she *needs* it. A woman's heart has the God-given desire to be wanted and loved. When a man focuses his attention on her, she will feel fulfilled in her marriage. She will gladly respect and follow you to the ends of the earth. She will trust you and love you deeply in return. *The Five Love Languages* book by Gary Chapman lists great ways to show how much you love her. But out of the five love languages, love has to be the focus because everything else comes out of that. Gifts, communication, words of affection, and appreciation all stem from a motive of love. "Love is patient and kind and does not boast" (I Corinthians 13). Where there is love, all these things will only increase. Appreciation, affection, and respect will abound in the home. "Love never fails." Bitterness fails, unforgiveness fails, anger fails, but love never fails. All those feelings fail, but love never fails.

Godly women are vital to the Christian family. Women thrive on love, so men love your wives. We have a Heavenly Father Who tells women how beautiful they are inside and out. This is how God views women as shown in Proverbs 31:10-31. Maybe she feels she hasn't always measured up according to these verses all the time. That is when it is up to the husband to make her feel better about herself. Women are often pleasantly surprised at all the good things people say about them. Though they don't always see it themselves, their husbands, family and others do. She works hard, cares for her husband, and her husband calls her blessed. He also is respected at the town gate. When the two complement each other in this way, their marriage is strong to the end.

One thing I have always admired was when I witnessed the spouse holding the hand of his/her dying life-long best friend. That speaks words of comfort, love, and gratefulness. That emotional cup is filled to the very end.

CHAPTER EIGHTEEN

Parenting Healthy Children

Children are a gift from the Lord; they are a reward from him.

Psalm 127:3 (NKJV)

One time I said to the Lord, "Lord, I would die for my son David." The Lord replied, "Yes, but will you live for him?" We not only provide for our children's physical needs but are called to care for their spiritual and emotional needs, as well. It has been an adventure raising these wild children of ours, and the adventures never end. Someone told me I should write stories of all the kids' crazy actions over the years, so here are a few. Maybe you can relate.

We were at Knoebles Amusement Park in Elysburg, PA. My wife was ahead of us in the log flume with the two girls. My son and I were in the flume behind them with me in the front seat. When my wife looked back, she saw David's legs up in the air. He had fallen out of the log flume. When I looked back to see if he was having fun, I saw him in the water. At first, I laughed, thinking this nine-year-old was playing around, but then I saw his look of fear. I jumped in after him and tried to lift him up, but the current was too strong.

"David. Listen. I'm going to lift you out of the water and throw you as hard as I can. OK?"

His eyes were still fearful, but I also saw he trusted me. He was so scared and cold he couldn't speak, so he shook his head "Yes."

I picked him up and threw him out of the water onto the ground, and then I jumped out. The people behind stopped everyone in their logs. They piled up like logs floating down a river! People were wondering what was going on. The ride was shut down. We were both soaked as we jumped the fence to get back into the park. Everyone stared at us. The police came. The park administrator had us sign a ton of papers.

"Why did you jump out?" I asked David.

He was too scared to tell the truth, so he took the fifth and remained silent. We figured it out though. He tossed his stuffed animal up in the air to play catch, and it fell in the water. He just had to go in after it!

Another time I had left my lighter on the grill from the night before. My two daughters got a hold of it. Trying to roast marshmallows, they accidentally lit the backyard leaves on fire, burning the lawn and the fence. The fire department arrived. Oh, we were the talk of the neighborhood that time!

Ashlee always liked slimy stuff. She smeared petroleum jelly all over the tub. When I stepped in, I slipped, ripping the shower curtain down. I yelled, "Where is Ashlee? I'm gonna kill that kid!" My wife said Ashlee had already left for kindergarten.

Another time, Ashlee's room reeked when I walked by. I found a rancid concoction of milk, shampoo, make-up, and lipstick festering behind her dresser. Another time she overdosed a baby kitten. We hadn't seen it for a day, so we assumed it was lost. We spent three days looking for that cat. We put posters all over the neighborhood. It turns out Ashlee gave her too much medicine. After three days of being behind a drawer in her room, the kitten finally woke up.

Mikala was my curious one. When she was four, she pulled the fire alarm at the foster care building. She also wanted to drive all by herself like a big girl. At the ripe old age of three, Dorothy pulled up in the driveway, leaving the car running. She ran into the house for a minute to pick up something. Mikala unbuckled her car seat and climbed into the driver's seat. Somehow, she put the car in reverse. The car rolled backward down the driveway and hit our neighbor's car. No one got hurt, but my neighbor wasn't happy. It's a good thing he was a Christian. I offered to pay for everything, but there was no damage except to our parenting skills.

Mikala's stories aren't done yet. We got a new puppy that wasn't potty trained and made a mess on the carpet in the basement. Mikala was two and thought it was play time. She put on her boots and did a happy dance in it, getting it all over the basement carpet. I was gagging

I'm in trouble! If I put a bandage strip on it, maybe that will fix it!

when I had to clean her and the mess. I had to throw that carpet out; we kept Mikala.

Now, my kids are all older and having kids of their own. I can laugh instead of cry. With all the stuff they put us through, there is no greater joy than watching them grow up into mature adults.

God has a plan for your kids. He will protect them from all the crazy things they do and put you through! Those are fond memories. Back in the day, I loved spending time with them. I loved having Mondays off to have time with the kids. We went to every park in Berks County. We went on zoo trips and visited family. A funny memory is a picture of my son David sleeping on the car ride home from Knoebels with one of those foot-long suckers stuck to the side of his mouth. These stories may remind you of all your funny family stories. Cherish them; make even more memories. Your family is not only worth dying for but worth living for.

WHAT CHILDREN NEED

"What boys need from their fathers growing up" was the topic at a men's conference I attended. Boys need reassurance, unconditional love, and security. Mostly, they need their dads to tell them how proud they are of them. I tell my son continuously how proud I am of him. That instills a healthy self-esteem. They never outgrow hearing that.

The word *encourage* means to *instill courage into another*. A father should encourage and instill confidence in his children. Scripture says fathers shouldn't exasperate their children but instead lift them up. Fathers teach love, strength, and courage to their sons who then develop healthy relationships with God and others. Fathers are to help their kids make it through life by teaching life lessons, faith, a strong work ethic, and so much more. Mostly, they instill confidence.

Likewise, girls need five things from their fathers to make them feel confident, loved, and secure.

1. They need to know they are beautiful inside and out. Every girl longs to know she is beautiful.
2. They need unconditional love. Daughters need to know their dads love them and hear these words, "I love you," and "I believe in you." This instills confidence.
3. They need you to show how happy you are that God gave them to you. "I'm so blessed to be your dad."
4. They need you to be inquisitive and interested in their lives. Ask, "What have you been thinking about?"
5. They need you to listen and pray for them.

Our culture has devalued the importance of fathers. Television sit-com dads are often portrayed as bumbling idiots who are uninvolved and know very little about what is going on under their roofs. They are disrespected by their wives and children. Men have been emasculated by psychology and pop culture and are not viewed as protectors, providers, or as strong leaders in the home. Sadly, young boys in the twenty-first century are being taught to be effeminate rather than confident. Some speak with femininity rather than their God-given masculinity. Young men need to be taught how to be godly men.

Young men who will someday be the God-appointed father and protector of their homes, must learn from godly fatherly examples.

They need to know how to lead so that the family feels secure under his leadership.

Young women desire to follow a strong Christian man who will take the lead, who loves God, and who loves his wife and family. Way too many fathers have neglected their families. The children then suffer from severe identity crises. The church has the opportunity to play a surrogate role in raising young boys and developing godly character. More than ever, the church needs to fill this gap for fatherless boys and girls and teach them who they are in Christ!

God has given us the family structure in Ephesians 6:1-3. Obey and honor your parents. Teenagers are in that in-between age of pushing the boundaries. They do this to see how far they can go. Testing their parents, they want to see if Mom and Dad care enough to pull them back. Teens might act like they want complete independence, but they are still insecure deep inside. They need to know Mom and Dad are there for them if they get in over their heads.

Proverbs 17:6b (NIV) says, "Parents are the pride of their children." Children won't say it, but they are proud of their parents. They love to see their moms and dads actively involved in life whether it is at church, coaching, throwing parties, or attending social events. They observe how we interact with the greater world and learn from our example how to socially interact. Children need to tell their parents how much they appreciate them and are thankful for all they have done for you.

Here are a few things children need to learn regarding their parents.

1. Accept their authority and recognize that authority has come from God. Parents know what's best for you; they have the wisdom and experience. Learn to submit to that authority. This teaches you how to submit to the Holy Spirit's leading and God's authority over your life.

2. Resist the temptation to argue with them over everything. Your parents love you and only have good intentions for you.

3. Treat them with respect. This involves not only what you say, but how you say it. You might be obedient, but the way you respond can be insolent.

4. Learn to serve your family. We taught our children to help and serve one another. This way they learn not only to be blessed but to be a blessing.

5. Value your parents' wisdom and decisions. It might be hard for a teen to believe, but Mom and Dad were teenagers once, too, and they probably did the same things you are doing. They know where your actions or attitude will lead. They know the end result, so listen to them!

6. As your parents get older, take care of them. They took care of you; now it's your turn to care for them. Even Jesus made sure his mother was cared for by the Apostle John as stated in John 19:26. Someday, they will be frail and not able to do what they once could. In spite of that, they will always be your heroes.

7. Watch that you aren't harsh with them. Many children become caretakers for their elderly parents. Be gentle with them. A long-time family friend that our children have known as Uncle Michael cared for his mother who had Alzheimer's for ten years. It wasn't always easy, but he cared for her till the end.

In the same way, fathers take care not to be harsh with your children by provoking their impressionable little minds as stated in Ephesians 6:4. Some of us had great fathers; others had bad fathers; still others like myself had no father. Fathers, instill courage in your children and other children whenever possible. The world needs positive role models.

FATHER'S SPIRITUAL LEADERSHIP

Fathers must confront conflict immediately. Jacob could have used a course in marriage, family, and ministry class. When I look at how his children turned out, I am amazed that they became the twelve patriarchs of Israel. They were a mess, and Jacob's parenting skills didn't help. Thank God for grace.

Jacob avoided conflict, played favorites, and was probably passive-aggressive. In Genesis chapter 34, we read where his daughter, Dinah, was raped, and he did nothing about it. Because of his silence and fear, her brothers decided to do something about it. Fathers need to be the ones who protect the family, not the children. Because of Jacob's inaction, his sons took the lead and slaughtered the townspeople. To Jacob's discredit, he was more concerned about his neighbors' reactions than his daughter's honor. It was only after his fear of retaliation that he went to God in prayer. God told him to leave. Jacob should have prayed to God right after Dinah was raped. He should have sought guidance from God and then confronted the situation head-on with courage. Instead, he let the matter fester, and it became even worse. Children should never have to be put in that position. Our children are not capable of handling conflict the way adults can. Their hearts might be in the right place, but their actions are often over-zealous.

We cannot sacrifice our family's needs on the altar of ministry. We cannot afford to care what our neighbors, congregation, and others think. We need to do the right thing by putting family first. Jacob's determination to assimilate into this pagan community cost him his relationship with his children. Granted, he had a small family, and in that day, small meant vulnerable. Little clans were wiped out by bigger nations. Jacob held onto God's promise of turning him into a great nation, but he lacked faith in trusting God to protect him in this situation. His indifference was hypocritical, and his children paid the price for his passivity.

Our families come first. We need to do the right things and trust in God to handle the outcome. Children need to know they are our priority. When my daughter Ashlee was nine years-old, a neighbor said something very hurtful to her. I was livid. It took all day to calm down and pray. The next day I went over and talked to her. It did not go over well. Her son was present when I told her that what she said to my daughter was very hurtful and harmful. She and her son got very defensive and began swearing at me then telling me to leave. Our friendship was never the same. However, I needed to let her know she overstepped her boundaries. It also showed my daughter that I would not leave it up to her to handle; that was my responsibility, not hers.

Fathers are there to protect children from abuse and let them know they are valued. Mom and Dad will risk friendships to do the right thing. On the other hand, we must not give our kids special treatment just because they are the pastor's kids. Other church people need to understand this, too. One Sunday school teacher said he didn't want to correct my children because they were the pastor's kids. I told him he needed to correct them when necessary and to do otherwise would be a disservice. Children need love, but they also need discipline. Discipline without love is harsh. Love without discipline is negligent. Discipline with love teaches children to be well-mannered.

CHAPTER NINETEEN

Raising The Prodigal Child

When he came to his senses, he said "How many of my father's hired servants have food to spare, and here I am starving to death! I will set out and go back to my father and say to him: Father, I have sinned against heaven and against you. I am no longer worthy to be called your son; make me like one of your hired servants." So he got up and went to his father.

Luke 15:17-20 (NIV)

We had to celebrate and be glad, because this brother of yours was dead and is alive again; he was lost and is found.

Luke 15:32 (NIV)

P arents aren't perfect. I have heard it repeatedly by children raised in Christian homes, "My parents raised me right; I went astray; I'm back now." They wish they never left the church. I don't know why some children become pastors and others prodigals. We can invest in our children, support them, and still they leave the church and embrace the world. Maybe it's because Christian children take advantage of the grace of God. They believe that just because their parents are Christian, they are safe to do what they want without consequence.

People confuse God's blessings with being right with Him. Just because things are going well doesn't mean we're saved. We still need to repent and ask for God's forgiveness. Psalm 145:9 says, "The LORD is good to everyone. He showers compassion on all His creation" (NLT). God is good to everyone — the saved and the unsaved — but we still have to do our part in coming humbly to Him and then begin living for Him. And, why wouldn't we? He is a gracious and loving God Who simply wants to bless us as we walk in obedience to Him.

In the Old Testament, a child was under the covenant of salvation as long as he didn't walk away from the law. Today, children are responsible to choose to accept Jesus as Savior at the age of accountability. It is at this time when they know right from wrong. However, many children in a Christian family may feel they are special to God and that God will "wink" at their sin. Sooner or later, however, God's patience runs out, His hand is removed, and they feel the consequences of their sin.

Prodigals never realize just how far they've strayed from God until they encounter a genuine move of the Holy Spirit. I have witnessed this in church services many times. They visit with their parents or come for a special service. The Holy Spirit begins to work in their hearts. They realize how far they've wandered from God, and conviction begins to set in. They finally *come to their senses* and feel God's presence once again. They missed it for so long they forgot what it was like. Then the tears flow, sorrow follows, and the result is a restored, joyful relationship with God.

Our role as parents to the rebellious child is to always provide a loving home, a place where the child knows Mom and Dad loves him/her no matter how badly the child has destroyed his/her life. "Teach your daughter or son that coming home from a failed relationship is better than coming home in a coffin" (*Facebook @Swizz*). Parents need to always leave the door open. There are exceptions, of course, when allowing them in your home will interfere with the safety of others.

I know some of the godliest parents whose children went wild. They got a taste of what they thought was the good life, and they ran with it. Love them, put them in God's hands, and trust Him to do what is best for them. Even with tears in your eyes, let God do His work to completion. God will bring them home.

I have ministered to many parents whose children were prodigals at one time. They rebelled hard and sometimes for a long period of time, but they came back to God. Now, as mature adult Christians themselves, they are taking care of their dying parents. I hear these stories all the time how they ran from God. They did vile things, but in the back of their minds, they knew they weren't living right. They were miserable in that lifestyle. They felt God's tug calling them home and finally they relented. I believe God's promise in Proverbs 22:6 (KJV): "Train a child in the way he should go; and in the end, he will not depart from it." Your son or daughter is not rebelling against you; they are rebelling against God. Just like you and I had to finally surrender, they have to make that decision for themselves. One thing I know for sure is that God wins every time! God is working. Mom and Dad, just love them, and let God heal your heart when your child breaks it. Always let him/her know he/she has a nice, safe, and loving home to come back to and is welcome any time. These principles can help steer our children in the right direction. Parents must have a Holy Spirit-filled home where love abounds so their children know what they are missing when they go astray.

Children observe everything. They are like little sponges, absorbing everything they see us do. Parents demonstrate relationships, whether good or bad. Children are not paying as much attention to what we say but what we do. If they see Mom and Dad kiss, hug, or hold hands with genuine love, they will feel secure. They will form healthy self-esteem and, in turn, know how to give and receive love to develop healthy relationships themselves. On the other hand, if they see their parents always fighting and back biting, they develop distrust.

Proverbs 22:6 gives hope to those with backslidden children, so never stop interceding, never stop praying, and never give up on them! God is setting things in motion for them to come back to Him in His time and in His way! If they disappear from your sight, remember they are never out of God's sight.

The Word of God tells us "not to be harsh with our children. Treat older men with respect, younger women like sisters, and older women like mothers." If we are to treat others this way, how much more lovingly, gentle, and caring should we treat our own families?

I had a hospice patient whose daughter was caring for her. She said her daughter had backslidden for a long time. I peered up at the daughter as she was nodding in agreement. I could tell it was a painful experience for her, but she wanted to give God the glory, so she told me all about it.

She was raised in a good and loving Christian home, but the cravings of the world got into her heart. She began to tell me, "I got into drinking, drugs, and clubbing. I was married but I wanted more. I slept around with a lot of men. My husband left me, I lost family, friends, and jobs. I was a mess. I knew I was running from God, but my heart was hard, and I did it anyway. Then my mother became ill."

Her mother looked at her and told her to continue the story. She continued. "This happened about twenty years ago when I was still living in sin. Mom was really sick, and I was by the bedside. I fell asleep. I had a horrible dream I was in hell! I was in a cage and couldn't see anything. The only time I could see was when the atmosphere lit up when someone was thrown into a lake of fire. The demons were sinister and had an evil laugh as people screamed in torment. It was pitch black; then a demon would suddenly appear right in front of my face and turn into a frightening creature. Then it would disappear. I cried out to God in my dream. I woke up by my mom's bedside, terrified and trembling in fear. I knew my experience was real and that I was going to hell if I didn't change my lifestyle. I prayed for God to spare my mom's life. I needed her so much. Mom was a godly-Christian woman, and I needed her to live."

She went on to say, "While I was having my dream, my mom was having a dream of her own; only a far better one. Mom dreamed she was in heaven." Her mom began to speak. "I went into heaven. It was beautiful and full of love. I saw Jesus. He was handsome. He was someone you just wanted to be near. He had on a white robe and purple sash. He asked me if I wanted to stay. I told Him I wanted to, but I needed to go back and be there for my children. "They need me."

Then I woke up. I was so happy! I noticed, however, that my daughter was crying. I asked her what was wrong. She told me about her horrific dream. I listened and knew that my decision to stay here was the right one. I then told her of mine. As we were sharing our dreams, Susan's heart began to change. She knew she was in a terrible place in her life and needed God. She asked God to forgive her of all of her sins, and she accepted Jesus as Lord and Savior."

Susan said, "That was twenty years ago, and I have been living for God ever since. Now, I am here caring for Mom. It is time for her to go and be with Jesus, this time for good." She looked at her mom and said, "I will see you again." I was profoundly moved by both of their testimonies. We held hands and prayed. She passed away a few days later.

I share that to encourage any parent with a backslidden child that God loves him/her more than we do, and He has the power to bring him/her back home. Your child may have to experience the fires of hell first, but God is allowing it to happen, so He can bring your child home for good.

HOSTILE HOME ENVIRONMENT

Tension in the home creates anxiety and fear in children. In Ezekiel 18:2 (ESV), it says, "The fathers eat sour grapes, and the children's teeth are set on edge." It is no wonder we have an epidemic of children who are on anxiety medication. The breakdown of the nuclear family has created fear, worry, and nervous conditions thrust upon our children. The traditional structure of the family has been under fire for the last forty years. The family dynamic has changed and not for the better. When the parents are under stress or marital discord, without God in the home, there is a greater risk for hostility. I am not saying this is happening in every family, but as a general rule, there is a lot of anger in homes these days. Children internalize these tensions and live as if they are on a never-ending roller coaster ride with their teeth clenched in fear. There is an epidemic of anxiety in the American youth because of the lack of godly parenting.

People tell chaplains some of the most horrendous stories of abuse. A man named Daniel told me how his father hated him, and how his stepmother molested him. To make matters worse they sent him to a Catholic orphanage where he was molested by staff. His father found out about it and took him back home. It was almost no better there because his father told him daily how much he hated him. Daniel had a difficult life. He never married and had difficulty with relationships. He especially didn't want anything to do with church. When Daniel came onto hospice, he never wanted me to pray with him, but he did appreciate the company. I had built a good relationship with him and began seeing him each week. After about three months, he opened up to me regarding all of the things he had been through. After breaking down and crying, he shared his hurts, disappointments, and difficulties in life. He did, however, have some positive experiences. He had always felt as if an angel were watching over him. He began to talk about his faith in God but not the church. His heart began to soften with each visit. He eventually let me pray with him and talk about God. The Holy Spirit began to work in his life. Then one day, he finally accepted Christ as his Savior. He now sits in chapel service where I preach every Sunday. He continues to suffer with bad memories, but God is healing many of those hurts as he grows in his relationship with God. A violent home destroyed the potential of a good life for this man. It doesn't have to be this way.

HEALTHY HOME ENVIRONMENT

A Holy Spirit-filled marriage produces a Holy Spirit-filled family. A District Council speaker once said, "We were missionaries in Africa. Mom and Dad did everything together. They loved each other. When we went walking in the evenings, we sang hymns. Mom and Dad loved each other, and we felt their love. I was blessed to be raised in such a good home." This man learned how to walk with God from an early age because of the influence of his parents.

My wife and I began having nursery Bible stories when our kids were small. As they grew, we switched to children's Bible stories until we graduated to selected Bible readings. Since they were born and through their elementary years, we had family Bible reading and prayer every night. Then our kids became teenagers. I thought they were old enough to have their own devotional time. Boy, was I wrong! One of the worst mistakes I made was to stop having family devotions. If I could rewind the clock, I would. The kids didn't take the initiative to have their own regular devotion time as I thought they would, and it showed. Don't make the same mistake we did. Have those family times all the way up until they are ready to move out of the house.

I've made my share of mistakes. Sitting at the dinner table one night, the kids began to act up. I thought to myself, *What am I doing here? Do I really need to put up with this nonsense?* The LORD corrected me saying, "It's because you stopped serving your family."

I was neglecting them for a short period of time. My workload was heavy, and a bitter spirit had crept into my heart. Thankfully, God convicted me of that bitterness. I couldn't allow it to grow any further. I changed my attitude with thankfulness. I began to spend more time with the kids and serve them. Almost every night I took them to the playground and spent time pushing them on the swings and catching crawdads in the creek. Things got better. When I changed my attitude, theirs did too. I was setting their little teeth on edge. I wasn't giving them the attention they needed. Children will act out if they are not getting the attention they need in the home. I made a commitment to God in the very beginning that no matter how bad things got, I would always be grateful for giving us these beautiful, crazy kids!

Sometimes, marriage and family come easy and sometimes not. It's work! I was raised by a single mother who did her best, but not having a father around limited my ability to understand what a healthy family was supposed to be. I had to learn. I had to practice on my poor wife and kids. Sometimes, I still don't know what I'm doing! Over the years, however, God has taught me how to be a good man, chaplain, and father. It took some doing, but with God's love, mercy, and grace, He continues to change me. Now, I am a grandpop. I sit with little Emily Adelaide Boyce (Marmalade) on my lap and sing, "Jesus Loves Me" and pray over her. My son and his wife do the same. We passed on a godly heritage that I pray will continue for generations because that's how it should be!

In 1900, A.E. Winship wrote a book (*Jukes-Edwards: A Study in Education and Heredity*). "The Juke-Edwards Story: A Contrast in Family Legacy" is an article written by Aaron Dunlop and published in thinkgospel.com. Dunlop relied on Winship's book to glean his study's main message that "family sins have serious and lasting consequences." In the study, two families were contrasted over many generations—one with a Christian heritage and one without. The statistics are astonishing, and it's a fascinating study.

In 1874, Richard L. Dugdale, an employee of the New York Prison Commission, found that "criminals in six different prisons...all descended from the same family." This led him to research five generations of this family—descendants, those who married into the family, and others linked to this family—some 1200 persons, whose traits were "idleness, ignorance, and vulgarity."

The second family's great-great-grandfather traveled from Wales to London and was a clergyman. This family's descendants were quite different. Here are statistics provided by Aaron Dunlop in his article.

Family One
- 310 of the 1,200 were professional paupers—more than one in four.
- 300 of the 1,200—one in four—died in infancy from lack of good care and good conditions.
- 50 women who lived lives of notorious debauchery.
- 400 men and women were physically wrecked early by their own wickedness.
- 7 were murderers.
- 60 were habitual thieves who spent on the average twelve years each in lawlessness.
- 130 criminals who were convicted more or less often of crime.

Family Two
- 1 U.S. Vice-President (Aaron Burr)
- 3 U.S. Senators
- 3 governors
- 3 mayors
- 13 college presidents
- 30 judges
- 65 professors
- 80 public office holders
- 100 lawyers
- 100 missionaries, pastors and theologians.

Evidence shows that raising children in a Christian home proves they will turn out better than in homes without God or morals. Statistics are in our favor. A framed quote on our bedroom wall is a good reminder each day. "A righteous man walks in his integrity and his children are blessed after him" (Proverbs 20:7). We do our best and leave the rest up to God. One time God said to me, "You serve me, and I will take care of your family." When we invest in our kids, the returns yield fruitful blessings. I believe that is a promise for all of us. Don't underestimate His power!

Parents are not perfect. We make mistakes, but we always love our children regardless of their behavior. We don't always like what they do or how they do it, but we always love them.

Mother Cohen was a woman of God and a hospice patient who informally adopted me as her white son. She was raised in a pastor's home. She continued that legacy. Her husband was a deacon (Deceased); she used to be involved in the church, as well. I sat with her when she told me, "Chaplain John, the world is tough out there. I don't care what they have done, but when they come into my home, I'm going to love on them."

She was one of the most loving, motherly examples I had ever met. She showed a mother's unconditional love without condemnation or judgment. When you left her presence, you felt good about yourself. She ministered to me more than I did to her! Ministry is like that sometimes.

Love is greater than being critical. I sat with Eric, a friend of mine who was having trouble with his prodigal son. He was upset that his son wasn't living for God. "I get so frustrated with him because he knows right from wrong. It seems my wife has a great relationship with him, but I am concerned about him, and it comes out." I sat and listened with empathy as I had learned this lesson first-hand. I told him to love him regardless of his lifestyle. Find ways to say how proud you are of him and be sincere. I finally said, "You have to love him, brother; your show of frustration with him is separating your relationship with him. Show him unconditional love, and your relationship will heal." Eric took my advice, and his relationship with his son is much better. Praise the LORD!

It is hard when the chaplain's children go astray. We worry what people think. We worry about our reputation. It affects our ego to the core. But your true friends will stand by your side. Forget what others think; the only thing to maintain is keeping that relationship a priority. The rest will fall into place. Love your children. They are getting beat up enough in this world, and they do not need any more condemnation from us. They need to know we are there for them and will never give up on them.

YOU DON'T HAVE TO BE SUPERMAN; JUST BE THERE

Before we adopted our son, David, I was terrified. As I read *Bringing Up Boys* by Dr. James Dobson on being a father, the Holy Spirit told me to put the book down. He said, "I am going to take you through every painful moment throughout your life when you wanted a Dad to be there for you." At first, I said, "No, I don't want to remember those times." The Spirit impressed upon me, "I will hold your hand through this." So, I put the book down and waited on God.

My mind recalled the all-star baseball game where all the other Moms and Dads were there for their sons, but I had no one. When I was named MVP (most valuable player) for soccer in the eighth grade, no one was there. When I got cut from the ninth-grade baseball team and didn't have anyone to talk to, I walked home alone, lit up a joint, and cried.

The old memories brought tears running down my face, but God spoke softly into my heart. "I was there with you during all of those times. Do you remember when your coach said, 'Good job, John'? He even played baseball with you on his days off."

I answered, "Yes."

"I was your father through him." He went on to answer all those times I felt alone. "I was your father through all of your coaches and male teachers, who encouraged you." He reminded me of when my coaches encouraged me on the ballfield or my teachers' guidance when I had problems. "Now, I want you to do that with your son. You don't have to be super Dad and have all the answers. Just be a good Dad, and be there for your son."

We don't have to be well-known or famous super-spiritual heroes. We are not here to make a name for ourselves or build a monument to ourselves. We don't have to live up to unrealistic expectations. We only have to be the man or woman God created us to be, and live life the best we can — to simply love and be there for them.

The convent in Reading, PA, asked me to preach their *All Soul's Day* service every year. It is a day to remember all the souls who have passed. Having gone to Catholic school, I shared how these nuns were godly mother-like examples to students without a mother. Some of the Catholic sisters influenced my life, loving me even though I was a troublemaker. They gave me guidance and a sense of morality with a hard work ethic to make it in the world. I told these retired nuns that is what many of them were to those of us who didn't have parents. They made a difference in the lives of the children they taught. Their lives were not in vain. I honored their memories because they were there for children like me.

Chaplains and pastors have the same ability to influence orphaned or foster children. These children are often neglected, misguided, and run wild. All they need is someone to love them, believe in them, and help them grow in the LORD. Kids today are starving for attention. Tossed about by all kinds of cultural influences, they are confused. They feel hopeless, neglected, and forgotten. Adults have failed to properly teach them for life. Chaplain ministries of foster care, adoption, and the church can spiritually adopt these children. We can be their mothers and fathers, taking the time to love them with God's love and pour value, direction, and purpose into them. This builds healthy self-esteem and character. We're called not only to be Fathers to our own kids, but to make room in our hearts for other children, like those who had done for me. This fulfills the gospel to care for the "orphans and widows of society." At least if they cannot get a healthy environment from home, we can offer it to them in ministry!

CHAPTER TWENTY

Wounds from Ministry

*And be ye kind to one another, tenderhearted, forgiving one
another, even as God for Christ's sake hath forgiven you.*

Ephesians 4:32 (KJV)

E veryone in ministry will suffer personal attacks. As a young
Christian in downtown Long Beach, CA, I was in line at a
convenience store. I felt the LORD wanted me to speak to
an elderly couple who were purchasing a bottle of alcohol. I followed
them out of the store.

"Excuse me," I said.

The old man turned around and said in a nasty tone, "What?"

The lady with him said, "Oh, he probably just wants to bum a
cigarette."

"No, ma'am," I said. "I felt God wanted me to tell you how much He
loves and cares about you."

The man waved me off. "Oh, get out of here," he said.

And they both walked away from me. I was absolutely dumbfounded.
That was not what I had expected to happen. I thought they would
listen and maybe even get saved. I was confused and didn't understand.
After all, God led me to talk to them, and I expected them to respond.
Why would God tell me to speak to them when He knew they would
reject me?

Then, I heard Him whisper to me, "You have to experience rejection
and hurt if you will do what I ask of you." I pondered what that meant.
My mind went to Jesus and His persecution and death on the cross.
As a young Christian, I began to understand that following Jesus was
going to be sacrificial.

THE COST

All ministers suffer when following God's call to ministry. I think of missionaries whose children died on the mission field, yet they remained faithful. There are many stories of godly men and women of God who lost finances, spouses, and children while doing the work of God. The hymn, "It is Well with My Soul," was written by Horatio Spafford. He composed the song from the pain of losing most of his wealth in the Chicago fires and shortly after the death of his four daughters in a shipwreck.

There is a cost to following God. There will come a time when you are faced with tragedy. The thing that matters most is your response. Will you give up and go home or persevere and choose to suffer? II Timothy 3:12 (NIV) states, "In fact, everyone who wants to live a godly life in Christ Jesus will be persecuted." The bottom line is that this world is evil, and evil people hurt good people. Circumstances will come against you, and people will offend you, hurt you, lie about you, slander you, or even physically hurt you or your family. When that happens, it is incredibly bewildering. We claim the scriptures, "No weapon formed against you will prosper," or "God has put a hedge of protection around us."

When I was sworn into the Navy, I took an oath to serve and protect my country from all foreign and domestic enemies. I weighed the cost and was willing to pay the price that I may have to lay down my life. After thinking it through, I took the oath.

Likewise, when we took our ordination vows, we made promises to God. We knew ministry meant laying down our lives, our pride, our will, and our resources. We promised to go wherever God called us to go and do whatever He commanded us. We understood the responsibility of ministry, weighed the cost, and accepted the call. We knew ministry would have a heavy price but had no idea at the time just how high the cost might be.

We may get wounded by sinners, but it stings more by saints. I had my first bad encounter with a congregational member only three months into the ministry. It upset me. Why would someone act this way toward their pastor?

Soon after the incident, I went to the Pennsylvania-Delaware District Council. Brother Thomas Trask, General Superintendent of the Assemblies of God, preached about getting hurt in ministry. After the service, I told him what happened. He gently touched my face. No words were spoken, but he felt my pain. God spoke through him to bring healing to me and probably other pastors in the service.

I can't recount all the times I have been hurt in ministry. At another pastors' conference, one preacher said, "I have been in the ministry for over thirty-five years. I have been hurt so many times that whoever hurts me again better watch out because I'm ready to go off." We all laughed, but we understood exactly what he meant.

If you haven't been hurt in ministry yet, don't worry. You will be. It will find you!

One minister went to the leadership of his denomination to be ordained.

"Do you believe in the devil?" he was asked.

"No," he replied.

"Well, we can't ordain him if he doesn't believe in the devil," replied one man.

Another older gentleman said, "Ordain him anyway. Within a few months of ministry, he'll believe in the devil."

WHAT DO WE DO WITH THE QUESTIONS?

God is Sovereign, and His will prevails. It's those low times we go through that become Job experiences. What do we do with all our questions? We feel like God has let us down. Trust has been broken, and relationships have been challenged, and now, doubt has replaced faith. What do we do? Where do we go? Who can be trusted?

Job was a righteous man. God blessed him with a wife, children, possessions, servants, wealth, and good health. Within a few days, everything was taken from him. His children died in a tornado, his belongings were stolen, his health crumbled, and worse yet, when looking for solace and consolation from his wife, she said, "Curse God and die." His faith, although shaken, was still steadfast. He said, "Be quiet, foolish woman. Naked I was born, naked I shall die, blessed be the name of the LORD.... In all this, Job did not sin" (paraphrased from Job 2:9-10).

We can be walking faithfully, abundantly, joyfully, successfully, and victoriously, and then out of nowhere, tragedy strikes. A death of a child, a murder, an accidental death, a heart attack, a stroke...your worst fear happens. The scripture, "That which I have dreaded has come upon me," (Job 3:25, NIV) has come true. Satan has persecuted you. For whatever reason, God has allowed this circumstance to happen. Your life suddenly turns upside down; your head spins out of control with so many questions. "But I thought...? Or, "...how could this happen?" Reality hits you, but your mind cannot comprehend it. You're in shock and disbelief. "This must be someone else's.... Or, "It just can't be...." But it is. It did happen, and it happened to you. What do you do now?

HEALING COMES THROUGH STRUGGLE

You grieve, mourn, and hurt for a while, but we go to God as the psalmist did in Psalm 73:17 (NLT). "Then I went into your sanctuary oh God, and I finally understood the destiny of the wicked." It is confusing when you see the prosperity of the wicked while the righteous suffer. The footnote of the *New Living Translation* says, "The psalmist affirms that God is good to the godly, but his own experience differs (73:3-12). Nearly overcome by his doubts (73:13-16), the psalmist meets the LORD in the sanctuary and gains a perspective that stretches beyond his life and renews his confidence in God (73:17-26).

Even in ministry, bad things happen even when you do everything right and live for the LORD wholeheartedly.

God is the only one who can heal you from devastating hurts. Running away from the situation will never help. You cannot run from God forever. It takes a daily surrender to His will and determination to not allow your heart to harden. Healing spiritual hurts takes time, but His love will cover and soothe your soul. Allow the light of His glory to heal you. You chose to let Christ be Lord a long time ago when you decided to "put your hand to the plow and not look back" (summarized from Luke 9:62).

I often use the story of the caterpillar at funerals because it has a good life lesson. A caterpillar struggles to climb out of its cocoon. A man walks by and, in his ignorance, thinks he's helping the caterpillar by creating an opening in the cocoon. The caterpillar wobbles out incomplete and deformed. The man should have left the cocoon alone and let the caterpillar struggle. By opening the cocoon too soon, the caterpillar did not have the opportunity to go through its needed struggle for completion. The caterpillar must push all fluid into its abdomen, thereby evolving its wings. Instead, this poor caterpillar wobbled the rest of its life and never became a butterfly.

Our struggles develop character and faith. We are not called to be spiritually crippled and wobble around the rest of our lives never fulfilling God's purpose. God has a plan for each one, and we can't stop halfway. Trials make us stronger, not weaker. We may feel vulnerable or insecure in the middle of the struggle, but when we push through, we are made more complete, more whole, more grounded, certain, confident, and our faith in God is even stronger than before.

My friend Reverend Anthony Jones preached a sermon entitled, "When you have a setback, take a step back, and then, make a comeback!" That is how grief is. We have a setback, and it feels like we lost and will never recover from that blow. So, when we have a setback, we need to take a step back, review the situation, re-evaluate, see what God is teaching through this situation, and then go on even further. You may have heard the saying, "When you feel like you are at the end of your rope, hold on tighter." But I say when you are at the end of the rope, let go, and let God catch you! It's okay to take a step back. God still has you. Stepping back for a while and taking time to process what happened makes us come back and draw closer to God than ever before.

God believes in you, Chaplain!

In Job 1:6-12, we see the account where Satan presents himself before the LORD. God asks, "Where have you come from?"

Satan replies, "Roaming to and from the earth."

God asks, "Have you considered my servant Job?"

The interesting note here is that Satan did consider Job because he saw God's protection over him in the spiritual realm. Satan probably considers us, too. God allows us to go through difficulties to test our faith and let us find out for ourselves what we are made of. He knew Job would even question Him, but He still put him to the test. God knew Job would pass.

During the testing, Job had to take a step back from his life. He thought his life was coming to an end. He felt God was getting ready to take him home. However, he grew through his pain, learned from his experience, and God blessed him even more the second half of his life. God used that experience to make Job an even godlier man. God had to deal with a deeper issue of pride in Job's life. Job wanted to question God, and when God finally appeared to him, Job put his hand over his mouth and had nothing to say. God took a good man and made him better.

Going through an emotional battle doesn't mean the end of your ministry or life; it's quite the opposite. He is preparing you to grow spiritually deeper. He considers you blameless, upright, and a man/woman who fears God and shuns evil. So, take courage Chaplain. God has confidence in you; have the same for yourself!

Be reminded that "We do not fight flesh and blood but against principalities and powers and rulers of this dark world" (paraphrased from Ephesians 6:12). Do not return evil with evil but evil with good. It is easy to get caught up in the evil of this world. We all have a choice: We can either allow revenge to pollute our souls and quit or remain steadfast and allow God to do the deeper work in our lives.

Matthew 5:8 (KJV) says, "Blessed are the pure in heart for they shall see God." Only the pure, the loving, the forgiving have a restful heart. We cannot see or feel God with revenge in our hearts. Mostly, our prayer life is hindered when there is unforgiveness or anger in our hearts. Forgiveness is commanded in ministry.

If you have been hurt in the ministry through no fault of your own, you are not alone. Many faithful men and women of God have suffered great afflictions and persecutions, sometimes giving their lives for the sake of the gospel at the hand of evil men. When we are hurt, we can turn to Him and allow His gentle love to heal those deep wounds.

HEALING FROM THE WORD

What do we do then with betrayal and hurt—from the wounds of ministry? Imagine your worst fear. The number one thing you never, ever wanted to happen. Will you still trust God? Will you still believe? Will we say as Job did, "Though he slay me, yet will I hope in him" (Job 13:15, NIV).

One of the biggest hurts in my life was when someone hurt one of my family members. Dorothy and I had ministered to this couple for months. We let them use our vehicle; we helped with groceries and finances. We prayed them through the death of their child—one of the most horrific experiences of their lives. We poured our hearts into these people. They ended up separating anyway.

My wife and I learned they did something very hurtful while we were ministering to them. Because of privacy, I won't go into detail, but it was a betrayal. When I found out, I was livid. We have been through a lot, but betrayal stings deeply.

When I need comfort, I quote my favorite scripture verse. This scripture reminds me of Jesus' compassion for hurting people. In Matthew 11:28-30, "Come to me, all you who are weary and burdened, and I will give you rest. Take my yoke upon you and learn from me, for I am gentle and humble in heart, and you will find rest for your souls, for my yoke is easy, and my burden is light" (NIV). God is our comforter, encourager, and the One Who comes alongside us to give consolation in times of great anguish.

This answer might sound too simple. Jesus is the only One to go to for healing a wounded heart. The day after it happened, the anger and pain had to be processed in my heart. Anger and hurt go hand-in-hand; I was feeling both. Hatred began to grow inside on top of the anger I felt. It was time to deal with these strong emotions. I asked God to help me forgive and get this bitterness out of my heart. Anger and unforgiveness steal everything and leave you with an open, festering wound. It will make you sick spiritually.

Opening the Word, I read Psalm 41:9 (NIV). "Even my close friend, someone I trusted, one who shared my bread, has turned against me." Immediately I thought of Jesus' betrayal. Jesus said, "The one who eats bread with me has lifted his heel against me" (John 13:18, KJV). Right then, I knew God understood how I felt. His presence began to soften my heart and reopen that which I closed.

I read a few more chapters the next day, but Psalm 42 began soothing my wounded soul even more. "Day and night I have only tears for food" (Psalm 42:3, NLT) "But each day the LORD pours his unfailing love upon me" (Psalm 42:8, NLT).

The following day I began to worship God with a full heart as I read Psalm 43-44 (NLT). "Rescue me from these unjust liars, for you are my God, my only haven" (43:1, NLT). "Let them lead me to your holy mountain, to the place where you live. There I will go to the altar of God—the source of all my joy" (43:3, NLT). As I became stronger, I began to put the hurt behind me. By the fourth day, I was fully restored. Psalm 44:3 (NLT) says, "It was your right hand and strong arm...that helped them, for you loved them."

By the fifth day, I preached a powerful message at church all because of God's restoration and grace.

We have to go to God as a child runs to his/her mom or dad after the child falls and gets hurt. Scared and crying, their parents take the child in their arms where there is love and safety. Daddy's strong arms provide strength and security. Mom's caring arms make the child feel warm, loved, and protected.

Relaxing in God's arms provides a calming reassurance that everything will be all right. He pours in the oil and the wine. Oil was used in the Old Testament to relieve pain and comfort the wound. Jesus pours out His healing and comforting presence into your wounds. When you allow Him into your hurts, He heals them from the inside out and does it perfectly.

Handle hurts with perseverance. Pick yourself back up, restore your love, and get back out there! Don't allow yourself to sulk, quit, or harbor bad feelings. You took the oath knowing you had to lay down your life, your ego, and everything else—most importantly, forgiveness. God will take care of you, but He needs you to take care of others. When we take the plank out of our eye, we can remove the splinter out of others. See clearly and love deeply. The world needs you!

I have been removed from hospital rooms simply because I walked in and told them who I was. I have been kicked out for telling people truths they did not want to hear. In my thirty-plus years of ministry, I have been dumped on, blamed, stolen from, lied about, slandered against, and betrayed. Those who knew me, however, stood by my side and supported me. Every time God has justified me in the presence of my enemies. God has protected me from abuse, justified me when lied about, and comforted me when I was deeply hurt. Dr. Kenzy's words grounded me during hard times in ministry when he told us students, "You will always outlast your enemies."

It's crucial to keep moving forward, growing, praying, and getting divine guidance and wisdom. Stand up straight with a strong back and a fortified spirit. Keep reminding yourself that if God is with you, Satan cannot defeat you. Don't fight people. Our real enemy is the influence of darkness overtaking a person. He uses them to attack you. Walk in boldness, divine anointing, and power. If something is wrong and the battle is worth fighting, ask God to go with you and before you so you can confront the situation head-on.

DEALING WITH CONFLICT IN THE CHURCH

Young chaplains and pastors will have people in the church who will try to harm them and divide the church. You do not have to put up with that kind of nonsense in the church. One person doesn't need to create confusion and disturbances. Watch that it is not swept under the rug; address the conflict before it gets out of control. One or two people can ruin an entire church. The twelve spies who went into Canaan saw the land flowing with milk and honey. However, ten of them created fear in the hearts of the entire Israelite community. Ten men negatively affected over 601,730 fighting men not to mention women and children (Numbers 26:51). If that can happen in a large community, it can happen in a church setting, as well. Deal with the conflict!

During a very difficult time at our church in Fleetwood, PA, I sought out my presbyter for help and guidance. It was right after about fifteen people left the church because of the changes I made. I was discouraged and talked with Pastor Bryan Koch over breakfast. He said, "John, I understand how difficult it is to make hard decisions. I had to release twenty-five leaders in my church because they went off on strange doctrines." Pastor Bryan protected his sheep and was not going to allow the church to suffer because of a few stubborn, disrespectful, divisive, and most of all, unrepentant people trying to take it over. We don't have to be ugly about it, but we do need to honor God's house when others try to divide it. When there is turmoil in the church, people want it peacefully restored. Sometimes, you have to remove Doegs from the church. It is uncomfortable until the issue is resolved.

When the conflict is dealt with, it brings peace for you and the church. Plus, respect is gained from followers. One thing to be mindful of. Be sure you're 99.999 percent right in your judgment of the situation! It must be righteous indignation guiding you, not a negative attitude, self-righteousness, or pride. We often make critical errors when we take things personally. When our emotions get involved, we are not objective and are easily angered and defensive. If it is a genuine problem, others will see it. Check your motives and talk with others. In the multitude of counselors there is wisdom.

If God is leading you to handle it, be prayed up and talk to the offender in love. The person may have a perfectly good reason behind his/her actions; perhaps it's just a misunderstanding. Maybe the person doesn't realize he/she is causing an offense. Hopefully, it will be something easily fixed.

As the leader, you don't always have to be the one to deal with the matter. There was a time when two congregants did not get along with each other. In this situation, I realized this was a matter the two of them had to work out themselves. Eventually they did settle their differences. As their pastor, I saw their conflict and prayed for peace. I don't think they will ever be close friends, but God did intervene, and the dispute was settled. We do not have to put out every fire in the church—just the ones that will burn it down!

"If someone asks for your cloak, give them your coat also," Jesus said (paraphrased from Matthew 5:40). There's a reason Jesus said to give them more than they asked for. He abundantly repays us for our kindness when we obey Jesus' words.

If you are married, you understand this principle. You don't call your husband the devil or attack him as an enemy. You let God deal with him. You let God punish or discipline him. He will listen to God and eventually come around; just be patient. Our problem is that we want instant satisfaction. It's hard to wait, so we fly off the handle. If your husband is a Christian, then he will hear from God and will eventually humble himself.

In the early days of our marriage, whenever I'd say something hurtful to my wife, she would say, "Sick him, LORD." And boy, did He ever. I would have the most miserable day! When I came home, she would ask how my day went. I told her it was miserable. She would gloat a little after I apologized, but we always made up. She knew how to trust God to fight her battles.

It's the same in the church body. If brothers or sisters offend us, we don't call them the devil or attack them as the enemy. We need to hear from God whether to let it go or talk to them. They are not our enemy. They are part of the body of Christ, and we don't hurt our own bodies. Our relationship with one another is more important than winning the battles. We need discernment when dealing with conflict.

As the spiritual leader, your church looks to you to do something about a disturbance. Sometimes, you leave it up to the LORD; other times you need to handle it, while still other times God uses church people to handle it. Leaders need wisdom from God to know what to do in these difficult times. Do we wait for God to fight the battle? Is God calling me to intervene? Do I let it go? These are the questions we wrestle with in prayer, and each one is appropriate depending upon the situation.

It is also always nice to witness a level-headed person solving a conflict peacefully. Everyone breathes a sigh of relief and is glad for someone to resolve an awkward situation. That is what a pastor and spiritual leader does. He/She becomes a peacemaker, and it doesn't always have to be the pastor.

A young hippie who recently accepted the LORD walked into church, but no one moved to give him a seat. So, being the hippie that he was, he sat down in the middle of the aisle. One wise deacon came forward to address the situation. Everyone seemed thrilled the deacon would swiftly handle this uncomfortable situation and escort him out. The deacon looked at the young man, but instead of asking him to leave, put his hand on his shoulder, and sat down on the floor beside him. They listened to the sermon together. Quiet repentance came over the congregation. Everyone settled down and turned his/her attention back to the sermon. That deacon was a wise man who handled the situation peacefully.

Some ministers think they must passively take abuse — to turn the other cheek, but this isn't always the case. Each situation is different. There was a time when I would keep my mouth shut just to keep the peace. The problem was everyone else had peace except me. I was being dumped on! With age comes wisdom. Now, I hold people accountable for what they say and do. At a service not too long ago, I noticed a lady I had never seen before sitting in the congregation. She got up and said something to two other ladies in the church. Their countenance changed to a look of hurt. One of the things God hates the most is "one who causes dissension among the brethren" (paraphrased from Proverbs 6:19).

After the service, I talked privately to the two people. They shared how this new person told them to stop talking during the pre-service fellowship. That was our church's time of fellowship. Besides, they knew to stop talking when the service began. This upset me. A new lady was coming to our church and causing disruption, discord, and hurt feelings. A conversation was necessary, although I didn't really want to do it. However, the situation had to be dealt with. Conflict in the church must be dealt with immediately, especially when it creates an atmosphere of tension.

Talking to the lady privately, I gently and politely told her my concerns. I explained that our pre-service fellowship was a healthy time for fellowship and socialization in our church. She did not receive it well. She excused her actions by saying her old church did it differently. I asked her to respect our time of fellowship prior to the service. I thanked her for coming and told her that she was still welcome to attend. She said she probably wouldn't be back. She went on to tell me how she also had to correct her other pastors on issues. Right then and there, I knew I did the right thing. I had learned over the years to trust my intuition and discernment. But God confirming it is always reassuring.

Nobody likes conflict, but God will take what we have and multiply the rest. We are not good at everything. He compensates for our lack of ability and gives us the words to say in confronting situations. The power of God is manifested in these circumstances. Step out in faith, and He will take care of the rest.

In an article about stress and burnout it says, "The stress that the average minister bears would bring most people to their knees" (*Stress and Burnout*). We are not most people. We are not supermen either, but what we are is Holy Spirit-filled chaplains that can face every trial with confidence. Love deeply, forgive wholeheartedly, and when you get rejected, handle it with grace and perseverance.

CHAPTER TWENTY-ONE

Ministry to Wheat and Weeds

Let them both grow together until the harvest. At that
time, I will tell the harvesters: first collect the weeds
and tie them down in bundles to be burned; then
gather the wheat and bring it into my barn.

Matthew 13:30 (KJV)

C haplains minister to everyone. Prison chaplains recognize that some congregants are genuinely there to worship while others are there to make a good impression to the parole board. Teen Challenge chaplains see the same thing. There are true worshippers, while others only try to avoid jail time. Some are sincere, while others play the system.

Churches have the same problem. That's why Jesus said to let them both (good and bad) grow together. If you try to pull the weeds, you will hurt the wheat. Let them grow together, and God will separate the wheat from the chaff at the end of time.

Weeds hurt believers. My lawn is mostly grass, but a few weeds are noticeable. A clump of grass comes up if I remove the weeds, leaving a deep patch of ugly, bare dirt. Sin is like those weeds and is ugly in any camp. There are times when Jesus confronted sin, while other times he left it alone. Jesus let Judas steal from the money bag even though He knew what he was doing. He didn't say anything. He also left him in charge of the finances. Judas knew better but didn't care. He knew the commandment "Thou shalt not steal," but chose to steal anyway.

Matthew, on the other hand, was a tax collector. He stole from people in his former life, but he chose to change. God turned him completely around. The same man who once stole from others could then write about honesty and integrity in his gospel (paraphrased from Matthew 5:33).

There will always be people we minister to who just don't care about spiritual things. They are not only weeds but poison ivy. They are like Doeg when Saul commanded his soldiers to put the priests of God to death in 1 Samuel 22:17-18. Saul's Israelite guards wouldn't dare touch the LORD's anointed, but then there was Doeg, the Edomite. There is always a Doeg! He neither respects the minister nor fears God. He is the kind of person who loves bloodshed. He gladly killed the priests of the LORD.

I met a World War II veteran in a nursing home. This man began to tell me about his experiences in the war. His stories were blood curdling. He loved to fight and kill. He told me about a time when he was trying to keep warm by hiding out in a cellar in Germany. He heard footsteps coming down the stairs. It was a German soldier. They swung their rifles around to shoot each other but suddenly stopped. They realized both would get killed, so they decided to have a knife fight.

I said to him, "I guess you won."

He said, "Yes, I actually like to fight. I fought people all my life and even killed another GI in a bar fight."

I asked him, "How do you feel about spiritual things?"

"I don't think about it much," he said.

"How do you feel about one day meeting God now that you are on hospice?"

"I don't believe in God," he said.

I tried to minister to him even though he had no fear of God or man. He died shortly afterward.

He died a cold and bitter man. He had no respect for others or God. Chaplains cannot pick and choose whom we pastor. The institution expects us to do our best; and we do. But even our best isn't always received. Nevertheless, God calls us to share the gospel with everyone.

A prison chaplain once told me he won many prisoners to Christ because he loved them regardless of their religion. Some were pagans in the worst way, but he didn't condemn or judge them. Many prisoners came to trust him, began going to church, and put their own faith in God.

There are some pre-sheep in our sheep pens. We must allow God to work on their hearts. I officiated a funeral one time for a man who eventually came to Christ before he died. He ruined his body from alcohol. When he died, I preached at his funeral. I preached the story of Ebenezer Scrooge, whose heart was full of greed and stinginess.

Everyone hated him, but they also feared him because he was so rich. We are all familiar with the story of the three ghosts of Christmas past, present, and future. Each ghost chipped away at pieces of his heart. The story later shows that Scrooge had been hurt by a woman he loved, closing himself off of ever being hurt again. By the end, he became saddened by how he had wasted his life. He wanted to make the remainder of his life worth living. His heart changed, and he became the most generous and loving man and even bought the biggest turkey for the Cratchit family.

Even though the family of this alcoholic man were Christians, he refused to submit to God or give his life over to Him. He even had a poster of a half-naked woman over his bed. With only a week or two left before dying, God finally broke through and he accepted the LORD. We all worked hard at helping this man find God. It took a long time, but God used us to speak words of love into his life. When he did accept the Lord, his whole countenance changed, and it was evident he genuinely loved the LORD and was telling other family members what God had done. He took that poster down, too! I love preaching these kinds of funerals. It took time. It took prayer and sharing God's loving grace and forgiveness until finally he surrendered to God and died peacefully. He was like Scrooge. God had to chip away at his heart one layer at a time. It takes a lot of patience ministering to people before you see fruit.

We were weeds, too, at one time. Our hearts were hardened. I used to make fun of television preachers. It never made sense to me and it looked stupid. But God saw through my foolishness, insecurities, and weakness and discovered the jewel in me. He had to remove the rough outer layers and peel me back to my most vulnerable self. I call it God doing a Nebuchadnezzar on people.

Nebuchadnezzar's heart was callous. He was hardened by war and killing. He gave the glory to his own gods of war. One day he saw

Daniel's three Hebrew friends defy the king's command to worship his idol as a god. He watched God deliver them from the fiery furnace. He saw the hand of God on them throughout his lifetime. Still, he did not repent. God gave him the mind of an animal and cast him into the wilderness for seven years. He grew nails like an eagle's and grew more insane by the day...until one day he couldn't take it any longer. Nebuchadnezzar looked up to God and finally acknowledged him as the LORD. God restored his sanity, as well as his kingdom. Nebuchadnezzar became one of the world's most influential evangelists by his treatise to all nations to worship the one true LORD and serve Him only. God changed his heart of stone and gave him a heart of flesh (paraphrased from Daniel chapters 1-4).

Toward the end of my chaplaincy ministry, I've ministered to more sheep than goats, to more wheat than weeds. There was a time when it was just the opposite. To be quite honest, it was frustrating, but that is where God had me and kept me for a long time. I grew and learned during that time. I patiently waited, sometimes endured.

In my early years of chaplaincy, I sat with many patients who were not Christian. It was hard, but I planted seeds when I could. Most of the patients were in nursing homes with dementia. It was difficult to see any fruit grow there, but I remained faithful during those dry times. It wasn't easy; in fact, it was boring and unchallenging, but it was a season of my life. Everyone has those seasons. Sometimes it's dry and aired, and other times it is pouring down rain. Thank the LORD, God is present in both.

WRESTLING WITH GOD IN YOUR MINISTRY

Jacob wrestled with God. He was in great distress because his father-in-law was attacking from behind, and his brother, Esau, was coming from ahead. He wrestled and fought with God all night long until daybreak. Now, that is tenacity! The angel of the LORD had to touch Jacob's hip socket to end the fight, but Jacob did not let go until the LORD blessed him. His name was changed from Jacob (meaning *deceiver*) to Israel (*one who wrestles with God and man and overcomes*). See Genesis 32.

Chaplains wrestle with God at times, as well. We may not like the ministry we are in, and we get bored and frustrated. Sometimes we find ourselves working in a secular environment with mission values and statements contrary to our own. Some work for companies whose sole mission is to make money. Granted, no company can survive without profits, but that is not our priority as chaplains. We are in ministry to give to others. We have basically taken a vow of poverty to go where God calls us to go. When things get difficult and we feel conflicted, we ask God, "Why?" We sacrifice so much, and we want it to be for the right reason, not just to make the company profitable, but we want our lives to be effective for the kingdom of God.

There will be times when you question your present state of ministry. God doesn't ask you to become stagnant there. God wants you to find the perfect fit for the ministry. He doesn't want us to be mediocre chaplains but exceptional ones. If you are not happy in your current position, pray that God shows you what branch of chaplaincy ministry He wants for you. Don't quit the chaplaincy; ask Him to show you what chaplain position is the right fit for you.

Hospital ministry was not for me; pastoring was not for me; but my giftings excelled in hospice ministry. It took me awhile to get there, but God used me in the process, and He is using you where you are, too. Don't give up. Don't quit. Realign yourself, and redirect your calling. You will eventually find the right fit, and the ministry will become a joy rather than a job.

Even when we are in the will of God, it may become so difficult that you want to leave. The time came when I prayed for the LORD to release me from hospice. At one time, we were the best hospice in the area. I pride myself on working with the best. However, there was a mass exodus of employees with interim administrators and staff members. Few stayed; many left. Morale was horrible. I was on the morale committee, but even my attitude wasn't good. We went from being on top to being mediocre at best. They had to hire temporary staff just to get through. We, chaplains, prayed for God to intervene.

Finally, He sent us an administrator who stayed through the hard times and fixed the problems. I was glad she came. We are back on top once again, and morale is great. Though I prayed to leave before, God kept me there. I had gone through personal difficulties before, but this one was different. This was a corporate one. I'm glad I stayed. After working there for nineteen years, we are still going strong.

There will be times when you beg and plead with God to release you, but He says, "No!" Be confident that God will see you through. It is easy to run away with everyone else, but it takes a person of fortitude to endure the storm. Pastor Michael Warner preached a sermon, "Bloom where you are planted." He said, "Find creative ideas to minister to people you work with because you never know what they are going through." This will renew passion for ministry.

God has taught me patience over the past thirty-five years of walking with Him. He has taught me to be patient with the weeds and the wheat, the hardships, and the easy times. I've worked in Christian ministries with the wheat and secular corporations with the weeds. He has matured me personally and professionally. Just because we are in the will of God doesn't mean we won't have hardships; we may even have more. If I am able to persevere through it, so can you!

CHAPTER TWENTY-TWO

The Chaplain as Spiritual Leader

Follow me as I follow Christ.

1 Corinthians 11:1 (KJV)

All chaplains should be able to say as Paul did in 1 Corinthians 11:1, "Follow me as I follow Christ." Chaplains are anointed men and women of God who carry within us the very presence of God. Never allow yourself or anyone else to diminish your calling. Be confident in who you are and where God called you to serve. Paul said to young Timothy, "Don't let anyone despise your youth, but set an example for the believers in speech, in conduct, in love, in faith, and in purity" (I Timothy 4:12, KJV). You, chaplain, are a spiritual guide for lost people; a counselor to troubled souls; and a leader who people look to for guidance, reassurance, and strength.

We all need people to look up to. We have all had influential spiritual leaders who demonstrated the love of Christ to us. They modeled Jesus in all situations. We've watched how they handled adversities and adversaries. We appreciated how patiently they loved us even when we made mistakes. They accepted us when we felt rejected. They were there for us at the most painful times of our lives.

Likewise, the people we minister should be able to look up to us as their spiritual leaders with spiritual authority—the highest authority there is—and with confidence tell them to follow our example. Our presence during their desperation is extremely influential. People look to us for comfort and direction. The chaplain may possibly be their last frantic plea for hope or help. Chaplain, you are their spiritual leader. Own that title, and walk in its authority!

CHAPLAINS ARE COURAGEOUS

Spiritual leaders are courageous. They go where others dare not. As the chaplain has proven himself in leadership, the company will give you more responsibility.

I was asked to speak at our general staff meeting during the COVID epidemic. Many healthcare workers were discouraged and even fearful. I quoted Joshua 1:9 (KJV), "Have not I commanded thee? Be strong and of good courage; be not afraid, neither be thou dismayed: for the Lord thy God is with the whithersover thou goest." As a Navy Veteran, I learned to prepare for war. I told them we needed to run to the battle, not away from it. This was a time for heroes, and we must rise and accept this challenge because this is what God called us to do, and He is with us.

I shared a story with them, which I had heard as a young pastor. Whether it is true or not, I am not sure. A priest and a doctor were called to help lepers on an island. They went into the town and began helping these poor people. They were helping a leper when the doctor asked the priest to hand him something, but the priest did not respond. The doctor looked up and saw that the priest was frozen with fear. He said to him, "Father, where is your faith?" That was a story that has always inspired me to go where others are too afraid to go.

After that inservice, I prayed for everyone. God set people free from fear and tension. Many came to me later or emailed me, thanking me for the words of faith, comfort, and strength. It was an opportunity to bring God's peace to this situation. After that seminar, I was asked to speak the same message of courage at other healthcare centers. My boss was grateful for the inspirational speech I gave and came to me later saying, "John, your peers and administrators have agreed that you will be Employee of the Month."

As we are led by the Holy Spirit and have the confidence of our administrators and fellow staff, they will not only allow your words of faith but welcome them. They will notice that *God is with this chaplain.*

That story of the priest and doctor also inspired me to be the first to volunteer to be one of the first responders to minister to COVID-19 patients. Psalm 91 gave me the scriptural protection I needed to face any fears. "For He will rescue you from every trap and protect you from deadly disease" (Psalm 91:3, NLT).

"No weapon formed against me shall prosper" (paraphrased from Isaiah 54:17). God has called us into ministry and promises that nothing can remove that call. Satan has no authority over you and cannot destroy you or your ministry. God moves mountains and grants favor because He has people for you to minister to both now and in the future. No person, no circumstance, no disease, not even Satan, can keep you from accomplishing God's will. Only when your Heavenly Father calls you home, is your ministry done on this earth. Then you will hear those wonderful words of the Master, "Well done, good and faithful servant, enter into my rest."

Ministry, in general, takes courage. It is vital to know that His presence and divine protection are there when walking into a situation wherever God leads. Maintain that childlike faith, knowing and believing in God's protection. Fear is a stumbling block. If there is fear, the gospel message would never have been preached; missionaries would not go, preachers would be too afraid to speak out, and evangelists would tremble. "For God hath not given us a spirit of fear; but of power, and of love, and a sound mind" (2 Tim. 1:17, KJV). Therefore, the chaplain cannot be fearful but rather bold and full of courage.

An old song by Unity Klan goes, "I went into the enemy's camp and took back what he stole from me." We are to trample on the enemy, not the other way around. We go into his territory and take back those who are lost. We go into areas where it is not safe so we can restore hope by letting others know there is a God who loves them. Yes, Satan will try to stop us with fear, threats, and even persecution, but has that ever stopped us from going forth? Often the reverse happens and causes us to become even more determined. We are called to be bold and go where God calls us believing "The gates of hell shall not prevail against it" (Matthew 16:18).

As we minister and pray with people, God speaks through us with words of wisdom or a word of knowledge to break a heavy yoke of discouragement or condemnation. People come to you beating themselves up for what they've done or said. As you speak into them, you see the tears flow. You watch their hands lift and receive forgiveness, reconciliation, and a restored relationship with God. You see God restoring faith and freedom right in front of your eyes. There is no greater reward than watching someone get set free from bondage. Don't let fear stop God's plan for your life and the lives you will touch.

CHAPLAINS ARE ESSENTIAL

I arrived at the hospital and was greeted by the nurses working at the front desk. They were taking temperature readings during the COVID epidemic. I introduced myself as Chaplain John. With a hesitant look on her face, she asked me if I were essential. She tried to dissuade me from going. I responded, "Spiritual care is absolutely essential." Amazed at my response, she waved me through. I got up to the COVID floor and put on a gown, gloves, mask, face shield, and booties for my feet; I went in. This man was all alone; his wife was not even allowed to visit him. With no visitors, this man was dying alone. He was nonverbal, but his body language told me he was anxious. After introducing myself and making eye contact, he began to calm down. Sitting with him for half an hour, I sang hymns, read scripture, shared Christ with him, and then prayed. When I left, his entire countenance had changed. He was peaceful. I called his wife afterward who was so grateful that I had spent that time with him before he died.

I eventually got COVID but had mild symptoms. Many quit during COVID, but many stayed. Healthcare workers were called heroes during that time. Maybe so; all I know is there were people dying of COVID, and I couldn't stand by and do nothing. Those patients needed spiritual care. This is what chaplains do on a regular basis. Chaplains are essential and are desperately needed not only to patients, but staff. The LORD is still asking, "Whom shall I send? Will you reply as Isaiah did? "LORD send me," in Isaiah 6:8.

DON'T BRAG ON YOURSELF

A philosophy in chaplaincy says, "Let your boss know how valuable you are to the company. Brag on your self-worth to them; if you don't, no one else will. Let them know what you are doing." Chaplains must prove their worth to the institution. They save companies thousands of dollars because of multiple pastoral interventions to staff members. They minister to co-workers when tragedy strikes. Chaplains talk people through conflicts at work and resolve differences between workers. They help people with depression and discouragement. Loving counsel is provided to the lowest on the totem pole to the highest CEO. Chaplains are no respecter of persons. They love everyone. They are the organization's pastor.

Therefore, we don't have to shout it from the mountain tops "how great I am." In fact, it's a turn-off when people brag about themselves. "Let someone else praise you, not your own mouth; an outsider, and not your own lips" Proverbs 27:2 (KJV). As chaplains, our work and attitude should speak for themselves. Actions of unconditional love, a non-judgmental approach, emotional, and spiritual support say volumes about who we are and what we do. Guided by the Holy Spirit, we make ourselves available and bring honor to God and respectability to the institution. Don't only do the bare minimum. Go the extra mile. Actions speak volumes.

Chaplains walk into some of the most chaotic, dangerous, adrenalin-filled, overwhelming situations. There may be a person so overloaded with grief that his/her normal coping skills are beyond the person's ability to endure, and he/she breaks down. This is where the chaplain is needed most. He provides a calming presence of security, reassurance, and hope. People will notice the presence of God in the Spirit-filled chaplain called into the emergency room in the middle of the night with his/her peaceful demeanor. They'll watch him/her settle a family down. They will recognize his/her worth to the organization. I have often walked into bad situations where emotions were running high. People were scared and anxious. After gathering them together, holding hands in prayer, the Holy Spirit filled the atmosphere. Afterward, there was a sense of God's peace, and the crisis was calmed. The nurse looked over and nodded her head, glad that I was there. When we are doing what God called us to do, we won't need to brag on ourselves; others will observe and see how needed you are and brag on you to your boss.

CHAPLAINS ARE PROBLEM SOLVERS

We work as unto the LORD and not for man. Go above and beyond the call of duty. The difference between a good chaplain and a great chaplain is hard work and perseverance. Good chaplains make excuses why they can't do something, while great chaplains find ways to make things happen. This is especially true when there is a death or emergency and we drop everything and go to the need. Your other patients will understand if you have an emergency because they know you will be there for them when it is their turn.

Chaplains are paid to solve problems. As chaplains, we work harder, pray more fervently, and allow God to give us creative ideas. When facing a challenge, pray about it, and have some solutions before talking to your boss. One chaplain used to constantly run to our nurse supervisor with questions and problems. She didn't know how to answer spiritual matters. Pulling him aside, I explained that when there is a problem to be addressed, have a few solutions so our boss can make a more informed decision.

Allow God to be the creative genius in your work. Take your battles, challenges, and needs to Him. He will give you answers you never dreamed of and help you make the best decisions for each situation.

Years before full-time ministry, I was a young cook in a nursing home. I had a dilemma. They had a chart system for every variety of diet and calorie count, but it was totally disorganized and confusing. I took it home with me and prayed over it, asking for God's help in organizing it better. God gave me a creative idea. I made a very easy-to-follow chart for everyone to understand. It was clear, concise, and easy to maintain.

A new dietitian was impressed by the diagram and said, "Mark did a great job coming up with this chart. We are going to adopt it in Corporate."

I said, "Mark didn't come up with that idea; I did." Seeing the look on her face, I continued with a grin, "Oh, let him have it. God will give me a million of these ideas."

And he has. God's creative genius will put thoughts in your mind, ideas in your imagination, and your boss and co-workers will recognize how vital you are. Our administrators feel secure knowing they don't need to worry about the pastoral care department because "our chaplains can handle it." Furthermore, administrators will do everything in their power to hold onto you because of everything you do.

Always leave the job better than when you got there. My mother told me when my father went to a person's house to paint, he was meticulous.

After moving all the furniture out of the way, he'd put down a drop cloth, do the painting job, return the furniture to its proper place, and vacuum the room once done. That is good customer service.

CHAPTER TWENTY-THREE

The Chaplain as Servant Leader

"...just as the Son of Man did not come to be served, but to serve, and to give is life as a ransom for many."

Matthew 20:28 (NIV)

T he model of corporate leadership looks like a triangle with the leader on top, while those underneath serve him. The lower you are, the less important you are.

Christianity's design of authority is the leader on the bottom serving upward, (Kenzy). In Mark 9:35 (KJV), it says, "And he sat down, and called the twelve and said unto them if any man desire to be first, the same shall be last of all and servant of all."

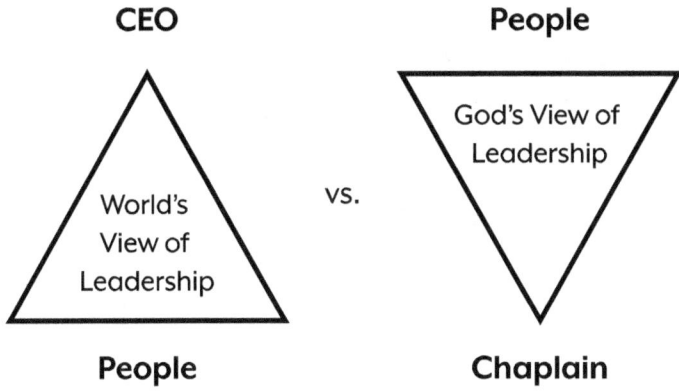

David Wilkerson prophesized over YCIBI. He called it the "school of the unlatched shoe," meaning students at YCIBI were called to a *foot-washing ministry*. We were not to be served but to serve. Some students left abruptly, complaining we were a cult because we worked so hard.

The school was not a cult. We worked hard. Students took the form of lowly servants and worked wherever there was a need. Dr. Kenzy always said, "Go where the need is." Ministry was not an option at YCIBI; it was included as a college course and graded on performance. Students ministered wherever God opened the door.

YCIBI developed spiritual confidence. The leadership put students at the forefront of ministry to develop leadership skills. As a young student, I was asked to be a part of a ministry to mentally handicapped adults at a local institution. The first night of ministry was very difficult. The odors were unbelievable. The residents hugged, touched, and breathed on me. I ran to the trash can and threw up! I told the leader I couldn't do this ministry. My excuse was, "It is disrespectful to the adults if I threw up by being around them." He told me to give it one more chance and said if I threw up, I was free to go, but if I didn't, then to stay. I agreed. The following Monday night, I returned. I still had a difficult time with the odors, but instead of throwing up, I just gagged. I acquiesced, "Okay, LORD, I'll stay." I stayed in that ministry for three years. I developed a deep love for mentally handicapped people. God revealed to me that when I meet them in heaven, they will have a sound mind and remember all that was done for them.

DON'T WAIT TO BE ASKED

Be a worker. Be the first to volunteer and lead by example. Don't wait to be asked twice. Whether your boss or co-worker asks for help, roll up your sleeves and serve. Be willing to do whatever the company needs. Be the first one to volunteer. Never feel above the scope of picking up a paint brush or helping move an office.

A chaplain friend told me a story about one chaplain who spent all his time in the office and neglected his people. When the chaplain ended his ministry there, his co-workers all turned their backs on him. There is a saying, "Our title gets us through the door, but it is our character that allows us to keep coming back." Our title as chaplain only goes so far; we have to earn that respect and never take it for granted.

In my younger chaplain days, I helped move the office from Conway to Myrtle Beach. I had a lot of energy back then and worked all day. I hung most of the poster boards, mailboxes, and bulletin boards. When we moved again years later though, I was older and didn't have the energy I once had. This time we had younger chaplains. I told them we needed to be an example. They gladly rolled up their sleeves and got the work done. Never, ever just sit there while everyone else is working. It is a poor example of chaplaincy.

Chaplains should be well-spoken of by coworkers. Our character defines our reputation and our reputation must be above reproach. "An elder must have a good reputation in the church and community." I Timothy 3:7 (NLT) says this regarding pastors, "Also, people outside the church must speak well of him so that he will not be disgraced and fall into the devil's trap." We ought to have a reputation of honesty, integrity, and hard-working, not just in the church, but in the community.

CHAPLAINS ARE PERSISTENT

Our patients are our customers. We work for them, not the other way around. When we leave a patient's home, the person should feel better than when we arrived. We should give the patient undivided attention, empathy, understanding, and a Word from the LORD to encourage his/her hearts. Under promise and over deliver. Exceed people's expectations. When we do these things, we will be valued, appreciated, and highly sought after. Your reputation will precede you. God will further open doors of opportunity. Prove yourself faithful in small things, and God will elevate you to even bigger ones. God will not only bless financially or positionally but with wisdom and understanding beyond your years.

Chronological age does not determine spiritual maturity. An individual may be chronologically ninety years-old but have the faith of a fifth-grader. While a young man, such as Timothy in the Bible may be young, he was wise beyond his years. Paul encouraged Timothy to not allow his age to be a deterrent. God called him, not the dominant co-worker who thought he/she knew everything and presumes to tell the young chaplain how to do his job. I've had nurses try to tell me how to do my job; it didn't work. God called you and you alone to be the spiritual leader.

NEVER LOSE YOUR LOVE

We have all met Christians who are critical, judgmental, and full of hell, fire, and brimstone. There doesn't seem to be much grace about them. What is going on inside shows on the outside. Christians with these attitudes have not experienced God's true goodness or love.

Some chaplains trust more readily than others. Our view of people will determine our relational successes. For instance, chaplains who have a lot of love in their hearts view people as friends and will have an easier time in ministry. But those who view others with suspicion and lack of love will have a more difficult time. I have met spiritual leaders who fight their way through ministry and leave a trail of hurt. If we think everyone is out to get us or wants something from us, our view will be guided by mistrust and emotional distance. That attitude leads to anger and a belief that ministry is a fight and that everyone is our enemy. Over the years, a hardening of the heart develops. These chaplains become disparaging after being hurt and burned too many times. However, chaplains who trust people and view strangers as friends have a successful ministry and leave a trail of uplifted people. The best spiritual leaders are those who never lose their love. They are secure in Christ and are not suspicious of others. We can never afford to lose our love and allow our hearts to grow cold. The older we get, the more love, patience, and gentleness should grow.

If the chaplain's personality is critical, he/she must ask God to help him/her grow. God is still gracious to use him/her, but He expects the chaplain to learn and grow in all areas. A critical spirit demands attention and needs to change.

We must remind ourselves that "it is kindness that leads to repentance" and "where sin abounds, grace abounds more." Since God is patient and loving with us, He wants us to be that way with others. The last thing people need is a critical chaplain. They are already beating themselves up and don't need any more condemnation and judgment from us. They need a chaplain who is full of grace and compassion.

People will gravitate toward a person who is full of love and the Holy Spirit and will love them no matter what. People will want to be around you because of the presence of God in your life and love dominates your life.

Being an introvert, extrovert, or anyone in between doesn't matter. God calls all kinds of people with all personality types. God looks at the heart and calls the individual. Those He calls into ministry all have one thing in common: a pastor's heart.

I was the third chaplain to visit one patient's home. I was on call that night when the patient died. The patient's son made an interesting observation and compliment. He said all three of you have different personalities. Bryan was the quiet one, Kirby talked to my brother about food, and you are the funny one. But there's one thing you all have in common. You all loved us. Each of you showed your compassion and care for the safety and comfort of not only my mother, but also for us."

God uses quiet chaplains, loud chaplains, and everyone in between. We are not cookie-cutter chaplains; we just need a big heart.

Spiritual Leaders Obey the Prompting of the Holy Spirit

I received a referral from a man who did not want to see a chaplain at first, but he agreed to see me because of the need for a spiritual care assessment. He was frail. Drugs and alcohol had destroyed his body, and now he had cirrhosis of the liver. I sat next to him and said, "I know you first declined a chaplain visit, but I am glad you agreed to see me. I read your history and understand what is going on with you." The Holy Spirit prompted me to go deeper with this man. "How are you doing spiritually?" I asked.

He told me he was Methodist but had gotten away from his faith. "I'm too far gone for forgiveness."

My heart was moved with compassion, and I knew God was getting ready to do something. "I don't know what you did," I said, "but I'm sure you did things you regret. I don't need to know what they were, but God is a forgiving God. No matter what you did, or who you did it to, God forgives."

His demeaner and body posture changed from being defensive to trusting me. He sat up and with a look of hope in his eyes, he asked, "Do you really think so?" He began to receive faith and believe the words of scripture I spoke to him. I reinforced God's forgiveness and love for him. The Word of God penetrated his heart, and he wanted to ask Jesus into his heart. We prayed the sinner's prayer together. When he opened his eyes, he felt clean and forgiven; he had a smile on his face and a peaceful appearance. He asked me to come back again. Unfortunately, I wasn't able to because he died two days later. Though this man had backslidden and caused a life of misery and suffering, he is now healed and walking the streets of Gold! 1 Corinthians 15:42 (NIV) reads, "So will it be with the resurrection of the dead. The body that is sown is perishable, it is raised imperishable; it is sown in dishonor, it is raised in glory, it is sown in weakness, it is raised in power; it is sown a natural body, it is raised a spiritual body."

Before the creation of time, God knew where and when we would minister. One Assemblies of God pastor's wife said to me, "We just moved here from Texas. God knew you were going to be here for us before we did. I am so glad you are here to help us through this time." When she said that to me, it increased my faith to how God works everything out.

I tell my patients, "God knew that you and I would be here today talking about these issues." God predestination us for divine appointments and good works. "For we are His workmanship, created in Christ Jesus unto good works, which God hath beforehand ordained, that we should walk in them" (Ephesians 2:10, KJV).

Chaplains must remind themselves that they are walking into a preordained situation when walking into the unknown. God knows the outcome already. Rely heavily on the Holy Spirit's leading to make the most of each visit. It's a reason to get up every morning and wait expectantly to see what God will do (paraphrased from Psalm 5:3).

CHAPLAINS ARE INFLUENCERS

The chaplain's spiritual authority influences people. Proverbs states, "As iron sharpens iron, so one man sharpens another." The chaplain's positive attitude rubs off on others in a good way. I met Carlo at an independent living facility. He was one of the most vulgar people I had ever met. Yet, he had a very endearing personality. He was like Dr. Jekyll and Mr. Hyde. One minute he talked about his sinful lifestyle, and in the next breath, he talked about how he helped people.

I often had to redirect the conversation to spiritual things, football, baseball, badminton—I didn't care—anything other than sex and alcohol. I saw him weekly. Little by little, Carlo's heart softened. The decent side started to become stronger and stronger. He was Catholic but open to the gospel. He eventually accepted the Lord as his Savior and began to change even more.

One day when I went to see him, he wanted to pray instead of me. This was his prayer. "Lord, I thank you for John. Thank you for coming to see me every week. I know you didn't have to, but you did. Your friendship, whether we talked sports, religion, or whatever is gratefully appreciated. This is what hospice is all about. I was so far away from my faith, I thought I could never come back. You helped me come back to God. Amen."

It took a lot of work, patience, perseverance, and spiritual baths after some of his visits, but it was worth it. Jesus said in Luke 15:10 (NIV), "I tell you, there is rejoicing in the presence of the angels of God over one sinner who repents." Some believe this verse refers to Jesus' rejoicing. What an awesome thought to know that Jesus rejoices when a person accepts His sacrifice for salvation. God is always working. Luke 4:18 (NIV) says, "The Spirit of the LORD is on me, because he has anointed me to proclaim the good news to the poor, he has sent me to proclaim freedom for the prisoner and recovery of sight for the blind, to set the oppressed free."

WISE USE OF TIME

A chaplain's time is valuable. There are schedules to keep, spiritual assessments to complete, meetings to attend, and patients to visit. When honoring God by being a servant leader and ministering to the need, He will give you the time needed to complete your other work. Pray first, work second. Keep your priorities in order. Brother Rick Schaffer, an Instructor at YCIBI, said, "I had such a busy day, but God wanted me to spend more time in prayer with Him. When I did, everything fell right into place. People on my schedule came to me instead of me hunting them down. I got everything I needed to get done because I put God first."

Allow God to be the LORD of your time. Some type A personalities have a complete meltdown when something interrupts the schedule. Chaplains must be flexible to drop everything and go where the need is, not where the daily agenda demands. God will make up the time for you if you allow God to be the LORD of your day. You never know what crisis lies ahead. Therefore, you must be spiritually ready and open to change. God will always give us the time we need to prioritize the job correctly. The ministry is not about us; it is about meeting people's needs by divine appointments that God has pre-ordained for us to do that day.

Let God be the LORD of your time when panicked. During my college days as a kitchen supervisor at Maranatha nursing home in Springfield, there was a Bible school student who always called off. I had to encourage her to trust God with her schedule.

"Why are you calling off so much?" I asked her.

"I have a test tomorrow and a paper to finish," she said.

I challenged her by saying, "First, people depend on you to show up. When you commit to do a job, you need to honor it. Second, if you trust that the LORD gave you this job, then He will help you in all your studies, your ministry, and your job responsibilities." So, she came into work for her shift.

The next day I ran into her on campus. She said, "After work last night, I sat down to do my paper, and God just gave me the words! I got it done in half an hour. I also did well on my test." She had learned to allow God to be the LORD of her time. If we honor our commitments, He will find a way to make sure we keep them.

Availability is key. Be willing to drop what you are doing and go whenever and wherever you are called, whether it is a stat admission, an emergency, or death. Ministry takes precedence over any other plans. Emergencies are the ministry. God will always make up the time lost. I have learned to let God be the LORD of my time. He has always given me extra time to make up for the time emergencies took.

CHAPLAINS NEED VARIETY MINISTRY

Listen to your spirit when it needs attention. Listen to your spirit's warning signs. It's like a flashing yellow or red light warning you of danger ahead that something is wrong. It is in times like these we need to stop, rest, and get our house in order. Chaplain ministry can be one dimensional, so it's imperative we balance our ministries with other things, especially things that we enjoy.

I performed hundreds of funerals over the years. At one point funerals were the only times I preached, and it started to affect me. I was the patient's chaplain and got to know that person and those closest to him very well. However, when the patient died, I rarely knew extended family. Nervousness was piling up after each funeral, but I didn't know why.

One day, all my inner turmoil came to the surface. I had an anxiety attack while giving a Power-Point presentation on compassion fatigue. When I tried to read my notes, the words were blurry and seemed to come off the paper. I didn't know what was happening. I couldn't control it or catch my breath. I thought I was having a heart attack. I was a mess!

Having an anxiety attack in front of a bunch of caregivers was the right place to have it! They felt bad for me and genuinely wanted to help. They were asking me if I was alright, if they could do anything, or if they could get me something. How ironic! I was there to teach them compassion, but I was the one receiving it. Nevertheless, I was embarrassed more than anything. Eventually, I regained my composure and somehow managed to get through the seminar. The lurking question remained. Why did this happen? I had to figure it out.

I sought Christian counseling and got the help I needed. Together we realized the only people I was preaching to were grieving family members who I really didn't know. I was always preaching to strangers in a formal setting with a solemn and serious atmosphere. I needed a change. I needed variety. I needed to preach to people I could build friendships with and be comfortable in a setting that was more relaxed and fun. I sought out Carole, who was the marketing director at an assisted living facility.

I had been ministering to our hospice patients there for over a year, so I asked her if I could preach there. Carole was there when I had my anxiety attack and was happy to help. She recognized not only my need to preach, but also the need for spiritual care in the facility. It was a perfect match and perfect timing from the LORD. I ended up preaching there every Friday morning for three years. It built my confidence back up, and I was free to preach Biblical messages on a variety of topics, not just death and dying. It was liberating! I enjoyed it and developed friendships with the residents. This was something that I needed to do for my own person spiritual and emotional health. Although it was more work each week, it was worth it. I never thought I would recover from that anxiety attack, but with God's help and the help of others, I got back up and have been preaching in facilities and churches ever since.

THE WORD OF GOD IS POWERFUL

Hebrews 4:12 (NLT) says, "For the word of God is alive. Sharper than any double-edged sword, it penetrates even to dividing soul and spirit, joints and marrow; it judges the thoughts and attitudes of the heart."

I never get tired of hearing a salvation message with a heavy anointing. People will respond. They understand with their minds while their hearts convict them of sin. They believe the word and respond in faith.

After my first year of Bible college, I attended a YCIBI graduation service. I sat next to a man who had recently entered the drug and alcohol program on campus. He was amazed at the preaching. At the end of the service, he looked at me and said, "Everything that preacher said is true." The power of the word of God broke through and he accepted Christ right then and there. That man went on to complete the program. I watched him grow as God transformed his entire life. It never gets old watching someone come to Christ. It inspires us to preach with even greater expectation! "So is my word that goes out from my mouth: It will not return to me empty, but will accomplish what I desire and achieve the purpose for which I sent it" (Isaiah 55:11, NIV).

Chaplains preach to all kinds of audiences. I have officiated funerals for a few hundred and as little as two. I have officiated at military installations with full honor guards. I have done services for high-ranking community leaders and have offered prayers at community memorial services. I've ministered to community leaders, judges, mayors, senators, professional athletes, and even pastors. From the poorest of the poor to the highest of the high, God's Word speaks.

It brings great joy when we preach a timely word to a receptive heart. When someone comes up to us after the service, whether a funeral or otherwise, and says, "Thank you chaplain; that message was for me." It means so much to us chaplains hearing encouraging words. It makes us feel that our work is not in vain and that our preparation of prayer and study were worth it. We know God called us there, but it is also nice to see the results of our ministry.

Some pastors use funerals as an opportunity to preach a hell fire and brimstone message. Most of the time, it was the pastor's own issue rather than the listeners. Over the years, I have developed my own style of preaching. I preach comforting words along with the hope of the gospel message. God's Word and His Holy Spirit will do the rest. I do not preach the same way at a funeral as I do in a congregation; nor should we. Our styles will vary, but the Word of God remains the same. Either way, preach with authority and with confident expectation that God is moving in their hearts.

Prison chaplains have opportunities the rest of us do not. They can disciple inmates over long periods of time. The same is true with other chaplains whose congregants are there for a short season of their lives, such as Teen Challenge, foster care, nursing home ministry, and any number of ministries. Unfortunately, in my line of ministry, my congregation dies every six months. I have to work fast! I don't have a lot of time. Fortunately, people who are dying are very open and honest with their feelings. They know their time is short, so they want to spend their last few months to be quality time with family, friends, and faith. I have found them to be very receptive to the gospel message.

Being a hospice chaplain has challenges other ministries do not. One of the difficulties of being a Holy Spirit-filled chaplain was watching others get healed at church but not my patients. I was at a small group meeting one night, and I vented my frustration. "I see people getting healed at church services; I pray for people in church, and God touches them. Yet, when I pay for healing for my patients, they die anyway. My congregation changes every six months." I was discouraged. They never knew the burden I carried or the frustration I felt watching others get healed when my people died. I was told by an older pastor that "the number one thing ministers struggle with most is discouragement." These friends of mine spoke words of faith into me. They reminded me that the work I do in providing God's comfort in times of great stress is a tremendous honor. Death is the ultimate healing, and we all die someday; it is inevitable. Even Lazarus, who was raised from the dead, eventually died. I was reminded of the holy atmosphere that fills the room when someone takes his/her last breath. It is a perfect opportunity for ministry. I needed their encouragement that night. Pastors and church members, don't forget your chaplains. Pray for them; support their work. This will be appreciated more than you will ever know.

I was further encouraged another time when I viewed my ministry from a different perspective. I looked at it objectively. I was out of work for a couple months due to a health problem. I was still able to preach at the Independent Living Center. A lady there told me her husband was on hospice. She said her husband's chaplain visited regularly, sang hymns, and prayed with him. As she was telling me this, I thought to myself, *What an awesome ministry.* Then it hit me that I had been in that ministry most of my life. Being out of work, I realized just how important hospice ministry is.

CHAPLAINS NEED MORE EXPOSURE IN THE CHURCH

Early missionaries were criticized by the church for dressing like the culture of the people they served. They also ate without utensils and adopted other customs, how dreadful! They never compromised the gospel, worked diligently and persistently. They eventually changed entire villages from paganism to Christ. We have come a long way in understanding the role of missionaries, and there is still some work to do in educating church members on what chaplains do.

Chaplains often go about ministry as unnoticed heroes. We tenaciously serve God and allow His Holy Spirit to do the work in people's hearts. People don't know what we do. Most people have no idea about all of the chaplaincy's various branches of ministry or their functions. People are inspired by hearing stories of chaplains' testimonies and everything they do. Churches need to be more aware of these who work in the trenches of chaplain ministries. The church needs to know what chaplain ministry is all about, as do church leaders. I would like to see chaplain ministries represented more at general, district, or even at sectional councils. Give your chaplains the pulpit. Let them share everything that God is doing in their ministries. You won't regret it!

CHAPTER TWENTY-FOUR

Wilderness Experiences

Then Jesus was led by the Spirit into the desert to be tempted by the devil.

Matthew 4:1 (NIV)

Matthew 4:1-11 shows Jesus' temptation by Satan in the wilderness. It was right after Jesus' baptism. Usually, the most difficult times aren't in the valley but when someone feels invincible. Pride fills the heart, making them the most vulnerable. After a spiritual victory or a successful church event, pride can fill a chaplain's heart. Thoughts like, "Look at me! Aren't I wonderful? I preached a powerful message, and many got saved, so now I'm going to reward myself" can lead to a swift downfall.

There is a joke of a man who went on a diet and lost twenty pounds. He was doing great, and then one day, he came to work eating a box of donuts.

"Why are you off your diet?" Everyone asked. "You were doing so great!"

He said, "Well, I drove by the donut shop and prayed, 'Lord, if there is a front row parking space in front of the store, then I'll know it's OK to eat donuts.'" It took me eight times circling the block before one came available. Thank God, the diet is over!"

It's a funny story with a good moral lesson. The joy of victory was overtaken by temptation. We can congratulate ourselves when we don't deserve it. In Luke 17:7-10 (KJV) we read, Will any of you who has a servant plowing or keeping sheep say to him when he has come in from the field, 'come at once and recline at table'? Will he not rather say to him, 'prepare supper for me, and dress properly, and serve me while I eat and drink, and afterward you will eat and drink'? Does he thank the servant because he did what was commanded? So, you also, when you have done all that you were commanded, say, 'We are unworthy servants, we have only done what was our duty.'" We are called to keep serving as unworthy servants. This attitude keeps us humble.

We are most vulnerable in times of victory, and that is when we must be the most careful. Jesus had come from being baptized by John when God said, "This is my Son in whom I am well pleased." Immediately, Jesus was driven into the wilderness.

Jesus was the Son of God but still had to go through trials, temptations, and difficulties. Jesus fasted forty days and forty nights. He was starving and thirsty, yet he was focused on pleasing God no matter how difficult it got. He was in for one of the toughest spiritual battles of His life. He was tired, hungry, and lonely, but God was with Him. Satan tempted Him by saying, "If You are the Son of God, turn this stone into bread." He tried to cause Jesus to use His power to fill His empty stomach. Jesus answered, "It is written: Man shall not live on bread alone, but on every word that comes from the mouth of God."

Satan tempts us when we are weak, as well as strong. He never relents. He tempts us to gratify ourselves with pleasures of sin rather than the joy of holiness. If God drove Jesus into the dry, barren land and allowed the devil to tempt Him in every way, then God will do the same to us. Those times of testing show us of what we're really made. We may fail at times, but that only makes us more determined. More often than not, we succeed and become strengthened in our faith.

Satan knew Jesus's vulnerability; he knew He was hungry, but Jesus refused to use His power for self-serving purposes. He refused to question God's faithfulness. Jesus entrusted Himself fully to His Father, Who would provide for every need. Even though He was hungry, His greatest need was spiritual food. Satan tries to satisfy us with sinful pleasures while God, "satisfies your desires with good things" (Psalm 103:5).

The greater need is always spiritual satisfaction. Satan tries substitutes, but it is never as good as the original. Quoting the Word of God from Psalm 91, helped Him through the temptation.

Psalm 91 reveals how God protects us in difficult situations. Satan tried to coerce Jesus to throw Himself off the cliff and the angels would catch him. Satan loves to misuse the word of God. He twists it, tries to confuse the context, but Jesus knew the word of God better than the devil because Jesus is the "Word of God."

Satan has authority over the kingdoms of this world and offered them all to Jesus if He would bow and worship him. Satan tried to appeal to his needs. Satan tries to appeal to our needs by giving us free stuff. Nothing the Devil gives is ever free; there is always a price to pay. He tried to keep Jesus from accomplishing the will of the Father. Satan's strategy was to get Jesus to abuse His authority and divert Him from the path of suffering and obedience that was ultimately fulfilled at the cross. Jesus resolutely said, "No. Worship the Lord and serve him only," again quoting scripture. Satan will tempt us to abuse our authority. God has placed us chaplains in positions of spiritual authority not to use our power for self-seeking reasons but to serve God. We chaplains need to be obedient even when it is hard. We must not be diverted by sensual desires but to keep our eyes on the cross, our calling, and our mission.

SATAN'S SCHEMES

Satan schemes to deceive us when we are tired, weak, lonely, or hungry. He tries to trip us by putting things in our paths to make us fail. He tempts us in areas where we are the weakest and wears us down with subtle thoughts.

Schemes are a deliberate pattern of events designed to take advantage and cause pain. When I was younger, I was being tempted to smoke while I was alone in my apartment. The temptation was strong for some reason. As I opened a drawer to put away clean clothes, there was an old pack of cigarettes. My eyes were immediately drawn to the pack. There's a reason Solomon says don't let your eyes gaze upon the wine in Proverbs 23:31. What our eyes take in goes straight to our hearts. We then begin to believe the lies that this sin will be satisfying. Billboard ads pop into our minds of the cowboy man smoking and feeling good; old thoughts of having a smoke after dinner began filling my mind.

Satan tempts with seductive words. "Come on. Drink. Party. Be social. Have fun." The next thing we know, we are no longer sober after years of sobriety or smoking after years of quitting. It doesn't matter how old we are or how long we have been walking with the LORD; we will always be tempted by sin on this side of heaven.

I saw those cigarettes and my pupils widened. Before I realized what was going on, I heard the inaudible words in my mind, "Smoke. It's cool and relaxing." It was as if I were in the wilderness all alone with no one around to see me. So, I took the pack of cigarettes, walked straight into the bathroom, and flushed them quickly down the toilet. Otherwise, I knew what the result would be. All the spiritual victory I had gained would have been lost. I would have to start all over again. Satan was trying to scheme me. He was setting me up. First, he knew I was doing laundry that day, and I would eventually open up that drawer and see those cigarettes. Second, the temptation was unusually strong that day. In fact, I hadn't thought about smoking for months. He was working hard, but God was working harder. Giving in to sin wasn't worth it, but my soul and salvation were worth the suffering of holiness. God wants us to persevere, endure, even if it means pain and personal sacrifice, if necessary. We must be willing to suffer physical agony for spiritual holiness. When you are being tempted in an unusual way, understand that the enemy is causing this to destroy your walk with God. When we persevere through, we maintain the spiritual high ground. After obediently enduring the testing in the wilderness, Jesus was then prepared for ministry. In order to defeat the enemy publicly, he first had to defeat the enemy privately. We must defeat temptations on our knees. Then, we are ready for what the world throws at us.

If you are in a time of difficulty, it will pass. As a shepherd boy, David learned how to handle difficult situations. It was a time of preparation for God's bigger things in the future. While tending the sheep, he killed the lion and the bear. You, too, are being prepared for the Goliaths that will come to challenge you.

Jesus showed us that there is power in obedience and prayer. Jesus went through all those temptations to be prepared for ministry. The question is are we willing? Are we ready to go deeper with God? Are we willing to go through fiery trials and temptations and still remain faithful? The old song goes, "No turning back, the cross before me the world behind me. No turning back, no turning back."

THE WILDERNESS IS WHERE WE GROW SPIRITUALLY

The wilderness is where spiritual leaders are prepared for ministry. Wilderness experiences help develop a fervent relationship with God. The worst enemy is not the devil but ourselves. When we practice conquering ourselves, we grow stronger. We experience new realms of spiritual growth and expansion.

Sometimes we are forced into the wilderness. Jesus was forced by the Holy Spirit into the wilderness after His baptism. There He faced every kind of temptation by Satan, and He conquered. The angels came and ministered to Him. The wilderness is where miracles happen.

Moses was forced into the wilderness eighty years altogether. There God spoke to him through the burning bush. He encountered God regularly. It was where he received the ten commandments and learned patience and dependence upon God. His reward for his obedience was knowing God as a friend. His face glowed because he was so close to God. The wilderness was where his life was changed forever. God was with him in the wilderness. There were millions of other people in the desert with Moses, yet none of them experienced God the way Moses did. Don't be in the wilderness without God. We find ourselves in the desert for lots of reasons. It could be in between ministry positions, grief, loss, health, or a death. God is with you; make sure you are with Him.

There are times we must go into the wilderness on our own to get alone with God. Paul willingly went into the desert, and he received revelation and wrote the Word of God. The Greek vernacular implies he went immediately without hesitation. He knew from Jesus' and Moses's experiences that the wilderness meant experiencing God's presence.

I am thankful for all the men and women professors, instructors, and teachers I had over the years who instilled wisdom, courage, and knowledge. But the Apostle Paul didn't receive a seminary degree. He didn't get his revelations from other apostles and teachers; he received it directly from God. Paul spent three years alone with God in the desert of Arabia. There is nothing better than getting alone with God and hearing Him for ourselves. Receiving an education from teachers is great, but receiving education directly from God is even better.

The wilderness is a place to get away from everyone else's voices and hear the voice of God for ourselves. God is in the wilderness, and it is where we encounter Him! He sends us there, so He can prune us, speak to us, and change us.

The wilderness does not have the distractions of everyday life. Sometimes, we need to get away from the TV, from food, from civilization, and get alone with God for direction, miracles, or simply fellowship with Him.

The wilderness is where spiritual battles are fought and won. The wilderness is a dry, arid place. It is a place where the strong survive, and the weak die. It is a spiritual survival of the fittest. It is a place we must occasionally go to fast, hunger, and thirst more for God.

Our weaknesses and sinful desires must die there. If we can say no to food, then we can say no to anything. Fasting replaces physical desires for spiritual ones. The physical needs are deprived for the spiritual strengths to emerge.

The best and the worst are revealed in the desert. The wilderness is a place of soul searching, weeping, and pruning, and focusing on God. God uses this time to reveal certain things that need to change.

Going through hard times can feel like a wilderness. You feel alone and abandoned. Everything was going great. What just happened? God, where did you go? Christians have bad days, too. Just like Job, God never keeps us there any longer than He needs to. We are often in the wilderness for a short season to teach us life lessons. We come out better than when we went in.

The wildness is also a place to get alone with God, so He can strengthen us. Our Christianity is often tested through health crises or financial hardships.

The wilderness is not a place to fear; it is a place to grow and wait for miracles to happen. Wilderness experiences help us see more clearly, be better refined, grow in our new natures, and experience new heights in our relationship with God. God uses those fiery furnaces of life's experiences to prepare and refine us to do an even greater work in ministry.

The wilderness is a place of change, so don't run from it. Embrace it, and let God do the necessary work that needs to be done. God reveals not only our weaknesses during those times, but he also emerges the best that is within us. When our will is lined up with God's, the impossible becomes possible when we allow Him to transform us.

FINDING GOD'S GRACE IN DESERT PLACES

Grace is the opposite of Karma. Karma is about getting what you deserve. Grace is getting what we don't deserve. Grace and forgiveness transform desires, motivations, and behavior. Hostility only breeds more hostility and contempt. Judgment kills, but grace gives life!

In Jesus' time taxes were on everything including food, clothing, and land. When a traveler went to the next town, taxes were imposed again; it was abusive. Zacchaeus was a sinner and tax cheat. He was getting rich while everyone else struggled. He collected not only for the Roman government, but for himself and the soldier behind him. "The three-hundred-pound soldier behind me will break your legs if you don't pay what I say," he might have said. Zacchaeus was despised by everyone. Without compassion, Zaccheus didn't trust anyone. He may have been picked on as a kid for being small. He had little man syndrome both inside and out. When he came into power, he exacted revenge on everyone. He was going to make others feel the same pain he felt. The problem with that is it never satisfies. Hate begets more hate.

When people allow anger, unforgiveness, or revenge to possess them, it distorts all rational thought, and they end up only hurting themselves. Satan encourages this sort of demented thinking. "Esau comforted himself with the thought of killing Jacob," Genesis 27:42. In some sick way, evil thoughts comfort people. By meditating or dwelling on these, they think it is soothing them when in reality, it is killing them spiritually. There needs to be forgiveness and a change of heart.

One day, Jesus came into town. Zacchaeus was a short man, too short to see over the crowd. Climbing a tree, he wanted to see Jesus. Jesus looked up and said, "Zacchaeus come down, for I am coming to your house for dinner." Zacchaeus was filled with hope. Jesus accepted him. Zacchaeus promised that he would pay back everyone he cheated four-fold. Jesus said, "Today, salvation has come to his house." Zacchaeus went from being physically small to a spiritual giant with one conversation with Jesus when He came into town. Jesus is still coming into people's towns and giving grace.

We often expect judgment or discipline from God, but then He surprises us with unconditional love and grace. God is so patient. Even in all my stupidity, making the same mistakes over and over and over again as a Christian, Jesus forgave me each time. I would have given up on myself a long time ago if someone treated me that way, but God never does!

God is loving and kind. He is kind to the ungrateful and wicked. His kindness leads to repentance. His grace disarms hostility, softening the heart of the sinner. Those who don't know Christ, and even some who do, expect anger, judgment, or retribution because of what they did. But when they receive grace, love enters, and anger dissipates.

Grace changes us. When one receives grace, he/she is more apt to give grace. When Jesus gives grace, it affects everyone. The whole family, and maybe even the community is changed. The more grace we receive from God, the more we want to give grace to others.

STREAMS IN THE DESERT

For those of you who are reading this book and have never accepted Jesus as your LORD and Savior, I want you to know that there is hope. Maybe you have been in the wilderness without God, and you're realizing you need God's help! Isaiah 35:6-7 says, "For waters shall burst forth in the wilderness, and streams in the desert. The parched ground shall become a pool; and the thirsty land, springs of water" (NKJV).

Without God, the wilderness is death! Zacchaeus, the thief, and others who walk in spiritual darkness need an encounter with Jesus. Everyone does! Going through life without God is death. The wilderness can be a great place for change when walking with God but a horrible place without Him. Without God you cannot expect miracles, divine encounters, or spiritual growth. You do not have the promises of God, His divine protection, or His Spirit inside of you. The only way to do that is to acknowledge your sin, ask forgiveness, let Him take away your sin, and fill you with His Holy Spirit.

God knows everything about you. Nothing is hidden from God. Allow yourself to be vulnerable and honest about your hurts. Go to Him in prayer, and tell Him everything. Then believe He can fix it. Sin, such as anger, unforgiveness, or anything else, can live in your heart. Allow God to have access to those areas, so He can heal you.

It's like a man who invites Jesus into his home. He shows Jesus all his belongings, his material things, his awards, and his accomplishments. He takes Jesus into the game room, the living room, and every other room in the house except for one.

Jesus points to that room and asks, "What's in there?"

The man answers. "Oh, Jesus, you don't want to go in there; it's a mess. There are things in that room I never showed anyone. I would be embarrassed if I showed you what's in there."

Jesus responds, "I already know what is in there. Let Me in so we can clean it together. Let's air it out, open the windows, dust off the furnishings, and make it look new."

The man trusts Jesus and allows Him to enter. Sure, enough, it's dark and dismal. The curtains are closed, and it has a musty smell. The man feels ashamed, but even with all the darkness in that one room, he trusts Jesus. As Jesus opens the windows, fresh air sweeps the house fresh and clean! The Holy Spirit fills the dark room of his heart with all God's presence. His light shines where darkness once dwelt. Peace fills his heart where anxiety once dominated, and forgiveness replaces sin. Shame is removed as Jesus accepts him. Jesus cleanses the soul, heals the hurts, and restores him to a full relationship with God. Nothing is hidden; everything is made new. God will heal your wounded heart and past hurts from what others have done to you. God forgives, and God heals!

Over the years, I have heard stories of how physical, emotional, or sexual abuse have wrecked peoples' lives either directly or indirectly.

I had been ministering to a lady in a nursing home for a few months. They were cordial visits with no deep significance. One day nurse Linda came to me and said, "Ms. Peggy opened up to me about her abusive past. It was beyond me, so I asked her if it was okay if you talked to her about it. She agreed."

Peggy began to tell me her story, but first she told me she was having pain in her arm. She said, "I was the oldest of seven children. When I turned eleven, my dad starting sexually abusing me." Unfortunately,

I was not surprised. For some reason, the community I was in had a lot of sexual abuse, and I heard more stories than I cared to. This one, however, was evil. I listened attentively. She continued, "The worst feeling of betrayal was that my mother held me down while he did it to me. If she didn't, he would turn on her. Then afterwards, he got all the children on the couch, opened up his Bible, and began preaching to us."

I sat there speechless. I told her I had never heard of anything so demonic in my life. That's when she said, "I called him the diablo—the devil. He did this from the time I was eleven until I was sixteen. At sixteen, I met a boy and ran away from home. I told my siblings I was leaving. They wanted to come with us, but we couldn't take care of all them. I had to leave them there with that monster. I felt terrible about leaving them there, but I had to get out. The boy I ran away with was older than me and took really good care of me. I loved him, and he loved me, but because of what my father did to me, I was unable to have children."

Surprisingly, she was not angry at God. She said she had always felt God's presence with her. At one point in her life, they even became Christians but had gotten away from their faith. "I am 90 years old now and on hospice. Every night of my life, I have nightmares of him. I see his face in my dreams. I just can't get rid of them."

Peggy was in a spiritual desert. Now alone and dying, she recognized her need for Jesus. I told her that her father used scripture to justify himself and used scripture as a weapon. I began to share God's love, forgiveness, and grace with her. After our conversation, I prayed with her. She said, "I felt a wave go over my arm."

I said, "I'm glad God is touching you."

I increased my visits and returned the following week. She said, "The last time you prayed for me, a wave came over my arm, and I have not had any pain since then." She said she was feeling better after our conversation but still saw his face every night in her dreams. After our talk, I prayed again. She told me that she felt that same wave over her mind. God was doing something.

I went back again, but this time she was beaming with excitement. She couldn't wait to tell me that after our prayer last time, she stopped having dreams of her father's face.

Peggy rededicated her life to the LORD. She lived another month with no pain, no horrific dreams, and the peace of God on her life. Then the nurse came to me one day and told me she was actively dying, so I went to be with her.

Peggy was laying there in her hospital bed. Her oxygen mask was on her face; she couldn't speak, but she smiled when I entered the room. I sat with her and told her that God was getting her ready to take her home. She nodded. I said, "Everything is going to be alright. Greet me when it is my turn." She nodded with a smile and died shortly after.

The wilderness can be a place of great torment, pain, and past abuse. I can't begin to explain why bad things like these happen. All I know is that it breaks the heart of God when it breaks the heart of a child. If you have experienced abuse, neglect, or any other kind of hurt, God is here for you right now to heal your heart and comfort your wounded spirit. Trust Him with your soul, and open up to Him.

Let Him take you out of the dry wilderness of life and give streams of living water to satisfy your soul. Will you let Him take the hurt that others have done to you and replace it with comfort and love? Will you decide today to follow Him? Will you also make a decision today to let God forgive you and give you grace even though you don't deserve it? Jesus says in Revelation 3:20 (paraphrased), "Here I am! I stand at the door and knock. If anyone hears my voice and opens the door, I will come in and eat with him, and he with me." Do you hear Him calling you right now? He is right there with you as you are reading this book. In a painting in our church is Jesus standing outside. There is no handle on the door for Him to walk in. The door must be opened by the owner of the house. Will you let Him heal you today? Will you let His grace overpower every sin caused by you or done to you? Encounter God in the wilderness today!

CHAPTER TWENTY-FIVE

Respect for Other's Spiritual Beliefs

Therefore, as we have opportunity, let us do good to all people,
especially to those who belong to the family of believers.

Galatians 6:10 (NIV)

My mother taught me to respect other people's religious beliefs. She said, "People hold their religious views very sacred, and when you reject their belief, you reject them." I have learned to respect other people's religious beliefs even though I disagree. We can respectfully disagree without rejecting the person.

Christians who come across as dogmatic and rude turn people off. We can challenge another's beliefs by asking questions without being a know-it-all. As a Christian chaplain, I seek to present Christ truthfully and in a nice, friendly, and wise way. Everyone loves to be validated. No one likes to have his/her religious beliefs attacked. It's possible to respect the person even if you disagree with his/her religion. Respecting other's beliefs does not mean we accept their religion, but it does show that we are open for meaningful discussion in a polite and intellectual conversation.

All religions are based on faith. For example, the Native Americans believe nature is alive and that lakes, the moon, and the earth are spiritual beings. Mormons believe they will one day be gods. If we are honest, some of our beliefs are almost unbelievable. Before we make fun of these religions, take a look at Christianity from the viewpoint of an unbeliever. We try to explain that the Holy Spirit impregnated a woman. Did the gods come down to have sex? How did Jesus die and be raised from the dead? These answers require faith and can be just as hard to believe as other faiths.

It can be challenging when the chaplain's Christian worldview contradicts others.

Listening to and loving people does not mean we always agree with them. There is a time and a season for everything under the sun. There is a time to speak up, and there is a time to keep quiet. We must be appropriate and gracious in our speech and attitude, not pugnacious. Being rude or obnoxious will never impress or compel others to Christ.

I was ministering to a lesbian couple this one afternoon. Neither were very religious, but they did say they were spiritual. The patient was raised in a Christian home. They believed in asking *The Universe* for direction. I quietly asked God to help me in this situation. I let them know we were there to help them through this terminal diagnosis. I shared that "we take a non-judgmental approach as we do not walk in their shoes of grief, loss, and stress." I told them we were just there to help. A tear flowed from the patient's eyes. At the end of the visit, I prayed for them to experience God's grace, peace, and love during this time. I ended the prayer, "In Jesus' name." We all felt His presence. I knew God was working on the patient. However, I was not going to go in there with an attitude of judgment, condemnation, and guilt. They had experienced that before. What they hadn't experienced was a pastor who loved them and did not condemn them. I left it up to God to do the rest. We never know what is going on in their hearts after we leave. That is the Holy Spirit's work.

What sets the Christian apart from all other religions is that God is the Ultimate Creator of everything. He is not the god of only a select group of people. He is everyone's Creator and God of all. The very first commandment is, "Thou shalt not have any foreign gods before me, no graven images or idols" (Exodus 20:3, KJV).

Chaplains cannot be all religions to all people. I have seen other chaplains try to fit in with the patient's faith group. It is disingenuous and comes across as unauthentic. We can only be the best Christian chaplain we can be, while remaining sensitive to his/her beliefs. I was called to a Hindu's death. I will not pray to their gods, and I will not compromise and dishonor my God, but I can offer emotional support. When I find myself in those situations, I simply let Jesus' love shine and offer as much comfort I can give. Chaplains are called to minister to people regardless of their religion. We can offer grief counseling, emotional support, and compassion but need to leave the spiritual matters to their clergy.

Unfortunately, many in the church think chaplains have compromised their faith because of ministering to those of other religions. The community, on the other hand, misunderstands us, as well and think chaplains believe in all religions. So, to all young chaplains, I repeat: Know your calling, and understand your role in Christ. Listen to the voice of God and not others, lest you will be confused. Lastly, be confident of your calling to this ministry because you will be misunderstood by both the church and the world. You will stand alone at times, but God is by your side.

Many religions have a strong philosophy about them. We know this because "God put eternity into the heart of man," (paraphrased from Ecclesiastes 3:11). Man has been trying to figure out who or what God is since the beginning of time. II Kings 17 talks about the Assyrian captivity. The King of Assyria invaded Israel and defeated them. He took the land of the northern kingdom of Israel. The king removed most of the Jews from the land and dispersed them to other countries. Then he put pagans in Israel. Pagans lived with Israelites. God sent lions to judge the people. The Assyrian king then sent one of the exiled priests back to find out what the god of that land required. Then it goes on to say, "And though they worshiped the LORD, they continued to follow their own gods according to the religious customs of the nations from which they came" (II Kings 17:33, NLT)

America is an eclectic mixture of Christianity, Buddhism, native Americanism, New Age spirituality, and atheists. When Christianity is compromised with other religions, people end up worshipping nothing, feeling nothing, experiencing nothing, and changing nothing.

Jesus came on the scene six hundred years later in Samaria and had an open and honest discussion with a Samaritan woman at the well.

AN ENCOUNTER WITH JESUS

Divine opportunities for ministry are often handed to us whenever God allows someone to cross our paths. In John chapter 4, Jesus asked a Samaritan woman for a drink. He then changed the subject from physical water to spiritual water. Jesus knew the spiritual carnality of this town, but He cared enough to take time to talk to her. He was getting her curiosity peaked (John 4:7,10). It's never about the obvious. It's not about the water; it was deeper than that. It's about Him meeting her spiritual needs (John 4:13-26; 39-42).

She sensed He was a prophet. Jesus continued to probe, delved into her life, and spiritually assessed this woman. He knew the history of the town of Samaria and that her beliefs were both Judaism and paganism. She had just enough knowledge of Yahweh, but to be on the safe side, she also was a worshipper of Baal, Moloch, or the Asherah. She believed she could only worship on that particular mountain, which is a belief of Baal followers. Baal was a fertility, regional god worshiped only in nature and specific places. Jesus probed deeper and had her intrigued in what He had to say. The Holy Spirit was drawing Himself to her through Jesus' words.

Droughts were common in Israel. Springs and rivers that ran all year were few, so the land relied on cisterns to catch and store the winter rains and wells to tap into underground water tables. In Jewish culture, *dead water* refers to standing or stored water. *Living water* refers to moving water like rivers, springs, and rainfall. Such water was precious. The Jews viewed living water as directly coming from God to supply all their needs (*NLT commentary*).

Jesus told the Samaritan woman about him being the Living Water. He prophesied that she had five husbands and then told her He was the Messiah. She was amazed and awed at His words, telling her about the prophets who came before Him. She became a believer that day, and many in the town believed. John 4:42 relates (NIV), Then "they said to the woman, 'Now we believe, not just because of what you told us, but because we have heard Him for ourselves. Now we know that He indeed is the Savior of the World.'"

Jesus spoke into this Samaritan woman's heart. Her need was not men. Her need was God. Jesus didn't judge her; He restored her. From that sacred conversation with Jesus, she and her neighbors were saved.

Jesus did not condemn this woman for what she did not know. She worshipped gods and other religions, but that was normal for her. He didn't judge her for being married five times nor shacking up with the man she was with at that moment. Jesus loved her as she was, but He wanted to show her a more fulfilling way of life. It was her faith that changed her. She had faith and went further by putting it into action.

Jesus then says, "Believe me, dear woman. The time is coming when it will no longer matter whether you worship the Father on this mountain or in Jerusalem. You Samaritans know very little about the one you worship, while we Jews know all about Him, for salvation comes from the Jews. But the time is coming. Indeed, it's here when true worshippers will worship the Father in spirit and in truth. The Father is looking for those who will worship him that way. For God is spirit, so those who worship him must worship in spirit and in truth" (John 4:21, NIV).

Christian chaplains have something that not all the other chaplains have—the Holy Spirit and truth. The power of the Holy Spirit can work miracles, signs, and wonders as we give Him freedom to work in and through us. But He also works through us with divine, supernatural wisdom and truth. Jesus didn't perform a miracle with the woman at the well; He used words. Much of the chaplain's ministry are words. Using divine insight to tell her about herself, Jesus talked about the water to begin a conversation. That was her primary concern. He continually referred to drawing water, using convincing words to persuade her. His loving kindness warmed her heart and built her trust. She saw in Him a genuineness that she probably never ever saw in other men. Something inside of her realized *this is truth*. She and the townspeople all believed.

Jesus proclaimed, "The truth will set you free." Most of our ministry consists of pastoral comfort and support. We need to hear from God in the middle of a crisis when emotions are running high and stress levels are at their boiling point. Family members might be tired and stressed out from all the extra work. Everyone is exhausted and grieving in their own ways: the patient and the family. Then the arguing starts. They begin to knit-pick at each other, getting stuck in the cycle of grief with no answers. No one knows what to do, and they are at their wit's end, feeling hopeless.

That is the time when the spiritual chaplain cries out to God. "Oh, LORD, help me here." God brings back to remembrance clinical training, the Word of God, life experiences, and a heart of and compassion for these people. Boundaries are discussed, identifying individual needs, and fears are revealed. Talking it out helps get to the spiritual issue and resolve the conflict underneath the surface. After all the painful truths are divulged, the visit is closed with prayer and faith. I often have asked those involved to give and receive forgiveness. A spirit of peacefulness often returns. God calls us to preach His words not only in "Samaria but unto the uttermost part of the earth" (Acts 1:8). The best miracle is bringing God's presence into the situation.

GUARD YOUR HEART

Many people in America claim to be Christians these days but have many beliefs. They say they believe in God but go to fortune tellers to consult mediums and spiritists who do more harm than good because that allows demonic spirits into their lives. They mess with Ouija boards and séances. They may even use scripture out of context to say what they want it to say rather than the truth. Some Christian churches have used crystals and "so-called Christian tarot cards." It darkens the council of God, (paraphrased from Job 38:2). Love cannot overflow in a compromised heart. A heart that says, "Well, I can sin, and it won't affect me." Or, "I can worship Jesus and another god" won't work. It's all or nothing with God; halfway doesn't cut it.

Our society has changed. We are not all Christians anymore. America, much like Samaria, has lost its way. Mixing false answers with faith will never work. People need answers to set them free. They are confused and need answers that make sense.

The Bible speaks for itself. We need to share the Bible unashamedly. When people ask me difficult questions like why God allows bad things to happen, I give them answers from the Bible. I explain the garden of Eden where evil came into the world through Satan. He is the one to blame, not God. Bad things happen because of bad choices resulting in sin, suffering, and disease. Be the mouthpiece, but let the Bible defend itself. I have found that patients listen inquisitively and often reply time and time again, "You know that makes sense. I never heard the Bible explained like that to me before." Sharing the Word of God in detail allows the Holy Spirit to quicken their hearts with faith. I have used the Bible to counsel Christians and non-Christians alike simply by stating Biblical truths. They may not have come to the LORD right then and there, but answers were given and seeds of faith were planted.

Preaching, evangelism, and pastoral care ministry sow the seeds into hardened hearts. Allow God to use your words, wisdom, counseling talents, and skills when you talk to people. Provide empathy and divine inspiration to breathe new life into a desperate soul. God needs you to be His voice, His hands, and His feet.

Chaplains have two responsibilities:

1. Keep from integrating into unhealthy spiritual beliefs.
2. Respect our patients and their spiritual backgrounds.

This doesn't mean accepting their beliefs as evident and trustworthy. You might think, as I did early in my ministry, *I see their point. Maybe I should think that way, too.* Don't make the same mistake I did. The secular world can seduce us if we are not careful. As a Spirit-filled chaplain, we must maintain that the only truth is God's truth. We must guard our souls and hearts and not get deceived by other subtle, deceptive spirits that are antithetical to your beliefs. Spirit-filled chaplains must maintain an uncompromised heart that is fully committed to the Holy Spirit's working in your life and ministry. When that happens, God will intervene on your behalf in every uncomfortable situation you find yourself. His Word will work powerfully, and you will see the fruit of your harvest.

CHAPTER TWENTY-SIX

America, The Churchless Society

*This is what the LORD says: "Restrain your voice
from weeping and your eyes from tears, for your
work will be rewarded," declares the LORD.*

Jeremiah 31:16 (NIV)

When my generation was growing up, our parents made us go to church. Catholic and protestant churches were full. Christianity had a positive influence on society. People knew right from wrong. The Ten Commandments were, for the most part, upheld and honored. Now, our country is in its third generation of unchurched citizens.

When I officiate a funeral and end with the LORD's prayer, usually the older generation are the only ones who know the words. The younger generation looks around confused not knowing what to say. One can almost tell what they are thinking: *What is that? I never heard that one before.* It saddens me. The Boomer Generation was different from the Greatest Generation. The Boomers dare not force our children to attend church because "We want them to choose for themselves what to believe." I have often heard the excuse, "I was forced, so I never forced my children to go." Really? Was everything our parents did wrong? Must we rebel against even the good things? Forcing a child to go to church is a good thing. Children are forced to go to school. Forcing children to read and write and obey laws and societal norms are good things so why not church? The Bible has timeless truths to make them better Christians and citizens. Simply put, Boomers got lazy and didn't want to attend themselves, so they used it as an excuse not to go. My generation did a genuine disservice to the next generation, and for that,

I am truly sorry. We left a spiritual void in our children, and the results have been disastrous.

Now the Boomers are grandparents. So, now there is a third generation of unchurched children. Using the Bible as an example, we see that each generation usually gets worse and drifts further away from God as time goes by.

NEO-PAGANISM

Israel, for example, gradually fell away from the laws of God. God designed sacrificial and fellowship offerings to bring people closer to Him and one another. It made for a healthy, moral, and civil society. As time went by, a new generation emerged and the book of the Law ceased to be read and obeyed. This caused Israel's moral and spiritual decline. Jeremiah was known as the weeping prophet because he witnessed firsthand what sin does to society. When Israel came out of Egypt, they were led by Moses, Aron, and later Joshua. They sacrificed offerings and worshipped only God. As years went by, other religions influenced them. They began worshipping the Baals, Asheroths, and Moloch. They became prosperous during this time and forsook Yahweh and relied on themselves and false gods, giving them the credit for their prosperity. By the time Jeremiah ministered from 626-585 B.C., Israel became so corrupt that God sent them into exile as punishment. They went from serving God to complacency, from complacency to nominalism. From there, it only got worse. During their backsliding, they became prideful and began worshiping other gods. They became completely apostate and wicked. This was the cycle of spiritualism in the Old Testament, and this is the same cycle here in America. After experiencing the full measure of God's wrath, judgment, and punishment, they repented only for the same cycle to continue.

Jeremiah was so overwhelmed by grief. He wrote in Chapter 8:18-19 (NLT), "My grief is beyond healing; my heart is broken. Listen to the weeping of my people, it can be heard all across the land. Has the LORD abandoned his people?" In verse 21, "I hurt with the hurt of my people. I mourn and am overcome with grief. Is there no medicine in Gilead? Is there no physician there? Why is there no healing for the wounds of my people?"

In Jeremiah 9:5 (NLT), "They all fool and defraud each other; no one tells the truth. With practiced tongues, they tell lies; they wear themselves out with all their sinning."

In Jeremiah 9:12 (NLT), "Who is wise enough to understand all this? Who has been instructed by the LORD and can explain it to others?"

The answer to that question in today's society is chaplains. Chaplains understand the times. Chaplains are wise. Chaplains are instructed by God and have the innate gift to teach others God's word. Chaplains have several things in common. First, they are not self-seeking. Most chaplains I have worked with are humble and unassuming. Second, we are gifted in evangelism. We love being around both the sheep and the goats. We are built that way. Third, chaplains are in the trenches and see first-hand what is going on in people's homes. We see how people live and behave. People are comfortable around chaplains because we are non-judgmental. People can be themselves in our presence; and we want them to be. Just like anyone else, chaplains don't like pretentiousness. We want people to be honest with us so we know how best to minister to them. Some can be too real.

I had a patient named Michael who was forty-five years-old with end stage alcoholic cirrhosis. He was an extremely intelligent man with a Master's degree in physics and mathematics. He was a scientist, but he loved the party life. He was a punk rocker in his day. During the third visit with me, he wanted to introduce me to something he was very proud of. He brought out his coke table. At first, I didn't know what it was until he explained this was where he cut up his cocaine and snorted it. I said, "Don't show me that. Are you crazy?" We both laughed. He left no stone unturned sharing his life story. It took me over a year of ministering to him before he finally accepted Christ as his Savior. I officiated his memorial service. Instead of the service being dark and depressing, it was full of hope. The family was grateful for all we had done while he was on hospice, especially becoming a Christian.

Who better than chaplains to understand the spiritual decay in America? Who better than chaplains are wise enough to instruct others right from wrong? We need to minister even when we are rejected. Lamentations 4:16 (NIV) says, "The priests are shown no honor, the elders no favor." The same is happening in America. Our nation is becoming increasingly hostile to Christianity.

There is a falling away from Christianity. General Superintendent Doug Clay of the Assemblies of God writes, "Closer to home, the number of Americans identifying as Christians continues to plummet according to Pew Research Center reports. In 2007, 78% of Americans claimed Christian affiliation, compared to 63% in 2021" (Influence Summer 2023).

I have seen this same cycle before in my lifetime. In the 1960s and '70s, satanic influences began emerging. The Satanic temple was built in 1966 in San Francisco by Anton Lavey. Movies, such as *Rosemary's Baby*, *The Exorcist*, and *The Omen* were popular. People were intrigued by the demonic and began having séances and using Ouija boards. The church was praying though! They were earnestly interceding. Then revival broke out. The Jesus Movement began. Young people were giving their lives to Christ because the world did not satisfy them anymore. Drugs, séances, Ouija boards, and movies left them empty and void of true peace. Revival spread all through the United States. Our God is a jealous God. He saw what was happening, and it grieved Him. He will not share His affections with anything other than Him. He put it into the hearts of Christians to pray, and pray they did because "where sin increased, grace increased all the more" (Romans 5:20).

Though we are living in the age of apostasy, people will once again turn to Jesus Christ though we have an increase in sexual immorality beyond what we have even seen before. However, we are in the cycle of Satanism and the occult; God will move again in America. With great repentance comes great revival! Once again people will feel the void these influences leave. Only Jesus can satisfy the soul. God loves our youth; He is jealous for their affection and will once again get their attention and change their hearts!

Right now, we are not living in a time of revival. We are living in a time of great lament and spiritual decline. We have watched our nation go from being blessed to being disobedient and defiant toward God. Our hearts break for our nation, children, and youth. We are the remnant who needs to stay holy. The time for nominal Christianity has passed.

Christians will be forced to stand against sin and make decisions as to what they will believe. We need to remain faithful in these dark days ahead. I am afraid our nation will only get worse before it gets better. But I do believe better days are ahead. I do believe God will bring revival to America once again. When the people have had enough of their fill of God's wrath; pestilence; and poverty, both spiritually and financially, they will cry out to God in their distress, and God will hear. He will answer. Hosea 14:4 says, "I will heal their waywardness and love them freely, for my anger has turned away from them." Reverend Doug Clay goes on to write, "Pentecostal/Charismatic Christianity is the fastest growing segment of World Christianity today." Most of the growth over the past century took place in the global South. Africans now constitute 35.7% of all Spirit-filled Christians, Latin Americans 30.3%, and Asians 19.5%, according to Zurlo in *Global Christianity*. This is cause for rejoicing. Unfortunately, there are worrisome statistical trends, too, especially the demographic expansion of Islam and the continuing decline of Christian affiliation in the U.S." (Summer 2023).

In the meantime, we need to pray, intercede, and remain the faithful remnant during times of persecution, hardship, and heartache. The Christian voice is important now more than ever. Though our words may fall on deaf ears, we must remain faithful. The Word of God remains the same regardless of what society dictates. Heaven and hell have not changed; we are all going to be judged by the same standards regardless of the time we live. Be faithful chaplains, be faithful Church! Plant those seeds because some will fall on receptive hearts. Christians are rising up and taking a stand. We have been silent far too long. God will move again.

HUMANISM

Godly mercy is replaced by social programs, handouts, and secularism. It removes any ambition to seek God and better ourselves. Hard work and ingenuity lose first-place with governmental handouts. It causes laziness and dependence on the state rather than trusting in God to supply our needs. Without God and His principles, the natural tendency is to replace it with humanism. Who needs God if we can do it ourselves? Government help is abusive. They give barely enough to survive and punishes people if they make more than they are supposed to. It takes away incentives to do better.

Secular society forgets about the innate human condition called "the sinful nature." Brother Anebal Delgado, an Instructor at YCIBI, used to say, "I wouldn't trust my flesh till it was dead for three days." Christians are honest about the human condition because we understand it is self-ish and self-centered. We know that good and evil will always be in the world, and utopia is unrealistic.

One of my elderly Baptist patients said to me, "It is in human nature to dominate and oppress one another." That's not bad for a country farmer. Humanists are utopian about human nature. They believe man is innately good and self-sacrificing. Yeah, okay! History says otherwise.

No Such Thing as Utopia on Earth

Utopians don't understand a fallen world. The ruler of this world is the devil. The spirit of the times or "zeitgeist" controls the thoughts and minds of the unbelievers and blinds them from seeing the truth (2 Corinthians 4:4). The gullible trust too easily and are swept away by lies. Jesus told the Pharisees, "You are of your father, the devil" (John 8:44, ESV).

Gullibility is nothing more than intellectual, emotional, and spiritual laziness. A gullible person does not take the time to think things through. Susceptible to any wind of doctrine, they follow the status quo because it takes too much effort to think. Gullible people believe whatever they're told without applying critical thinking or even mere curiosity. Americans are becoming a nation of illiterate adults who don't know truth from fiction, superstition from spiritual truths, and have zero discernment from God. Instead, we have rehearsed phrases, emotionalism, and empty euphuisms taking the place of intellectual thought. I call it the *age of emotionalism*. Rise up America! Where are the scholars of our day who oppose collective thought? Where are the leaders shouting from the mountaintops with words of wisdom and common sense to go against the status quo?

When Adam and Eve sinned, they brought sin into the world. Sin created shame, so they hid from God. They saw their nakedness and vulnerabilities. For the first time, their eyes were opened to sin. Because of sin, God told Eve she would give birth in pain rather than in joy. He told Adam he would work the land with toil and sweat rather than with joy and energy. They lost their blessings because they allowed themselves to be deceived.

Our people are being deceived by morally bankrupt leaders. It is being replaced by intentional godless social programs that can even be called diabolical. You cannot truly care for your fellow man with natural love. Our best love is still selfish. Humans can be the vilest of all of God's creatures with the capacity to justify cruel actions.

If we continue to replace Christian principles with humanistic ones, the prophetic words of John Adams will come true: "Our Constitution was made only for a moral and religious people. It is wholly inadequate to the government of any other."

Theocracy cannot work either. People will mess it up every time. Jesus was the only one who heard directly from his Father and always did what His Father asked Him to do. Jesus walked with God because He was God. He is the only One Who ever made truly selfless decisions to honor God in every way. We may try, but we will fall short every time. Sometimes, we get it right; other times not, but Jesus always did.

In the early days of this country's beginnings, a theocratic government was attempted by Governor William Bradford, a puritan. He quickly found out you cannot run a secular colony like the church. Theocratic government never works on this side of Glory; in fact, the opposite happened. While some worked extremely hard, others became lazy drunkards as they depended on hard-working people to support them. The hard-working people stopped working so hard, and the lazy people became lazier. Bradford decided to stop this theocratic/socialistic lifestyle because it negatively impacted everyone, both collectively and individually (Beliles and McDowell).

Bradford tried the socialistic, theocratic style of Barnabas, who laid down the deed at the apostles' feet to a plot of ground to give to the poor. The early church gave as everyone had need; no one went hungry. But Barnabas did not give up his home, personal belongings, and everything else lest he would be homeless and poor himself. The church would then have had to be burdened with taking care of him. The early church gave out of their excess and other times sacrificially. They trusted in God to take care of them, not man. One cannot run the world as the church. The wicked will always abuse the good.

GOD GIVES EVERYONE TALENTS

Jesus holds us accountable for the talents He gives us. In Matthew 25:14-30, a parable tells about the master of the house giving a bag of silver to three servants. The amount was given in proportion to their abilities to wisely make more. The servant to whom he gave five bags gained five more. The master was full of praise. "Well done, my good and faithful servant. In handling this small amount, I will give you many more responsibilities. Let's celebrate together" (verse 21, NLT). The servant who had received two bags invested those two and gained two more. Again, the master was pleased and gave him many more responsibilities. But the servant who the master gave one bag of silver began blaming the master for being harsh and deceitful. He was afraid, declaring, "I hid the money." His master replied, "You wicked, lazy servant! Why didn't you at least deposit the money so I could gain interest?" Then he ordered that the money be taken from this servant and given to the one with ten bags of silver. To those who use what they are given well, even more will be given, and they will have an abundance. But from those who do nothing, even what little they have will be taken away. "Now, throw this useless servant into outer darkness, where there will be weeping and gnashing of teeth" (Matthew 25:28-30, NLT).

I wonder though, did the lazy servant lay on his death bed still blaming everyone else for all his woes? Did he spend his whole life blaming others for his misfortunes and problems because he wouldn't apply himself to knowledge or hard work? He climbed into an attitude of self-mortification and self-pity. He lied to himself with thoughts of *It was never my responsibility. It was always someone else's fault; my boss is unfair.* Now, on his deathbed, did he look back and despise his life of loathsomeness? What a way to live! What a way to die!

In the movie *Pappion*, Steve McQueen stands before the judge in his dream. At first, he declares his innocence of a crime until the judge says,

"The crime you are held guilty of is a wasted life." He replies, "Guilty, guilty, guilty," as he walks away, a condemned man. In Proverbs 5:11-12, (NIV) it says, "At the end of your life, you will groan when your flesh and body are spent. You will say, 'How I hated discipline! How my heart spurned correction!'"

God will hold all of us accountable on the Day of Judgment for the gifts He has given to us. God will ask each one us what we have done with the talents we were given. There will be no room to blame Him or anyone else. Your soul will be revealed before Him to see. There will be no hiding behind a fig leaf. Only a face-to-face encounter with God. Sad to say, that lazy, loathsome person will be cast into outer darkness, apart from God suffering in an eternity of heat, pain, and absolute agony. What a pitiful ending to a pitiful life.

Spiritual gullibility affects every generation. This master held his servant accountable for his laziness. The movement seen in America to socialize the government creates an atmosphere of governmental dependence. That lack causes a moral, spiritual, and financial decline. It sucks the life and spirit right out of man, replacing God-given curiosity with intellectual sloth and a lack of individual creativity.

Communism, socialism, totalitarianism, and dictatorship stifle and kill the human spirit and God-given freedoms. Proverbs 25:2 (NIV) says, "It is the glory of God to conceal a matter; to search out a matter is the glory of kings." God has put into man's spirit a desire to investigate, advance, and imagine to use his mind to gain knowledge in medicine, science, technology, and so much more. He was given the ingenuity to put a man on the moon; physical sciences to discover laws of dynamics and physical principalities; and properties to explore the mysteries of the universe. God has given doctors, chemists, and pharmaceutical sciences to cure diseases and comfort the ills and sicknesses in society. He has given man the curiosity, the ability, and the desire to search out the things God already knows. It is exciting and invigorating to create something out of nothing; removing roadblocks and solving problems is the spirit God put into man.

God has given each of us a spiritual bag of silver. This bag is precious and costly. It represents our willingness to be creative. In fact, this bag of silver represents our character and what we do with the responsibilities, spiritual gifts, families, professions, and callings that God has entrusted to us. Don't surrender for an easy life, and don't let anyone take it from you.

HOLY SPIRIT-POWERED LIVING

Willpower only has enough power when a person is emotionally motivated to change. Willpower is based on emotionalism, which is always temporary. However, when someone receives the Holy Spirit into their lives, it becomes more than willpower—it is God-power working in them. Prayer changes us. It connects us with God. He sparks an anointing of supernatural motivation to be passionate about life. His presence causes our hearts to explode with joy and excitement.

Jesus calls us His friends, not servants, and He wants to impart more of Himself into us. When God speaks, it is permanent. His words stay with us giving us an internal desire to accomplish each task. He does not allow us to give up! Sister Carol Record preached a sermon one time entitled, "Throw Another Log on the Fire." When we find ourselves burning out, we need to turn up the heat.

Use the supernatural power of God to minister to suffering people. While working in the hospital, I was known as the *coma chaplain*. Three times during my tenure at the hospital, I prayed with people who were in a coma. While praying for one man, his hand twitched. The family saw it and looked at me in astonishment. "He hasn't moved since the incident, and his fingers just moved!" The man woke up from the coma that same day. God brought two other people out of a coma state and awoke after praying for them.

We have heard the nay sayers, "Then, why don't all the faith healers go into the hospital and heal the sick people?" We are! Spirit-filled chaplains are in the hospitals! We are out here touching people's souls, laying hands on the sick, anointing them with oil, and helping restore them to wholeness.

Not anyone can come off the street and go door-to-door in a hospital praying for people. That is taking advantage of a person's private time of recovery. We had two women going door-to-door in The Williamsport

Hospital, praying for patients. Staff members told me what they were doing and asked me to talk to them. They were Pentecostals, whose hearts were in the right place, but they did not have permission. Their mother was in the hospital, and while she was there, others in the room asked them to pray for them. They continued this after their mother's discharge. I informed them they were not allowed to do this, but if they would like to go through the proper channels of training, they could volunteer. I felt bad about telling them to stop; after all, they were my own people, *Pentecostal*. If a person wants to be used by God, they must go through the proper channels.

Chaplains are not fly-by-night. We go through a rigorous training process of Clinical Pastoral Education. My internship was two years, and that was after four years of Bible college and three years of seminary. God has developed character, patience, and maturity within us to function as an agent of God in a secular setting. That is no easy task!

When we allow God to do the work in us and in others, He will take us from being good to being best! He calls us to do specific works, and He will multiply what we are unable to accomplish by ourselves. While I was in Pentecostal/Charismatic seminary class, the professor shared a story that has impacted my life to this day, and I want to share it here. He was talking about ministering to the poor.

Father Richard Thomas, a charismatic priest, who received the Baptism of the Holy Spirit, changed an entire community. In his book, *A Poor Priest for the Poor — the Life of Father Rick Thomas* by Richard Dunstan, entire families squatted at a local dump in Juarez, Mexico. Their food, clothing, and even debris helped build their shacks that came from the dump. God called this man to start a ministry among these people.

On Christmas Day as they were handing out food, more and more people came. They were overwhelmed with how many had shown up. The workers got tired. The woman cutting the ham got tired and needed a break. The bags of candy for the children never ran out. When they got back to their ministry in El Paso, Texas, they realized they only had enough to feed 150, yet they fed 300.

Sure enough, God did provide. In the natural realm, they should have run out, but as Jesus multiplied the loaves and fishes in the first century,

He also multiplied Christmas dinner in the twenty-first century. As time went on, the Priest built relationships with the local business owners. Eventually, these businessmen hired men and women from the dump and taught trades. One by one, they began to leave the dump and buy decent housing for their families, and all because one man responded to the voice of God.

Proverbs 19:17 (NIV) says, "Whoever is kind to the poor lends to the LORD, and he will reward them for what they have done."

EFFECTS OF POVERTY

"Poverty is linked with negative conditions, such as substandard housing, homelessness, inadequate nutrition, lack of child care, lack of access to health care, and unsafe neighborhoods.

Chronic stress associated with living in poverty has been shown to adversely affect children's concentration and memory. Children living in poverty are at a greater risk of behavioral and emotional problems, such as impulsiveness, difficulty getting along with peers, aggression, anxiety, depression, low self-esteem, and attention-deficit /hyperactivity disorder (ADHD)" (*American Psychological Association*).

We not only need to pray but act. "Pray the LORD of the Harvest would send forth workers. For the harvest is plentiful, but the workers are few" (Matthew 9:37-38, NLT). If we respond to the call of God regardless of the risk, then we can change our communities.

Surrender your will and let God do His work. Surrender desires, finances, fears, and even failures. Let your need of God's desire be matched by His abundant provisions. We need to pray for another revival, so this generation can see waters parted and people healed and delivered by a genuine shekinah presence of God.

When I attended the revival in Pensacola, Pastor Steve Hill quoted a local police officer who witnessed people in his community throwing guns, drugs, condoms, and other paraphernalia onto the alter and giving their lives over to Christ. He said, "More laws won't change our community, but this certainly is."

The Bible speaks to real-life situations. The reality is that there is a great deal of pain and suffering in the world. Only God can change a person, but He uses us to help Him do it. This generation of unchurched people need to hear the gospel message. They are ripe for harvest because they are weary of pessimism, sarcasm, emotionalism, and a genuine lack of truth.

Matthew 9:35-38 (NLT) complements the Great Commission. "And Jesus went throughout all the cities and villages, teaching in their synagogues and proclaiming the gospel of the kingdom and healing every disease and every affliction. When He saw the crowds, he had compassion for them because they were harassed and helpless, like sheep without a shepherd. Then he said to his disciples, 'the harvest is plentiful, but the laborers are few. Therefore, pray earnestly to the Lord of the harvest to send out laborers into his harvest.'"

The harvest is always plentiful. There are people who are in misery right now who desperately need our help. Some are suicidal, some feel unloved, and others feel abandoned and alone. The message of the gospel will never lose its power regardless of the times. It is a timeless truth that holds up the banner of hope. I don't believe the world is lost and hopeless; there is always hope. God is still working!

"Those who sow in tears shall reap with joyful shouting. He who goes to and fro weeping, carrying his bag of seed, shall indeed come again with a shout of joy, bringing his sheaves with him" (Psalm 126:5, NLT). We chaplains sow with tears. We give to God all we have by sowing and sowing and sowing until we are weary at times, maybe even tearful. But there is that day when we see the results of those seeds take root in receptive hearts. As we share restoration, love, and hope, they begin to believe, their faith grows, and there is another changed life. Even Amos 9:13 declares the plowman will overtake the reaper. As we preach or share God's Word in any circumstance, we will witness before our eyes people turning from sin and turning to God. Instantaneously, they are changed! I believe the best days for the chaplaincy are ahead of us to fulfill the Great Commission. In the article by Doug Clay, he goes on to say, "Pentecostal/ Charismatic Christianity is the fastest growing segment of world Christianity today." Zurlo writes in *Global Christianity,* "We must pray for a fresh outpouring of the Holy Spirit on our ministries and for people in our churches to receive the baptism in the Holy Spirit."

I plead with the Remnant to fall on our faces in prayer for God to move again. I challenge us to pray with tears, a broken heart, a repentant spirit to intercede for our nation. It begins with us. Every great revival began with prayers of tears. Let us put aside all distractions and get a burden for lost souls and revival. According to His own Word, He promises to bring revival. "If my people, which are called by my name, shall humble themselves, and pray, and seek my face, and turn from their wicked ways; then will I hear from heaven, and will forgive their sin, and will heal their land" (2 Chronicles 7:14, NIV). Too often we read this scripture as a cliché' without letting it deeply penetrate into the core of our soul. As you read this, I pray God quickens your spirit. I pray He moves you with compassion. I pray He renews your burden, so we see people as God sees them, and allow His heart to be our heart. To believe God's Word when He says He will hear, He will forgive and He will heal. I challenge you to put the book down right now and pray. God will move your heart with compassion for lost souls.

CHAPTER TWENTY-SEVEN

Be True to Yourself

For when I kept silent, my bones wasted away through my groaning all day long. For day and night your hand was heavy upon me; my strength was dried up as by the heat of summer.

Psalm 32:3-5 (ESV)

Chaplains are trained to tone it down in order to minister in a pluralistic setting. Dr. Kenzy called it *abusive*. I felt abused at times because I had to learn to *fit in* to be a chaplain. Don't let the yeast of the professional, liberal chaplaincy mold you into its image. Don't tone it down; turn it up!

The evangelistic chaplain is needed and necessary. That is what I strive for and hope you do, too. Recognize your calling. Never lose that mandate to win the lost. Be on guard to never lose the passionate evangelistic fervor of your true self. Thankfully, I am in a place where I have the freedom to lead people to the Lord. I do so in my own personal style. My mission statement is "to minister the compassionate love of Jesus Christ through pastoral care."

Seasons of growth and learning come and go. Desert places are necessary if we are to remain in the will of God. Some of the hardest, most challenging places of ministry were not in the wilderness but in the center of God's will. His grace was sufficient, and I learned through trials, failures, and successes. I was taught the dos and don'ts of ministry through the school of hard knocks. That was where God stretched and built my character.

In the movie *Jaws*, Hooper, played by Richard Dreyfuss, was harassed by Quint, the typical bully sea captain played by Robert Shaw. Hooper finally had had enough and sarcastically said, "I can't take this abuse much longer." There may come a point where you just can't take it anymore because you're not being true to yourself as a Christian chaplain. You can't keep silent any longer.

Jehoiada, who was a zealous priest had enough. In II Chronicles 23:1, it says, "In the seventh year of Athaliah's reign, Jehoiada the priest decided to act." Athalia was a wicked queen in Judah who worshipped Baal. Jehoida had had enough of this evil woman and decided to boldly take a stand against her. He appointed priests to anoint Joash and kill anyone who opposed him. When Athalia found out, she shouted "Treason, treason!" Jehoiada had her put to death and then had all the Baal temples and idols of the false gods destroyed. He groaned under her authority until he couldn't take it any longer. He decided to act. There comes a time when we have to act.

In my chaplain ministry, I also reached a point where I also had enough. I was tired of conforming to the liberal ideology. I had to find my true self within the chaplaincy. It was time to follow my own path.

A preacher noted at a seminar, "When we start out in ministry, we get closer and closer to the bull's eye in ministerial positions." As time goes on, we learn, grow, and gain more experience in the ministry, getting closer and closer to the bullseye. There are many positions in ministry that are spiritual stepping stones. I was where God wanted me to be, but my gifts were not yet fully matched with my maturity. These are places where God develops us and prepares us for positions of leadership. It takes a while to get there, but when we do, it is what baseball players call the sweet spot.

God loves to honor, elevate, and reward His anointed ones who remain faithful and work diligently. He took a shepherd boy and made him king; He took a brash immature Joseph and turned him into a prince. All throughout church history, God took the humble, the useful, the teachable and honored them to positions of power and leadership. It takes a while to get there, but when we do, we are ready.

SWEET SPOT

When we find that sweet spot in ministry, it feels good! Our supervisors and peers alike trust us and respect our wisdom and counsel. It is not because of our position that people respect, but rather our character, experience, influence, and maturity they appreciate. When God develops us from the inside out, there is no need to pretend to act like a chaplain; we are chaplains. We become genuine and true to ourselves and calling.

During a radio advertisement for our organization, I was grateful to acknowledge, "I thank hospice for giving me the opportunity to fulfill God's calling in my life." I finally found where I belonged and have been with the company for nineteen years. I look forward to seeing God work in me here until I retire if it is His will.

Never lose your zeal. If you give up who you are or compromise your values, beliefs, or doctrinal positions just to fit in, then leave; in fact, run! Requiring compromise is an abusive and unethical thing to make a chaplain do. Chaplains must never compromise their beliefs in order to minister to others of different religions.

Compromise kills the spirit. A mechanic cannot cut corners or the car becomes unsafe and even dangerous enough to kill. That's why mechanics need to be certified, doctors need licenses, and chaplains need to be endorsed.

NAVAC (The National Association of Veterans Affairs Chaplains) has a wonderful guide for spiritual care. I personally adopted these core values for my own life.

NAVAC CODE OF ETHICS
National Association of Veterans Affairs Chaplains
(Presented here with permission from the NAVAC.)

PREAMBLE

The National Association of Veterans Affairs Chaplains (NAVAC) is an organization of individuals with an interest in providing spiritual care for our Veterans, their families and staff through various Department of Veterans Affairs facilities and programs. As such, members of NAVAC will hold true to the tenets of the organization which provides for their ecclesiastical endorsement in a VA setting.

The mission of NAVAC is to provide highly qualified chaplains with various levels of certification.

The end goal is that persons providing spiritual care in VA settings will be professional and well qualified through education, training and experience.

NAVAC understands that we live in a pluralistic society with varying understandings of religion and spirituality. Under no circumstances will NAVAC nor its members discriminate against others on the basis of race, color, religion, gender, national origin or sexual orientation.

The maintenance of high standards of professional competence and moral and ethical conduct is a responsibility shared by all NAVAC members. Members are accountable to one another to maintain the ethical and professional criteria established by NAVAC.

Each person of the National Association of VA Chaplains is individually responsible to uphold these tenets in coordination with their endorsing agency.

The following Code of Ethics is set forth to inform our membership and those with whom we work of the values, principles and expectations of the organization.

CODE OF ETHICS

1. I will hold in trust the tenets of my endorsing agency, carefully adhering to its guidance in order to maintain endorsement by that body consistent with functioning in a pluralistic setting.
2. I will provide spiritual care to all persons in a religiously and spiritually diverse environment.
3. I will not engage in discussion or behavior that intentionally disparages another person's faith system or lack thereof.
4. When I am not able to provide spiritual care because of differences in belief, I will seek to find another provider who can meet those needs.
5. I will provide for the free exercise of religion and spirituality for all whom I serve.
6. When conducting interfaith worship or speaking at public ceremonies, I will seek to find common beliefs and expound upon those commonalities.

7. I will respect the faith traditions of those persons I supervise. I will exercise due diligence to ensure I am not requiring tasks that violate the beliefs or morals of the person or their religious body.

8. I will maintain a disciplined personal ministry which includes spiritual practices that help me to remain focused on my specific calling.

9. I will only accept additional responsibilities if they do not diminish my primary obligations or cause conflicts of interest.

10. I will defend my peers and those I serve against discrimination based on factors including but not limited to race, religion, color, age, national origin, disability, gender or sexual orientation.

11. I will follow the policies of my employing institution regarding patient confidentiality, sharing private information about those whom I serve only according to those policies, my endorser, or as required by law.

12. I will not attempt to proselytize persons who hold beliefs other than my own. I will show grace and kindness to all.

13. I will strive to preserve the dignity and honor due every human being regardless of physical, mental, emotional or spiritual condition.

14. I recognize that the office of "chaplain" often comes with certain authority or power whether assigned or perceived. I will hold that authority to be sacred and will not abuse it for personal gratification, nor use it in such a way as to denigrate the life of another human being religiously, emotionally, physically, sexually or in any other manner.

15. I will promote professionalism and honor among my peers in order to preserve the integrity of the vocation to which I am called.

16. If I encounter an ethical dilemma not addressed in this code of ethics, I will contact the NAVAC Board of Directors. The NAVAC Board of Directors will put me in contact with the appropriate subject matter expert for me to obtain guidance. (https://www.navac.net/sermons and NAVACBCC@gmail.com)

These guidelines are the best I have come across for ministering to patients, as well as protecting the chaplain's personal beliefs. We are to provide spiritual support to everyone regardless of his/her religious beliefs. It does not mean we have to compromise our beliefs to do so.

When I first started my ministry in hospice, I asked a hypothetical question to one of my superiors. "Do I have to do a funeral service for a Satanist?" He said, "Yes." I knew right then and there this guy, who was a social worker, had no idea about our role as chaplains. We are to never compromise our religious beliefs in order to minster to someone of a different faith. The first NAVAC code of ethics explicitly states, "I will hold in trust the tenants of *my endorsing agency*...in order to maintain endorsement by that body." The Assemblies of God has doctrines and beliefs that cannot be compromised. These tenants are there to protect the chaplain's spiritual integrity. No institution can force the chaplain to do something contrary to his/her beliefs or his/her endorsing body.

KEEP YOUR PASSION

Don't ever lose your passion. Be comfortable, content, and free to be yourself in the setting where God has called you. God wants us to be joyful, useful, purposeful and utilize the spiritual gifts He has instilled in us. We should not feel frustrated, stifled, or suppressed. At our seminary graduation Dr. George Wood said, "It is not your work that makes you fulfilled; it is our relationship with God that makes us fulfilled. Out of that relationship your ministry will be joyful."

God has called you specifically to be a chaplain in some area of ministry. Sometimes that means finding the right chaplaincy ministry fit.

Chaplaincy is not for everyone but neither is pastoring, missionary work, teaching, or any of the fivefold ministry gifts. God has called each one of us in the body of Christ and gifted us with specific tasks to fulfill His will. I have a pastor/evangelist friend who did a unit of CPE and said the chaplaincy was not for him. He said, "I'm praying for these people when I know they are not saved and going to hell...I can't do this. I need to evangelize them." I have a different view. I recognize my calling in the broader picture. In fact, I do feel like I am evangelizing them. Galatians 6:10 (NIV) says, "As we have therefore opportunity, let us do good unto all men, especially unto them who are of the household of faith." We are called to do good to everyone. If we chaplains can do this by sharing love, hope, and comfort, then we are doing what God has called us to do.

Chaplaincy can be confusing to the church. That is why the Spirit-filled chaplain must know himself, his calling, and that his identity is in God and not what others think. Trust in the LORD with your calling. Proverbs 3:5-6 (NIV) says, "Trust in the LORD with all your heart and lean not on your own understanding, in all your ways submit to Him, and He will make your paths straight."

ADD VALUE

The chaplain is sometimes a light, sometimes counselor, pastor, teacher, or friend. I like what Chaplain Paul Ray said in his "Network of Leaders in Healthcare Ministry." "The chaplain's calling is 'to add value daily' in people's lives." A chaplain must seek to add value in whatever way or means possible, and then leave the rest up to God. The LORD will work the rest of the matter out after the chaplain leaves the patient. Give Him everything you have, and allow the LORD to use your two mites or multiply the loaves and the fishes. Let Him multiply your small contribution because God knows how to get through to a person's life better than we can. You are the catalyst to get it started. God will take the seed you planted and make it grow. We need to trust God for the growth in the lives of each person we bless. You water...but only God makes it grow.

When you're in a ministerial position where there are not a lot of opportunities to share the gospel, but you know that is where you belong, then stay! You may have no idea of the quiet impact and influence you have in other people's lives. Only God knows the heart of man. He is using you to be effective. II Peter 1:8 states, "For if these qualities are yours and are increasing, they keep you from being ineffective or unfruitful in the knowledge of our LORD Jesus Christ" (ESV).

One person at the hospital said to me, "I love it when you visit on this floor. You are a light to us." Some missionaries spend years on the field and end up with a few conversions. But those few converts start the fire. Years later, after the missionary dies, communities are transformed by the gospel because of his or her sacrificial lifestyle. Missionaries stay and minister where they know God has placed them even when they don't see fruit. It must be the same with chaplains. Stay even when you don't see fruit. You don't have to see it with your eyes but know in your heart that you are doing what God called you to do. On that day when God rewards us, then and only then, will we truly see the spiritual impact we have had in the lives of those around us. Think about your calling like a link in a fence. You do your part and let God do the rest. Someday it will all come together. Don't get caught up in the fruit of the ministry; get caught up in the work of it.

I Corinthians 3:6-8 (KJV) says, "I have planted, Apollos watered, but God gave the increase. So then neither is he that planteth anything, neither he that watereth; but God that giveth the increase. Now he that planteth and he that watereth are one; and every man shall receive his own reward according to his own labor."

Before I got saved, many men and women talked to me about the gospel. They were links in the chain; then one day, I made that vital decision to follow Christ. I believe that on Judgment Day, all those who witnessed to me will be rewarded and share the impact of all those I have touched in ministry. I believe it is the same with us chaplains. We will be rewarded far more than we think. We will be rewarded for our labor, not the fruit. I also believe the reason we are not judged until the end of the age is because the influence we leave behind will continue long after we are dead.

A hospice chaplain may often sit with people who do not want spiritual care but appreciate someone to talk to and give companionship. For me, that is okay. I can handle it. However, if that was all I did, I would not be true to myself or comfortable with that calling. That was the kind of ministry I had with dementia patients. It was boring. I cried out to God daily to release me, but He didn't. He kept me there for a season of six years to grow, learn, and be patient. The growing pains were hard but worth it! During this time, I officiated more funerals than I cared to, learned patience, and developed spiritual and professional skills. Don't give up! Let God do His work, so you can do His work. You may have dry years of ministry. It will seem boring, redundant, and unfulfilling. However, after God has seasoned and prepared you, and you are finally in that perfect place, you will appreciate it more because you never gave up, and He rewarded you for your faithfulness. Keep chasing that bull's eye. Ministry only gets better!

CHAPTER TWENTY-EIGHT

When the Chaplain is Persecuted

Finally, be strong in the LORD and in His mighty power. Put on the full armor of God, so that you can take your stand against the devil's schemes.

Ephesians 6:10-11 (NIV)

We often think persecution is only for those on the mission field, but chaplains get persecuted, too, right here in the USA. Persecution is defined by Oxford as "hostility and ill-treatment, especially because of race, political or religious beliefs. A Persistent annoyance or harassment."

Chaplains walk into situations where there is outright disrespect, contempt, and even hostility directed at them. Most of the time it has nothing to do with us. They are angry at God and take it out on us. Sometimes we're even met with demonic influences.

Chaplains are not exempt from persecution. Jesus said in John 15:18-19 (NIV), "If the world hates you, keep in mind that it hated me first. If you belonged to the world, it would love you as its own. As it is, you do not belong to the world, but I have chosen you out of the world. That is why the world hates you."

Be reminded. "We do not fight against flesh and blood but against rulers, powers and spiritual beings in high places" (Ephesians 6:12, NIV). When it comes to persecution, we cannot respond in the flesh. When people revile you or are spiteful towards you, you will be given a supernatural anointing of grace to endure. *Foxes Book of Martyrs* describes a man being burned alive. It tells how he felt a closeness of God unlike any he'd experienced while being burned at the stake. God gave him the courage and faith to endure.

Luke 6:27-28 (NIV) says, "But to you who are listening, I say, love your enemies, do good to those who hate you, bless those who curse you, pray for those who mistreat you." Jesus said on the cross, "Father, forgive them for they know not what they do."

Pat Robertson related a segment of an older lady's testimony. Her church was surrounded by a mob that wanted to harm those in the church. She said, "If they only knew the love of the LORD the way I do, they would not be doing this." If we respond with anger, we have already lost. Our reward is in our blessing, not retaliation.

THE KINGDOM OF DARKNESS

Persecution is bound to come when working for the LORD. When stepping on the kingdom of darkness's domain and principalities, demons will fight back hard and with contempt.

I had an encounter one time, which I believe was a demonic attack. A patient made it clear from the beginning that he did not want to talk about spiritual matters. So, we talked about his interests and began to develop a good relationship. Eventually, he opened up and shared some of his beliefs. Some of these were a little odd, but I respected him and listened. He began to talk about his beliefs in great detail and about how demons had often visited him. He believed in the ancient worship of Egyptian gods, as well as Baal worship.

He went on to say, "Some demonic spirits cause fear while others remain passive." He was normally a quiet-spoken, passive man. As the conversation progressed and he felt comfortable sharing his beliefs with me, I, in turn, felt comfortable sharing mine. It was clear this conversation was meant to be a monologue and not a dialogue. While I was sharing how Christ changed my life, his entire countenance changed. He leaned back in his chair. His body language became stiff and rigid with an angry disposition. I had never seen anyone change so quickly. His voice deepened, and he said, "That's enough! I'm done talking with you. You need to leave. Now!" It honestly took me by surprise. I thought we were having a cordial conversation about our beliefs. Normally, I am very discerning to the demonic but not this time. I think God shielded me, so I could share the gospel with him.

I'm not one to shy away from confrontation, but when I looked into his eyes, there was a spirit about him that meant business. I honestly thought if I said anything more, he would have physically attacked me. I knew I was not fighting flesh and blood, but a demonic spirit. I apologized for upsetting him and that was not my intention. He told me once again to leave. I walked away leaving him in God's hands.

The spirit in him was confronted by the truth of the Gospel. His passive spirit rose in extreme-demonic anger and was not about to be silent any longer. As I drove away, I thought about it some more. That demon did not want the name of Jesus spoken. The scripture says, "For this reason also, God highly exalted Him, and bestowed on Him the name which is above every name, so that at the name of Jesus every knee will bow, of those who are in heaven, and on earth, and under the earth, and that every tongue will confess that Jesus is LORD to the Glory of God the Father" (Philippians 2:9-11, CSB). That spirit was not about to bow to Jesus; but someday it will.

My spirit was very troubled when I left there. I might be big and tough on the outside but inside I'm sensitive. We are emotional people and wear our emotions on our sleeves. As much as we try to cover it, it still bothers us until we deal with it one way or another. Sometimes, it's talking to a colleague, but this time I needed God. When I finally had time alone with God, I went into study and prayer. I began to think about all the other times I had been personally affected in my thirty years of ministry. As I dwelt on all those times, I got even more discouraged. Spiritual depression came over me. I was in spiritual warfare. I lay there in bed feeling like Elijah, "Woe is me. I wish I had never been born." David wrote in Psalm 69:9, "The insults of those who insult you fall on me." I began to get weighed down spiritually and felt like I was done. I just couldn't take anymore. Then God showed up!

John Arroyo's words suddenly came alive in my spirit, "Did God change His mind calling me into ministry?" I had to answer loudly into my spirit. "No. He did not. Nor was I going to change my mind." My calling as a chaplain began stirring again. I began to think of Nehemiah's burden and how he was harassed and mocked. My soul needed to revive again. As God touched Elijah, God touched me.

Elijah was worn out when he was running from Jezebel. She wanted to kill him, so he ran into the wilderness and eventually fell from exhaustion. An angel woke him up and said to eat and drink. He laid down again and slept some more. The angel woke him up a second time and he ate and drank. He was energized and ran in the physical and spiritual strength of the LORD for forty days and forty nights (1 Kings 19:1-18).

God has ways to rejuvenate us, as well, maybe through rest, counseling, or variety in ministry. He is faithful and helps us get back up after being knocked down. There are consequences from demonic encounters. I also had a demonic dream that night. The spiritual battle continued. The next morning, I woke up very ill with all the symptoms of COVID-19 but tested negative for the virus. I believe it was a demonic attack on my body. Satan mimicked the symptoms, but it didn't work!

I believe I was demonically attacked and physically afflicted by a strong and ancient spirit, but "greater is He Who is in me than he that is in the world." Ministry has a way of knocking us down, but God has a way of picking us up. "For a righteous man may fall seven times (meaning infinity) and rise again" (Proverbs 24:16, NKJ).

From that encounter, I realized just how important it is to put on our spiritual armor. I put on my spiritual helmet and began to take charge of my thoughts and regain control of my mind. God began to speak to me, building me back up as I continued to armor myself with all the other weaponry. I rose victoriously. I told myself, "Not woe is me, but woe to any spirit that gets in my way!" Spiritual battles make us stronger.

Rely on God's power when you're feeling wiped out. You can be victorious. If you believe God has called you to work as a chaplain, then no man or demonic power can remove you from God's calling. You might be persecuted, shamed, or slandered. You might lose heart for a while. You might think your ministry is dead, but resurrection is on its way. He reminds us of His Word, and we rise yet again with power, love, and a sound mind. New life is right around the corner as long as you never, ever, ever mouth the words, "I quit." You have responded to God's call, and there will be times of weariness, doubt, and tears as we cry through the times of wilderness and disillusionment. But by staying true to God's calling, we keep moving forward.

I saw this patient one more time. He was physically declining and needed a staff member to sit with him. Lucky me, I was the only one available. He agreed for me to come but not talk about spiritual matters. I prayed earnestly before I got there for God to armor me with his power and protect me from harm. I had hoped I would get another opportunity to share Christ, but I could tell it was not welcomed. He made his choice. Unfortunately, he died without ever knowing the Lord. The sad truth is that many die without Christ. Matthew 7:13 (NIV) says, "Enter through the narrow gate. For wide is the gate and broad is the road that leads to destruction, and many enter through it. But small is the gate and narrow the road that leads to life, and only a few find it."

If you feel discouraged and defeated, it's okay. Every minister has been there. You will rise again. God will "never leave you or forsake you." He will rescue you. Do not minimize persecutions; they are real and have the potential to be detrimental. Don't gloss over them. Face and defeat in the battleground of prayer!

Don't do ministry by yourself. We need pastors, friends, and chaplains to pray for, encourage, and fellowship with us to maintain a healthy attitude. Surround yourself with those who understand your ministry. Balance your life between ministering to the ones who take energy from you and those who give energy to you. Pastors, pray for the chaplains in your church. Invite them out for coffee and encourage them with prayer and a listening ear. They undergo an enormous amount of stress that many in the church are not aware. Chaplains are often the forgotten and misunderstood heroes in our denominations and fellowships. Please don't forget them!

SPIRITUAL DEBT

Keep depositing into your spiritual bank because you will be making withdrawals daily. Spiritual debt leaves a hole. CPE, Bible college, and seminary have helped chaplains prepare and withstand the demands of chaplaincy work, but not everyone is trained and as educated as we are. I have a saying about nurses. "Nurses can handle any type of fluid that comes out of the human body except for tears." Nurses are taught to take care of others but not themselves. Self-care is vital in ministry.

I tell our staff regularly, "If you want to stay in healthcare for the long haul, you must take care of yourself."

People will hurt us intentionally. First, they do not know the LORD; secondly, they do not know you. Some only want to hurt and do you harm and feel absolutely no remorse. We live in an antagonistic world where hostile people will attack physically, verbally, emotionally, and spiritually.

When my wife and I took our children to the town pool, my daughter, who is Mexican by descent, ran in front of a lady. I noticed her expression of frustration and that look of prejudice. My initial thought was to slap her, but then I thought this is something we have to learn to deal with. I told my wife about it. Her response was, "We have to move!" I laughed and said, "Honey, prejudice is everywhere; no matter where we move there will always be prejudiced people." I went to work and talked to my chaplain friend, Chris, who was African American. I asked him how he dealt with prejudiced people toward his children. He said, "When my daughter came home from school one day after experiencing some name calling, my wife and I sat her down and talked to her. We told her there will always be ignorant people in the world who don't know you. Mom and Dad know you and love you; furthermore, God loves you, and we will always love you no matter what others say or do." I asked him how she responded. He said, "It made her happy. She ran out the door and played with her friends and never talked about it again."

My four year-old daughter, at the time, never even noticed it, but I did. Jesus said, "Forgive our debts as we forgive our debtors." A debt is something of yours that someone else took. This can refer to money debt, but I'm talking about a spiritual debt—a piece of our soul taken away. This kind of debt leaves an empty hole inside. It takes us off guard and penetrates deeply into our core being. A spiritual debt is when someone deliberately offends us. To forgive is to fill that hole and repair the damage.

Nehemiah had a calling from God. News that Jerusalem was plundered and the gates were burned down burdened his heart. His heart was moved by God to do something about it. He prayed and fasted until he felt led to ask the king for assistance. The king had compassion and gave Nehemiah everything he needed to rebuild the walls of Jerusalem.

Nehemiah had many challenges both from within and without the community. He persevered and built the wall in just fifty-two days. It doesn't take us that long to rebuild our spiritually broken walls, but it does take work.

As Christian leaders, we must care for our spiritual walls that are continually in need of repair either because of abuse or use. Those in ministry will be persecuted. We will get depleted of spiritual resources and have days where we are in desperate need of prayer and repair. Our bodies are the temple of the Holy Spirit. Sometimes our temple needs a full restoration; most times, it only needs maintenance. Take care of your temple so that the presence of God's Shekinah glory is glorified in us.

Nehemiah rebuilt the walls (Nehemiah 2:17, NLT). "Let us rebuild the wall of Jerusalem and end this disgrace." Many of the people came alongside and helped, while others did nothing. Still, his enemies opposed him outright. It's easier to focus on those who oppose us than those who are for us. We allow the offenders to live rent-free in our heads, repeatedly replaying the hurt until we talk ourselves into discouragement and depression.

The book of Ester is a perfect example of Mordecai living rent-free in the head of Haman. Haman had everything a man could ever want. He was second in power next to the king. He had riches, honor, power, and prestige. But there was one man who refused to give him honor. That was Mordecai. This rivalry goes back five hundred years earlier. Haman's intense hatred of the Jews comes from 1 Samuel 15 describing Israel's vengeance upon the Amalekites especially King Agag. Haman was a descendant of the Amalekites and possibly of the royal lineage of Agag. Samuel killed King Agag, and Haman resented the Israelites his entire life. He held onto this grudge from centuries ago. Now, it was his turn for revenge. We all know how the story ends. Haman's blood lust ended up being his own downfall (*NLT Commentary*).

In II Corinthians 4:9, it says, "We are persecuted but not forsaken." Jesus was forsaken on the cross so that we would never be. He obeyed His calling so that He could do the opposite—rescue us. That's why He came. Chaplains are His sheep, too. He cares about us just as much as everyone else. If you have been thinking about quitting the ministry, you are not alone. Most every pastor, chaplain, or minister I have ever met had those same thoughts at one time or another. Ministry can be just as hard as it is fun. There are seasons in ministry that are more difficult than others. That is when we need to remember Jesus leaves the ninety-nine to go after that one lost sheep. Sometimes that one lost sheep is the chaplain, who needs a gentle reminder of God's love in the arms of Jesus.

Satan wants nothing more than to have you quit. Don't give him the satisfaction. He is the one creating chaos, but God is the One Who will create order once again. Don't be discouraged. Don't seek revenge; don't allow bitterness to draw you away from the ninety-nine. Stay in the flock, and let Jesus be your Good Shepherd, leading you to still waters and restoring your soul. Enjoy life. Don't let people or ministry steal or rob your joy. Don't allow trivial and temporal circumstances keep you weighed down by worry and fear. God knows what you need, and He will take care of you.

WALK IN THE FULLNESS OF THE HOLY SPIRIT

I was talking to Mrs. Sally Slater, a Pentecostal patient on hospice. She shared with me that she often speaks in tongues to receive more power. She said, "It sounded as if one of the words was Yeshuuua." She said it sounds like the Hebrew name for Jesus. She said, "When I speak in tongues, I feel closer to Jesus as I feel I am calling on His name." Pentecostals speak in tongues. We do not understand the words, but God does. Romans 8:26 (NLV) says, "And the Holy Spirit helps us in our weakness. For example, we don't know what God wants us to pray for. But the Holy Spirit prays for us with groanings that cannot be expressed in words." We are called to ask God to help us interpret what we are saying. In 1 Corinthians 14:13 (NIV) we read, "For this reason anyone who speaks in a tongue should pray that he may interpret what he says." As I was having this discussion, I told her that when I speak in tongues, two of the words sounds like "Shaddia and Kai." She told me to look up its meaning, so I did. Shaddai or El Shaddai means "The All Sufficient One," while Kai has many different meanings throughout the world. To the Hawaiian culture it means "Sea." In Welsh, Scandinavian, and Greek roots it means "Keeper of the keys; Earth. In my ancestry in European roots, Kai means "warrior," (www.verywellfamily.com). Putting these two words together means that God is more than enough" and "He is my warrior." I don't have to control everything or worry about the future. I know that He will take care of everything. A peace comes over me when I pray knowing that God will provide for all my needs and will fight all my battles for me. This is a promise, not just for me, but all of us who put our faith in Christ. As we abide in Him, he removes fear, worry, and anxiety. Therefore, when we pray "in the Spirit," we feel strengthened, peaceful, and comforted. I often pray for illumination after I pray in tongues. Often, I get a spiritual breakthrough, a word of wisdom or supernatural knowledge comes to my mind. I would encourage every reader to seek out the Baptism in the Holy Spirit and to speak in tongues to empower you and your ministry in supernatural ways. Arm yourself with the full anointing of God.

CHAPTER TWENTY-NINE

Maintaining Holiness While Suffering

In all this, Job did not sin by charging God with wrongdoing.

Job 1:22 (NIV)

The theme of suffering is a crucial element in the work of hospice chaplaincy. Early in my ministry, I wanted to rescue people, solve their problems, and ease their pain. Chaplains receive their CPE training not to be rescuers but rather to simply be with people at the worst time of their lives. Some things are worse than pain to the body; it is pain to the soul. Job experienced both. Demonic attacks will come, but how they are handled makes all the difference. Job shows us how. He remained faithful even when he did not understand the whole picture. He grieved and questioned why, like any of us would, but he remained steadfast in God's goodness.

Job not only went through physical pain but spiritual and emotional torture. People mocked him and blamed him for having sin in his life. They refused to stand in his presence and no longer gave him honor. Enemies attacked him, friends betrayed him, and his wife told him to curse God and die. His body was covered with worms and painful sores; he had demonic night terrors, and he finally reached the point of total exhaustion and regretted being born. Job's reputation in the community was destroyed.

Job did not know what we know now about suffering. He didn't understand that Satan is the destroyer and not God. The devil roams to and from seeking to kill, devour, and destroy for no other reason than because he is a murderer, thief, and liar. Job suffered for a reason. God wanted to bring about a greater good (Job 42:7, NLT).

Satan must have used these tactics on people before with great success. "Take away everything, and he will curse you. Afflict his body, and he will curse you" (Job 1:11, 2:4). How many people today still curse God when bad things happen to them? They renounce their faith because something bad happens. They curse God to His face because He does not heal them. Job did not react that way. Job's response to persecution is a great example for all of us to follow. In Job 1:20 (NIV), it says, "At this, Job got up and tore his robe and shaved his head. Then he fell to the ground in worship and said: 'Naked I came from my mother's womb, and naked I will depart. The LORD gave and the LORD has taken away; may the name of the LORD be praised.' In all this, Job did not sin by charging God with wrongdoing."

Not all the people we minister to are like Job. People blame God for the acts of Satan or the cruelty of others. They've allowed their souls to be polluted by lies. Chaplains display God's loving-kindness and patiently listen as others blame God. The patient might curse the day he was born, asking, "Why does God allow evil to happen to good people and bad things to good people?" We gently journey with them in their pain while we are praying earnestly inside for God to give us the words or actions to help comfort them. They are fighting God because their world was rocked to the core. Their faith was rattled. They struggle to get answers. Some come back; some don't. It is their wrestling match with God.

One of my patients was a truck driver. His wife was a Christian, but he was not. He had been in a terrible accident, flipping his truck over and severing his leg below the knee. He was in an upside position for a few hours, waiting for help. Thankfully, the severed leg was caught in his seatbelt, creating a tourniquet that kept him from bleeding to death. As he hung there alone for hours, waiting for someone to pass by, God began to deal with him. He regretted all the years he wasted apart from God. He asked God for another chance and gave his heart to the LORD hanging midair in his seatbelt. He survived the accident. Though his body was deformed, his soul was made whole. He lived many years afterward, actively involving himself in his church and as a faithful follower of Jesus Christ. God got his attention through suffering. God did a deep and cleansing work in his heart through divine circumstances. His name is written in the Lamb's Book of Life, and he is now in heaven with God for all eternity.

People must go through pain and suffering. We watch God turn people upside down, inside out, and every other way to get their attention. It is not our responsibility to know why, nor is it our responsibility to rescue them from what God is doing in their lives. This is their battle, and they have to do the wrestling themselves.

The book of Job teaches us to accept suffering and be faithful through it. "God has made a mockery of me among the people, they spit in my face" (Job 17:6, NLT).

Spitting in one's face was worse than slapping one in the face. It was considered a punishment by God (Numbers 12:14). They spit in his face because they assumed he sinned. We call that *secondary wounding*. When one is already hurting only to have someone, especially one we love and trust, to come along and hurt us even more hurts. That's when Job stood alone with God in his own integrity. He longed for the day God would justify him.

It is said *reputation is everything*. I don't believe that. Character is everything. Reputations can be slandered, but character lasts forever. Jesus abides with us in the secret shelter as we hold onto our integrity while suffering. God eventually changes curses into blessings and slandered reputations into positions and places of honor. "Though I walk in the midst of trouble, you preserve my life" (Psalm 138:7, NIV).

WHY DO WE SUFFER?

The Apostle Paul answered the question as to why we suffer. "Not only so, but we also glory in our sufferings because we know that suffering produces perseverance, perseverance character, and character hope. And hope does not put us to shame because God's love has been poured out into our hearts through the Holy Spirit who has been given to us," (Romans 5:3-5, NIV). We know He will bring us through.

Do people suffer because of sin? Did they do something to deserve this? God allows tragedy into people's lives for various reasons. The book of Job does not give an answer as to why bad things happen to good people. Suffering's purpose is to pull out the unfruitful parts of people's lives and replace it with grace and growth. He prunes. Job summed it up nicely when he said, "I had only heard about You before, but now I have seen You with my own eyes" (Job 42:5, NLT).

BLESS THOSE WHO CURSE YOU, PRAY FOR THOSE WHO MISTREAT YOU (LUKE 6:28, NIV)

The apostle Peter wrote his first epistle (I Peter) in the early 60s A.D. He was writing from Rome to the persecuted Christians in what is now modern-day Turkey. Back then, it was known as Pontus, Galatia, and Northern Asia Minor.

People of that day thought the early Christians were strange and superstitious. They thought they were cannibalistic because they said they ate and drank the body and blood of Jesus. These men and women were ridiculed by society for being different and not doing the things they were doing. The Christians were tempted to retaliate by being harsh. They were tempted to compromise their faith because of the grief it brought.

Peter wrote in his letter to them to turn these obstacles into opportunities to be a witness for Christ. He admonished them to use these situations to grow further in their faith. He reminded them of Jesus' example of refusing to condemn those who reviled him but rather entrust ourselves to God.

Think about Jesus' response when he was persecuted. He was accused of all kinds of evil as He stood before the Jewish council. Nothing could be proven, so they made up lies about Him. Jesus remained silent. He then stood before Pilate and remained silent for the most part. He listened as people lied about him and said evil things about Him. Yet, Jesus did not respond. Pilate was shocked. An accused person usually defends himself and will go to court to restore his reputation. Pilate told Jesus, "Don't you know I can send you to your death?"

Jesus responded, "You would have no power over me at all unless it were given to you from above."

Jesus entrusted Himself to God and no other. He knew that God was bigger than the Rome. He knew who He was and the reason He came to earth. Jesus understood He would be hated, lied about, and cruelly murdered. Yet, He endured because of His mission to save us from our sins. He knew He was innocent and didn't have to prove Himself to anyone. Jesus knew His Father knows all truth, so He didn't have to justify Himself to any man.

For a person to stand silently and take insults and abuse is not natural or easy. Our natural reaction is to fight back. Peter reminded these Christians to suffer even when they knew they were being lied about and abused. He told them not to react in the old way of doing things but respond in the newness of the Holy Spirit who dwelt within them and gave them the power to do so.

These early Christians obeyed God. They knew the cost of following Jesus. They refused to serve in Rome's military because that meant worshipping Ceasar as a god. So, they refused. They refused to go in the service; they refused to go along with their neighbors in drunkenness and sexual depravity; and they suffered the consequences.

Christians today continue to suffer the consequences for following Christ. God blesses the Christian who suffers under unjust treatment. In other countries, the law forbids worship to God. These brothers and sisters are being martyred for their faith because they worship God anyway. Some may fall away but many will not.

Twenty Egyptian Coptic Christians were killed in 2015 by the Islamic State. Nineteen were Christians; one was not. The man who was not a Christian saw the other's faith. He saw their courage and gave his heart to the Lord right then and there, and then he was beheaded. These twenty men knew who they were in Christ. They knew there was more to this life than the physical. If they would just endure temporary pain, they knew they would be with Jesus in heaven in just a few short minutes. God stood by their side. They knew their captors wouldn't listen, so they gave no excuses, did not revile back, or try to explain their point of view. I believe in their hearts they were kneeling before God and not because their captors made them. They suffered temporarily but were glorified for all eternity. "For I consider that the sufferings of this present time are not worth comparing with the glory that is to be revealed in us" (Romans 8:18, ESV).

Holiness in times of suffering does not weaken the church; it makes it stronger. Remaining faithful under persecution pleases the heart of God. In I Peter 2:20 (NIV), it says, "But how is it to your credit if you receive a beating for doing wrong and endure it? But if you suffer for doing good and endure it, this is commendable before God." God is pleased with you if you suffer for doing good. *Pleased* means to have favor. When you are persecuted and then suffer for a good work, God's favor—His unmerited grace—rests on you.

I was not a Christian in my first years in the Navy. My superior was a man I hated, and he also hated me for various reasons. After becoming a Christian, my attitude changed. God gave me a supernatural love for him and everyone else. The guy did not like that I had become a Christian and made my life even harder. He was my superior as a petty officer and abused his authority. He gave me the worst jobs possible and even hurt me physically one time; but I never retaliated or turned him into his superiors. I knew I was being persecuted for my faith, and I was going to let God handle him. Even when he barked an order at me, in my heart, I'd respond *Yes LORD; I am not working for man but ultimately for God* (Colossians 3:23). I was suffering unjustly, and I knew this was commendable to God. I never refused an order but always replied "Yes." He was so hateful that he mocked me and God by making the most vulgar gestures as I would say the evening prayers over the ship's loudspeaker.

Then God's judgment came. God saw my situation and fought the battle for me. While in the Philippines, he slipped and hit his head on the diving board, knocking himself unconscious as he went into the water. He would have drowned if it had not been for some other men who rescued him. They retrieved him, dragged him to the surface, and gave him CPR and mouth-to-mouth resuscitation. He spent three days in the hospital. When he returned to the ship, he never bothered me again. God dealt with him. There are times we are persecuted for actively being involved in preaching the gospel, other times just because of who we are. Either way, we are to endure with holiness.

God sees what is going on. "Father, forgive them, for they know not what they do" needs to be our prayer, too. This is a hard thing to do; nevertheless, God calls us to endure, and let Him fight the battle. You may not see justice right away. The point is to silence your accusers as you show them an attitude of God's love with patience. In our culture as Americans, this is hard to do. We have rights, but the Bible tells us that sometimes we have to give up our rights if we want to follow Him (1 Corinthians 8:9-13).

CHAPTER THIRTY

The Chaplain's Devotional life

See what great love the Father has lavished on us, that we should be called the children of God! And that is what we are!

1 John 3:1 (NIV)

THE NEED FOR REST

As I write this section, I am sitting at the Assemblies of God camp-ground in Honea Path, SC. When I woke up, God told me to rest today. I came here to work on my book and even though there is much editing to do, God said "rest," so I did. I spent time with Him first. He spoke to me, saying, "I love you with a deep love...more than you can ever fathom." I taught my kids that the most important thing you can learn is to listen to God speak to you. Listen to Him tell you how much He loves you, is with you, and hear those sweet words, "I love you and care for you." Your heart will be full to overflowing, and you will feel a deep and fulfilling joy.

I didn't realize how tired I was. This COVID pandemic took a lot out of me. This time alone with God was necessary, so God could refresh my body and my soul. I slept in today, went fishing, took a nap, and now, here I sit at a picnic table writing by the river. What a peaceful and serene atmosphere! It reminds me of my home in Pennsylvania. I feel at home here. After long spiritual battles, make sure you refresh yourself. Take time for you. Invest in your soul. Then you can go back to ministry and help restore others.

JUST BEING WITH HIM

John wrote in the book of Revelations 1:10 (NLT), "It was the LORD's Day, and I was worshipping in the Spirit." John took the day to worship

Jesus. Take special times just to be with HIM. Take time to worship in the Spirit. Just you and God, no one else. When you do, He will take you into spiritual places and reveal heavenly experiences.

Brother Lawrence said to *practice the presence of God*. When we listen to God, He tells us what we need to hear. He knows what needs to be spoken into our lives. Sometimes I go to prayer with my agenda. Instead, God surprises me with something I never thought about but needed to hear, words like "I love you," "I love your wife," "I love your children." "Love people." "Forgive." "I am with you." Or, He brings someone to my mind to pray for, and so on. It changes my entire outlook when He reveals Himself to me in special ways. I meditate on those words, so they go deep into my soul. I repeat them over and over again until I fully receive these words, and my heart is overwhelmed with gratitude. Stay in prayer until God is done. When finished, we are prepared to go out into the world and be present with people and help them in their time of need.

I no longer have a sanctuary to go to spend time alone with God. When I pastored, I would often leave my office and spend time upstairs in the sanctuary. I love spending time with God in His house, so I built an altar in my home. I always wanted an altar in my house but could never have one. My children are moving out one by one, and I finally have an office again after twenty-four years. I painted the room a beautiful maroon color with a wood railing around the room. In the closet, the holy of holies is where the altar is. I bought a table and overlaid it with white lace and a maroon satin banner. I placed two candlesticks with lights in them that run on batteries when I go in to worship. I have a Bible on a Bible stand. My communion set and a Menorah are also on the table. Above it is a cross with a purple roble draped over it and an angel above. This is where I go to read, pray, study, and write. When it is time to worship, I light the candles and play praise and worship music. My wife sometimes has to knock on the door to make sure I'm okay. I love the presence of God. It is where I go to speak face-to-face with Him. When I come out, I feel like I'm glowing. Then my wife asks me to take out the trash! She keeps me grounded.

One time we were staying at a friend's house. I had to preach that morning and when I walked into the living room, our host said, "Here comes the man of God." I turned to my wife and asked her why she doesn't say that to me when I walk into our living room. She said, "Because I know you." Keep it real chaplains! Have that special place to commune with God.

I was beating myself up one day, thinking I was a failure. I went to prayer and felt God speaking to me, saying, "Receive my love." My first thoughts were just like Isaiah, who said, "I am a man of unclean lips and live among a people of unclean lips." In His presence, I felt so undone. I felt dirty and stained with sin just by being in His presence. I said, "I cannot receive your love. I'm unworthy; I don't deserve your love." Almost immediately, Satan spoke up in the other ear saying, "Then, don't." When spiritually attuned, you recognize your Master's voice, and I knew that was not of my LORD. The LORD kept repeating, "John, receive my love." Yielding to Him, I said, "Lord, help me to accept your love."

As I lay in bed in an attitude of prayer, God gave me a vision of a silhouette of a man on the cross. I knew it was Jesus, but it looked bronze, dark, and lifeless. As I looked closer, the LORD began to move His head. Jesus was speaking, but I couldn't hear Him. Then the words came to me, "Father, forgive them for they know not what they do."

My own thoughts condemned me. The words of Jesus spoke louder into my heart. "Father, forgive them for they know not what they do." I began to understand. He was talking about my weaknesses and intentional sins, and my hard heart. I entered into His holiness, and opening my heart, I began to receive His love and forgiveness.

In my vision, the image on the cross became more alive. Blood ran down from His head onto His cheeks. I saw Him in agony while remaining steadfast in His mission. His body became more and more black until it turned into charcoal. Then it shriveled into a ball and went into the ground. I knew Jesus carried the sins of the world onto Himself. Nothing happened for a while. I wondered where He went.

Then a bright light began to shine, like a beautiful sunrise on the horizon without a cloud in the sky. Jesus appeared in the sky. He had wings on His back and a smile on His face. He was calling anyone to come and enjoy being with Him. His smile was so radiant and welcoming. He was thrilled to reach out His hands toward anyone who would respond. I knew then I was forgiven and accepted. I was loved unconditionally by a man willing to go through pain and suffering so that I could find salvation and joy in Him.

I couldn't reach or touch Him. He faded into the clouds, and I saw Him no more. The vision was humbling, yet exhilarating! I know He watches over me. And He calls to me daily, so I can enjoy "just being with Him."

These are visions, words of affirmation and love that He wants to speak into every one of us to encourage us. Love motivates, and that is how He gives us spiritual strength to go higher. Spending time with God is essential. Those are the times He reveals His plan, His will, guidance, or He just loves on us. Spending time with Him satisfies the soul.

BATTLING THE ENEMY WITH DISCERNMENT

Satan wants to destroy our relationship with God by creating chaos. The enemy wants us to focus on physical life rather than spiritual life. That old devil never stops attacking our relationship with God. His focus is to create an atmosphere of fear.

As a young Christian, I went to our usual prayer room on the ship. I was alone when God showed me my first vision. I sat in the middle of the room with eyes closed in meditation. I saw a black panther circling me. Its eyes were full of hate and evil. He stared, circling, looking for a weak area to lunge forward. I did not give him one. I knew it wanted to kill me. I kept my eyes on him, giving him no opportunity to harm me. It started to crouch, ready to lunge at me. Then the vision ended.

I have been disliked before but never to the point where someone wanted to kill me. The beast in my vision hated me and wanted to mortally wound me. It was frightening! There is a real enemy of our soul, mind, body, and spirit. Recognize that Satan hates you. He hates your children; he hates God and everything that represents God. If he could, he would kill you and everyone you love; that is how intense his hatred is. There is a real spiritual war going on around us, and we need spiritual eyes to recognize the enemy's lies, deception, schemes, and madness behind the scenes. There is a spiritual realm all around us; it is another real world, and we must be mindful of it.

Peter knew the power of Satan. Satan wanted to sift Peter earlier in ministry and get him to turn away and lose his relationship with God. Peter would have fallen if Jesus had not prayed for him. Jesus then told Peter, "When you are restored, strengthen your brothers." Peter found strength in the words of Jesus and fully committed himself to God.

Thirty years later, Peter wrote two epistles informing the church Satan was still prowling around like a roaring lion trying to destroy us. Peter remembered that experience and never forgot the diabolical nature of the devil. He never forgot he was almost taken out of the ministry and almost lost everything if it were not for Jesus interceding for him. Jesus is interceding for us all the time. Romans 8:34 (NIV) says, "Christ Jesus, who died—more than that, who was raised to life—is at the right hand of God and is also interceding for us." It's nice to have friends pray for us, but when Jesus Himself prays for us, we are going to win! Because we know He is on our side and that He is for us; it gives us the confidence to overcome any attack that Satan throws our way. We have the victory in Him. Peter learned how to defeat the enemy and walk in the power of the Holy Spirit. The enemy prowls around you looking for weaknesses and vulnerabilities, and even if he doesn't find any, he will attack anyway. 1 Peter 5:8 (KJV) says, "Be sober, be vigilant, because your adversary the devil walketh about as a roaring lion, seeking whom he may devour." My friend, Pastor George Vastine, preached in a sermon that "Satan imitates God. He roars but has no authority. Don't be afraid. We have another lion behind us. He is the Lion of Judah, who roars louder and is stronger than anything that comes against us!"

We look at things in the natural with our physical eyes. We have five senses—we see, touch, smell, taste, and hear. But Christians have another sense. Not a sixth sense (that sounds creepy), but God gives discernment. Through discernment, God reveals things in prayer as we seek Him. This takes a conscious effort if we want to understand His will for our lives. We must reach beyond physical sight and go deeper into the spiritual realm to find God's will.

I was preaching one morning at the chapel service at YCIBI. I told the students there are times when we can put a fleece before God, but there are other times you may have several options, and you need discernment to know what to choose. At that time, I was candidating at several Assemblies of God churches. I had three offers and a fleece wasn't going to work in that situation, so I prayed and fasted. God began to make it clearer what church to take. At first, I had a peace, but then I had a joy. As I continued to pray and seek God's will more and more, joy filled my spirit about the church in Fleetwood, PA. I pastored there six years, and that is where God blessed us with three beautiful children.

Proverbs 14:12 (NIV) says, "There is a way that seems right to a man, but in the end, it leads to death." The enemy likes to lead us into things that look good, but they can often be harmful. The enemy attacks the five senses. He is subtly deceptive by steering our minds to the wrong things. Satan attacked Adam and Eve, "Look at the apple. Gaze at its beautiful color. It will taste good; it will open your eyes. Feel it; touch it. Hear the sweet sound it makes when you bite into it. Smell its fruity goodness and taste how sweet it is. It will make you feel good."

All the while, the Holy Spirit inside screams, "NOOO!" Listen to the still small voice of God speaking, "No, it will destroy you." But if we are strong spiritually, walk with God consistently, and listen to His voice, we will have spiritual discernment to recognize the dangling apple for what it really is. If our spiritual man is not strong enough, then our sensual man will win and listen to the enemy's voice to satisfy the flesh.

"So, the LORD God said to the serpent, 'Because you have done this, cursed are you above all livestock and all wild animals! You will crawl on your belly, and *eat dust* all the days of your life'" (Genesis 3:14, NIV — *emphasis mine*).

I believe God is telling him the *dust* he will feed off from is man's sinful nature. "God formed man of the dust from the ground. And then breathed life into him" (Genesis 2:7, NIV). Genesis 3:19, (NIV) says, "You are dust and to dust you shall return." Without God dwelling within, we are just dust bunnies. We are the *walking spiritually dead*. When we are born again from above, accepting Jesus into our hearts, we become spiritually alive and full of God.

Satan feeds off our flesh. He stirs up its sensations. As a horse jockey puts out a carrot to the horse, Satan puts out temptations to us. He dangles pride, prestige, and self-glorification and then feeds off the sinful nature of our desires. When we bite the bait, the enemy promises sensual fulfillment but, in the end, leaves us empty and away from God. Sin is a thief; it only takes and gives nothing back. "In the end she is bitter as gall.... Her feet go down to death" (Proverbs 5:4-5).

Adam and Eve shared a wonderful relationship with God until Satan tempted them with pride and power. They both partook in the sin and ate the forbidden fruit. Their eyes were opened to good and evil, sin and righteousness. For the first time, they felt shame and hid from the presence of God.

Don't fall for the devil's schemes. He is a liar and will never change. A Cherokee legend tells the story of a little boy and a rattlesnake. A little boy was walking down a path, and he came across a rattlesnake. The rattlesnake was getting old. He asked, "Please, little boy, can you take me to the top of the mountain? I hope to see the sunset one last time before I die."

The little boy answered, "No, Mr. Rattlesnake. If I pick you up, you'll bite me, and I'll die."

The rattlesnake said, "No, I promise. I won't bite you. Just please take me up to the mountain."

The little boy thought about it. He finally picked up the rattlesnake, tucked it close to his chest, and carried it up to the top of the mountain. They sat there and watched the sunset together. It was so beautiful. Then after sunset, the rattlesnake turned to the little boy and asked, "Can I go home now? I am tired, and I am old."

The little boy picked up the rattlesnake and again tucked it close to his chest, holding it tightly and safely. He carefully held the snake all the way down the mountain and took it to his own home, giving it some food and a place to sleep.

The next day the rattlesnake turned to the boy and asked, "Please, little boy, will you take me back to my home now? It is time for me to leave this world, and I would like to be at my home now."

The little boy felt he had been safe all this time, and the snake had kept his word. So, he promised to take it home as asked. He carefully picked up the snake, tucked it close to his chest, and carried it back to the woods to his home to die.

Before he laid the rattlesnake down, the rattlesnake rose up and bit him in the chest. The little boy cried out and threw the snake on the ground. "Mr. Snake, why did you do that? Now I will surely die!"

The rattlesnake looked up at him and grinned, "You knew what I was when you picked me up" (www.northerncherokeenation.com).

As the leopard cannot change his spots, the devil cannot change his nature. John 10:10 reminds us, "The thief comes only to steal and kill and destroy." Satan *only* comes to do these things. That is his only purpose; there is nothing good about his intentions. God has only good intentions for us. He says, "...I have come to give life, and life to the full."

LIVING ON THE WORD

We have all sinned and understand that horrible feeling of separation from God. We try to hide by avoiding church and other Christians. Our own condemnation beats us up. Sometimes, we want to run away from God in shame, but they are the very times we need to run to Him the most. God, in His mercy, covers us with grace. When we feel like hiding, He says, "Come to Me and let me forgive you." Go to church anyway. Experience God's loving on you instead of condemning you. What an incredible feeling of love and freedom to receive! That is the wonderful thing about God. He doesn't feed off us like the enemy does — He lets us feed off Him, which is His Word.

God provides strength as we feed on His life-giving words. "Man does not live on bread alone but on every word that comes from God." Spiritual strength comes from His Word. Our God promises blessings, forgiveness, a right standing, and a right walk with Him, no matter how we feel. We have peace with God by faith even when we're not at peace with ourselves. Our walk with God is not about feelings but faith.

BE PREPARED AND STAND STRONG

A painting in my home pictures a man standing on top of a lighthouse while raging waves crash down below. If he were to fall, he would drown, but his face has a look of confidence. The strong tower would hold him secure, even though there are deadly waves down below. His faith is in the strong lighthouse. When the storms of life assail, we can stand strong and tall with God by our side. And no matter what comes against us, God will fight our battles if we quietly trust in Him. Proverbs 18:10 (NLT) says, "The name of the LORD is a strong tower; the righteous run unto him and are safe." We are safe and secure because we stand in Him. Nothing can move us when we trust in Him.

Peter admonishes us to "gird the loins of your mind" or essentially, *be prepared*. Spiritually speaking, the mind is where we stand or fall. In Peter's day, a man had to tuck (or gird) the hem of his long robe into his belt before he could work or run. He had to be prepared for the work ahead. In the same way, Peter tells us to "gird up the loins of our mind"—be prepared for whatever we are running into.

When faced with a decision, we must ask ourselves these questions.

1. Is this what I want, or is this what God wants?
2. Are my desires getting in the way of this decision where I can't hear God through the anxiety of the moment?
3. Do I need to take a step back and really evaluate this, being patient and waiting on God for the go ahead?
4. Do I have a peace about this?
5. Do I have a spiritual joy in my heart about this decision, and do I know for sure God is giving me the go ahead? Do I have confirmation?
6. Am I running away from my current ministry?

I speak from experience. We have to be careful. "Do not be anxious about anything, but in every situation, by prayer and petition, with thanksgiving, present your requests to God. And the peace of God, which transcends all understanding, will guard your hearts and your minds in Christ Jesus" (Philippians 4:6-7, NIV).

Prepare your minds for action. With humility in our hearts, we win battles on our knees. Place yourselves under God's authority, not your own nor anyone else's. The only time to listen to someone else's advice is if he/she is praying over our situation and there is a mutual feeling of God's will. The collective prayer of the Apostles said, "It seemed right to the Holy Spirit and to us." Then you know it's God's will.

Don't let emotions get the best of you. Emotions can be deceptive, but the promises of God are always true. He has our best intentions in mind when others do not. God will lead in the right direction.

God will also rescue you from making mistakes. If you think you made a mistake, pray about it. Know that God loves you and, in His mercy, will take care of you and lead you back in the right direction and make everything work out. If you find yourself out of His will, you will not have a peace until it is resolved. He will help you figure out what and where He wants you to be. He factored in our mistakes, and He is big enough to get us back on track. Romans 8:28 (NLT) says, "And we know that all things work together for good to them that love God, to them who are called according to his purpose." Seek Him in prayer; He will reassure you and guide you.

Our responsibility is to be spiritually fit, stay alert, and keep our minds fixed on God. Then He will make all things clear even when things don't make sense at the moment; God will make it clear.

SPIRITUAL GROWTH

While in seminary, I wrote a short paper on Richard Rolle, one of the church mystics. His story encouraged me to keep going even after multiple setbacks in ministry. It is a story about a young monk who never gave up serving God, nor did God ever give up on him. The book entitled *The Fire of Love and the Mending of Life* is about God's love holding us together all throughout our lives. God's love and forgiveness kept Rolle from quitting. He had many issues, including lust. As a young Monk, a woman came into his room for confession. As she confessed her sins, she caught him looking at her chest. In embarrassment, he ran out the door as she yelled at him, "You wouldn't know what to do with them anyway."

Rolle almost gave up on ministry. He felt ashamed and asked how God could use a sinner, such as he. Feeling God's love come over him, he kept on moving forward. God's love mended him, molded him, and shaped him over the years. Now, as an older Monk, the same scenario happened. A woman came into his room to confess her sins. However, this time, as she was confessing her sins, he made eye contact the whole time. He was more concerned about her soul than her body. God grew him into the man of God he knew he could be. Richard saw his flaws, but God saw what he would be.

Ministers often think they need to be perfect and shocked when undesirable feelings, desires, lusts, wants, or jealousies prove we are only simple human beings. Ministers are no different than anybody else. His love bends us, shapes us into seasoned men and women of God. It does not happen overnight; so, don't give up!

As God works on the average Christian, He works on ministers and chaplains, as well. Just as it takes many years for a tree to grow, so it is with the spiritual growth of the chaplain.

Everyone has weaknesses. For some, it is lust; for others, it is power, prestige, recognition, or more. God created you; He knows all about your weaknesses, and He will pick you back up after a fall and love you to completion. If others don't forgive you, don't worry. God does. "Forget what is behind you and strain toward what God has for you." Start out strong but finish even stronger. Let God build you, and don't ever quit!

God wants to make us into something good, productive, and useful. Our new nature in Christ should cause us to grow and move forward rather than stay comfortable. Hermit crabs' bodies grow but their shells don't. Their body gets very uncomfortable when the shells become too small for their bodies. Its instinct is to get another covering. It is vulnerable for a few seconds when it comes out of its shell into another, bigger one. But now it can grow. Its nature is to grow, so it seeks a new shell. Like the Hermit crab, we must continually shed ourselves of our old nature, seeking God's divine covering for the new growth in life.

Some people desire to remain in their small shells where it's safe and familiar. Though being cramped and tight will stunt their growth, they choose discomfort over growth.

A Christian's new nature causes us to want to grow. God may make it uncomfortable for us to stay where we are and prod us until we can't resist anymore. When we enter the unknown, we discover how much better it is than staying where we were. Seeing God do new and exciting things and experiencing new horizons will cause a growth in faith.

Be brave and courageous. Be willing to continually step out of the familiar and comfortable and risk following God's leading. His rewards are worth it, and He'll never fail.

CHAPTER THIRTY-ONE

Preventing Compassion Fatigue to Those we Minister

All praise to God, the Father of our Lord Jesus Christ. God is our merciful Father and the source of all comfort. He comforts us in all our troubles so that we can comfort others. When they are troubled, we will be able to give them the same comfort God has given us.

2 Corinthians 1:3-4 (NLT)

WHO IS AT RISK?
Anyone who works in providing care for others is at risk. Psychologists, psychiatrists, mental health professionals, healthcare workers, chaplains, nurses, caregivers, firefighters, police officers, first responders, and those working directly with trauma. People at risk often have low levels of support both personally and professionally. They have high stress and lack proper coping skills. They bottle up their emotions and avoid caring for themselves; they are at high risk.

PREVENTING COMPASSION FATIGUE TO THOSE WE MINISTER
Compassion fatigue as defined by Merriam Webster is "the inability to react sympathetically to a crisis, disaster, etc., because of overexposure to previous crises, disasters, etc. Compassion fatigue sets in when one begins providing care out of duty only, rather than compassion. It is understandable how this can happen especially when a family member has to give up their lives twenty-four hours a day seven days a week to care for their loved one.

Patients know they are a burden too. I shock my patients and family members when I agree with the patient in telling them that they are a burden. Let's be honest; it is difficult to care for someone all the time. But I finish by saying that "it is a burden of love." I tell them, "Your family is willing to do it because they love you and want to provide as much care for you as possible during this time." However, when the caregiver ceases to love, bitterness and anger set in, producing resentment and regret.

CAUSES OF COMPASSION FATIGUE

Compassion fatigue can be caused by trauma. After the Rwandan War when the Hutu slaughtered the Tutsi, four Assemblies of God missionaries resigned. The leadership did not understand why they suddenly resigned. They traced it back to the trauma of witnessing one million deaths. Compassion fatigue can also be caused by prolonged exposure to violence. The Assemblies of God studied this carefully and strategized a plan to help missionaries overcome and prepare for the experience of trauma.

War and killing has the potential to harden soldiers for the rest of their lives. I had a patient retell this story of when he was in a battle in Korea. He went to Catholic school and even considered the priesthood. He said, "I always believed in God, but even to this day, my heart is hardened by war and trauma, and I have post-traumatic stress disorder. He said, "There were fifteen men pinned down by a sniper. The Chinese were lined up ready to attack. The battle raged. We each saved one bullet for ourselves because we were not about to be captured and tortured. Thirteen died. Only another soldier and I survived. The other guy ended up in a mental institution, and I lost my faith in God. When I was assigned to another company, and the priest came by to bless us, I wanted no part of it." To this day, he refuses to love, has no compassion, and refuses to let anyone into his heart.

British poet Alfred Lord Tennyson wrote this poem, "In Memoriam," after he lost a dear friend.

> I hold it true whatsoever befall;
> I feel it when I sorrow most;
> Tis better to have loved and lost
> Than never to have loved at all.

Going through trauma or loss makes it hard to trust or love again. Someone once said, "Grief is the cost of loving too much." To be honest,

I would rather love and feel alive than go through life never wanting to love or risk getting hurt. Is love worth it? Is opening ourselves up to others worth it, or do we go around with a closed heart and never allow anyone in ever again, so we don't get hurt? Love is worth it because LOVE IS LIFE. Life without Love is an existence and is itself death. By loving we do open ourselves up to possible hurt, but more often than not, we experience affection more.

Compassion fatigue can be caused by showing compassion to people over a long period of time with little or no results. It is repeated exposure to unresolved problems. This is exhausting to the caregiver. Mental health care workers can get frustrated with clients with mental illness because they have the same issues forever. Likewise, when caregivers provide care to dementia patients, the problems not only persist, but they get worse. Police also can get desensitized over time dealing with homelessness, domestic violence, murder, and so much more. They see the worst in human nature, and there seems to be no end.

Compassion fatigue can also take place because of past experiences with caregiving. They don't want to relive that difficult period again. Caregivers can have the fear of re-experiencing grief. Perhaps they cared for their mother for several years before she died, and now they are asked to care for their father. In their minds, they begin reliving the ups and downs of caregiving and do not have the capacity to provide care for their terminally ill father. A dreadful feeling comes over them, and they do not want any part of caregiving.

False expectations can cause compassion fatigue, such as believing others should behave the way we do. Caregivers get frustrated when their expectations are not lived up to. This happens when one person is caring for a family member, and everyone else in the family deserts him/her. It hurts and, he/she is disappointed. However, it is worse when expectations are placed onto others. An example of this might be, "Well, I never acted that way; why do they?" Or, "I would never do that; why are my siblings not helping me?" Not everyone is as responsible as the one family member who cares for the Mom or Dad. Sometimes, the caretaker doesn't have the time or resources because he/she cannot afford to take off from work. Also, plainly speaking, not everyone wants to help; most people would rather someone else do it.

When the expectation for others to help you are not met, it leads to family discord. They are setting themselves up for bitterness and long-term unforgiveness toward other family members. They often tell me, "My brother says he can't take off work, but neither can we, but we are doing it anyway." I then empower them in saying that God put them there. He made circumstances available for you who has the time to be the caregiver. I have heard many times, "I just retired." Or, "I'm in between jobs right now, and I am so glad it worked out this way." It is reassuring to realize that God caused your availability to happen, and He chose you because He knew you could handle it. Now, do the best you can by keeping an attitude of compassion, so you don't take it out on the patient or family members. Too many families have years of resentment over this issue. Compassion fatigue can linger even after the crisis is over because of the toll it took on the entire family.

MORAL CONFLICT

We are Trinitarian. We have a body with which we physically feel things. We have a soul, which is our will and emotions and with which we express ourselves. We have a spirit that is eternal. When our bodies are tired, it affects us physically and emotionally. We are tired and maybe a little cranky. When our soul is stressed, it affects us physically because of worry or fear; and we are weighed down by life's burdens. In my experience, the worst is when one's spirit is hurting because it affects the body, mind, and spirit.

Proverbs 17:22 (NLT) says, "A cheerful heart is good medicine, but a broken spirit saps a person's strength." When one's spirit is sick, it cries out, "Help me!" Like a physical pain, the body warns us that something is wrong. Maybe a person feels like God is punishing him/her and feel abandoned by God and under His thumb. Some people may think God hates them and there is no redemption. The amount of suffering they are encountering is enormous. They can't sleep, can't eat, can't pray, and are in desperate need of a divine breakthrough.

A broken spirit can occur when there is a moral conflict. A moral conflict occurs when there is a war within a person of right and wrong. I once read a story about a nurse who gave a patient potassium chloride instead of sodium chloride. The patient's room was dark, and she did not want to turn on the light to disturb the patient. She assumed the vial she filled was sodium chloride, but shortly after administering the medication, the patient became comatose. They were not sure this patient would survive. She realized what she had done right away but struggled to tell the truth. Her Christian faith was a constant conviction on her conscience to come clean, but she was scared. In the meantime, the patient was in the balance of life and death. The consequences of her telling the truth and him dying meant possible jail time for her. Her faith gave her the courage to confess. Thankfully, the patient survived. She was fired but had a clean conscience.

SYMPTOMS OF COMPASSION FATIGUE

Compassion fatigue causes a decline in job performance. Mistakes are made, punctuality suffers, morale suffers, and personal relationships decline. This happens when Dad comes home from work absolutely fatigued by carrying the weight of the world on his shoulders. His family notices, and they see the toll it is taking on him. He hasn't been happy for a while; he doesn't laugh as much; he sits in his chair all depressed instead of spending time with his wife and kids.

I often use these two illustrations at a funeral service. There is a statue of Charles Atlas holding up the world on his shoulders. He is straining by carrying all the weight of the world on himself. Then there is a picture of baby Jesus holding up the world with His little finger. At a funeral service, sometimes we have to re-prioritize our lives. Death makes us think about how we are living. Not only are you grieving today, but there are times when it feels like you are carrying the weight of your world on your shoulders, which God never intended us to do. We carry worry, fear, insecurity, financial pressures, and it gets heavier and heavier. Today, God is saying, "I'm here. Let me come alongside of you and help you with your world. You don't have to carry it alone. I am here for you." Then I quote Matthew 11:28 (NIV), "Come to me all you who are weary and heavy laden and I will give your rest."

Other symptoms of compassion fatigue are that one's personal health suffers. People become addicted to drugs or alcohol to numb the pain. Depression, fatigue, and even a reckless attitude sets in. Try not to isolate from others. Other people give us energy and strength. It keeps us from the temptations of the evil one. When people isolate, sometimes they are susceptible to self-medicate. That's why some people turn to substance abuse to cope with their pain. However, self-destructive coping mechanisms are harmful to self and others. People self-medicate to replace relationships or suppress the issues beyond the surface. Unless we deal with the underlying issues, they remain unresolved. Others reenact the story over and over in their heads like a video tape that they can't shut off. They become sleepless, restless, and are thinking about their ministry even on their time off.

Worry is another form of compassion fatigue. Worry always takes and never gives back. It is a thief stealing energy and creating stress, irritability, and fear. Worry doesn't change anything; it only creates more anxiety. Jesus has a remedy for worry: faith! In Matthew 6:25-33, He tells us He will take care of all our needs. We cannot add anything by worrying except more frustration. He says in verse 30, "O you of little faith." He gives us a soft rebuke. In other words, "Don't you trust in me?" After all I have done for you, are you going to doubt me now? Stop it and believe! (My words). Too much worrying causes emotional fatigue.

CORPORATE RESPONSIBILITY

Corporate leaders need to rely on their team of professionals who are trained and qualified in counseling. Chaplains and other support services are there to help their administrator's and executives. They can't do it all; therefore, they need to surround themselves with people who are qualified to handle organizational trauma and grief. Managers and leaders need to invest in their people for a healthy work environment so employees feel valued. This will solve the problem of "a culture of silent suffering."

High stress jobs can create emotional and adrenaline overload. Organizations can even be the cause or at least contribute to compassion fatigue. If an organization avoids caring for its people by creating a "culture of silence" where stressful events are taboo in open discussion, then people are then afraid to express their opinions for fear of corporate shame. Conflict, grief, loss, disasters, and any number of stressors not openly discussed or avoided make employees feel uncared about and disrespected.

Corporate sin can be a moral conflict. There will be times when you do not agree with a policy or a decision of your workplace. You have to decide whether to stay or leave. God may release you; He may not. Each person has to make that decision to stay on board or leave. It must be done prayerfully rather than emotionally.

Chaplain's help co-workers from becoming hardened in their professions. We need to emphasize that our jobs do not become our world view. For instance, people who deal with victims of rape, incest, and violence can become cynical and distrustful of the world and the people around them. We have to be careful that our jobs do not affect our attitudes toward the world. What we do is a microcosm of the rest of the world. I work hospice; therefore, I can't always be thinking of death or I would be depressed. There is a bigger world out there than our focal point of prison, sick people, or anything else.

SOLUTIONS FOR COMPASSION FATIGUE
WAYS TO HELP FAMILY MEMBERS

I encourage siblings who are not able to be there physically of the need to be supportive of those who are. They need to support them financially. Help pay for a caregiver to give your sister a break. Look into respite stays. Offer to care for the patient temporarily. Take the patient to your home for a few days or even weeks. If you are local, come over for a few hours a week to give your sibling a break. I remember how difficult it was when our children were little. Those few hours family or friends watched our children were invaluable, and I appreciate them to this day.

DON'T OWN SOMEONE ELSE'S PROBLEM

Caregivers have to make sure they don't own other people's burdens lest there become two victims: the patient and the caregiver. One doctor told a caregiver, "There are two victims here: the patient and you. You are suffering, too!" Another caregiver once said, "Will there be anything left of me when this is over?" Caregivers need to be engaged enough to be empathetic yet distant enough to be objective.

With emotional overload, some people become overly engaged while others become overly disengaged. I was on call one night in the hospital when a man came into the ER who was unresponsive. I escorted the family to the side conference room for privacy. I had prayed with the family and stayed with them, waiting for the doctor to come in and tell us how he was. This third-year resident doctor came in without compassion or emotion and stated, "Your husband died; sorry for your loss," and walked quickly away. I sat there with the family who had multiple questions. That doctor made the situation worse by his callousness. I know doctors are busy, but if he would have taken a few minutes of his time to show some sympathy and answer questions, that family would have felt much better than the way they did. This doctor, unfortunately, learned very early on how he was going to deal with death; by disengaging emotionally. Fortunately, I provided enough pastoral care to not only help them in their grief, but also their anger at the doctor.

The impression we leave, whether good or bad, is magnified because of the intense emotional state families are in. They will remember our care, whether good or bad, for the rest of their lives. Let all health care professionals make it a positive and comforting one.

Be Present

When you are with your family, be present with them. And when you are with a patient, don't be thinking of home. People need you to be actively involved while you are with them. They both need you, so be cautious of bringing emotional work home and bringing home stress to work. Don't give anyone your emotional leftovers!

Seek Help!

Some deal with stress in unhealthy ways. They sit alone after a day's work with a bottle of alcohol in their hand. Self-destructive behavior is not a good coping skill. Alcohol, drugs, or any other type of addictive behavior is a sign of needing help. Some suppress their emotions until it begins to come out in a negative way. There are things you cannot "pillow talk" with your spouse about. Unfortunately, those of us in crisis ministry don't have easy going jobs. We have high-energy callings filled with adrenalin and trauma. So, when we come home from work all wound up, are lying in bed, and can't sleep and our wives ask, "What's wrong?" you can't tell her you just had to scrape up body parts off the cement. Or you had to deal with an abused child. Or you had to deal with an emotional death. If your spouse can handle it, then fine; otherwise, share it only with others who can handle those kinds of conversations. Know who you can talk to and who you can't. Find people you trust with your deepest hurts, thoughts, and feelings. Talk to people who will not judge you. When I come in from being on call, I often have a hard time sleeping. It takes me about two hours to wind down and rest my mind. If it really affected me, I will talk to one of the other chaplains the next day. We all need support.

I was working with veterans who suffered from Post-Traumatic Stress Disorder. One man, told a friend of his that he had to kill in combat, but the person he told it to could not handle it. He finally confided in other veterans who did understand and found comradery and support. There was a veteran who refused to come to my support group for combat veterans because I was not a combat veteran. I thought about it later and concluded that if I had to experience every form of trauma just to be able to identify with counselees, I would be too messed up to help anyone! Counselors are trained in principles and systematic styles of counseling. Though the trauma varies, counseling principles remain the same. Don't reject the chaplain who is there to help you! God sent that person as a gift to find healing. Accept the help.

People deal with stress differently. Kelly, a lady I've worked with for several years, told me the way some emergency medical technicians coped with trauma was to sit around, have a few beers, and see who had the worst experience that week. Most men don't like to talk about their feelings, but this was their way of coping with it in a non-counseling atmosphere. That was their way of getting their feelings out in the open and dealing with them directly. One time my kids were joking around with me and went a little too far and hurt my feelings. My daughter,

Ashlee, always the sensitive one, said to her siblings, "Dads have feelings, too, you know!" Men have feelings and need to talk to others about their stress, so they don't end up letting it out in unhealthy ways. There are times we even have to hold back anger and maintain professionalism. For example, when I worked in the emergency room, a drunk driver hit and seriously injured another driver. Since it was a small community hospital, both parties ended up at the same hospital in the emergency room and only a few rooms apart. The drunk driver was still drunk and inappropriately kept coming over to the grieving family. The men in that family were ready to hurt this guy; the atmosphere was tense and increasingly hostile. I had to remove him several times before security arrived. To be honest, I wanted to rip into him myself, but as the Chaplain, I had to remain calm, professional, and keep the peace.

THE HOLY SPIRIT'S HEALING POWER

Deal with your feelings before they will deal with you. People who experience trauma can be healed by the power of the Holy Spirit. A friend of mine was in Iran during the Vietnam War. He was involved in black operations over there and suffered from PTSD. He came to a small group ministry I had been leading for combat veterans suffering from PTSD. We used the book, *The Combat Manual for Christians.* There was one chapter where the veteran was told to re-experience the trauma of war that he struggled with the most. Bob relived the sights, sounds, smells, feelings, thoughts, and every detail he could recall regarding his trauma. It was extremely difficult for him to recall the horrors of war but he got through. It took him two weeks on that one chapter. He often had to lay the book aside for a few days to handle the flood of emotions. During that chapter, he attended a military funeral. When they shot the rifle salute, he ran into the woods. He called me on the phone while sitting there on a log shaking. He talked to me about what he was recalling. I sat and listened as he shared his fears and flashbacks. We prayed and discussed how this was a different time and place and that it was not Iran. The ceremony was over, and he went home.

As I look back, I realize now how courageous he was to dive back into the time period of his life and relive those experiences. The following week we resumed the small group. He recalled certain foods that reminded him of Iran and how the smells brought back memories. We worked on his prejudices and anger toward the Arab people. He had to let go of bad thinking patterns — especially that they were not trying to hurt him anymore.

He shared that every time he saw an Arab wearing his head scarf he felt threatened, became paranoid, and felt like he almost had to be ready to defend himself. After attending that small group, he received a great deal of soul healing. Those few months of working with him on his issues, relearning healthy thinking, and the comforting and loving presence of the Holy Spirit completely delivered him from reliving traumas and having bad dreams. Bob became an ordained minister after that and is now a chaplain of a fire department in South Carolina! God did a Holy Spirit cleansing in his soul, and He can do that for anyone suffering from trauma. Bob only wishes he had done this thirty years ago.

HEALTHY SELF-TALK

Caregivers have to remind themselves that these are God's children, and He loves them. If He loves them, so must we. My Christian caregivers often say, "I wouldn't be able to do this without God's strength." Others say, "Mom took care of me, and it is now my ministry to take care of her." It really is about our attitudes and what we say to ourselves. Even the best of us can succumb to caregiver burnout.

People need to distinguish between rational and irrational thinking. Irrational thinking is when a person may feel guilty for something he/she had no control over, such as survivor's guilt. In war time, some soldiers feel guilty having survived when so many of their friends died. They internalize self-blame.

Rational thinking is when a person sees the situation clearly, whether good or bad, and can still function in a crisis. For instance, if a person is in a car accident, and it is his fault, and someone dies, that person can maintain rationale without dissociation. Perhaps the car accident was because he didn't fix the brakes. He is honest with himself, accepts responsibility, and moves on in life living with the disaster he has caused. Carrying grief forever is just as bad as suppressing it.

When a person's spirit is ill, we need to help him/her identify the problem to deal with it. Chaplains, pastors, counselors, or sometimes just a close friend, can help a person identify it and let it go! The important thing is to catch it before it becomes a problem in someone's personal or professional life.

CHAPTER THIRTY-TWO

Prevention of Compassion
Fatigue in the Chaplain

*Then because so many people were coming and going that they
did not even have a chance to eat, he said to them, "Come
with me by yourselves to a quiet place and get some rest."*

Mark 6:31 (NIV)

SOLUTIONS FOR COMPASSION FATIGUE FROM MINISTRY

Early in my Bible college education, we had to read a book about
ministry burnout. I will never forget this story of this man who took
a position as the counselor in a church. He was excited, of course, as
most people are who start out in ministry. At first the sessions weren't
too difficult. He basically ministered to families in the church.

Eventually, the church grew, and he had to hire on more staff to
help. However, he began taking on more difficult cases. Congregants
asked him to begin seeing relatives outside the church. He began to
be burdened with divorce cases, custody battles, pedophilia, prisoners,
and violence. He found himself ministering to people outside of his
calling. He also took on all the hard cases, so his staff didn't have to. He
wanted to protect them from burning out. He was protecting everyone
else but himself. He said he began to burn-out. The joy of the LORD
was gone; he was exhausted all the time; he had nothing left to give. On
his tenth year of service to the church, they gave him a three-month
sabbatical. He took this time to re-prioritize his life. He took his family
to the beach. The first week he slept. His children wanted to play but
his wife told them that daddy needed his rest. The second week came
by, and he began socializing a little more. Each week got better and
better. He began playing with his kids and enjoying his family and his

life. His joy and peace were returning. He said that by the third month, he was rejoicing on the beach with his hands lifted to God in praise and thanksgiving. He was restored.

Upon returning to church, he set up boundaries, which he had not done before. He began to refer clients to more specialized counselors and spread his workload onto his staff. He only counseled people who attended church and were willing to allow God to work in their lives as he provided Biblical counseling. The remainder of his ministry was joyful and fulfilling. I will never forget that story.

We can learn a valuable lesson from this man's testimony regarding ministry burnout. Compassion fatigue takes place over a long period of continued stress, lack of self-care, overstepping boundaries, and the idea that "only I can handle this." We have to let go of perfectionism and accept the help of others. The thing I appreciate most about working in healthcare is relying on other team members for help. I have a doctor I can refer to, or a nurse, a social worker, or aide I can call to assist or even hand off something that I am not trained in doing. Some things are outside of my expertise. Utilize others and trust others to help you. Let God raise up people you can trust to work with on the ministry team, and let go of controlling everything.

PASTOR's SUPPORT

Support groups are a great way to help people talk about common experiences in a safe and non-threatening environment. We chaplains learned the value of trust in Interpersonal Relationships (IPR) in our Clinical Pastoral Education Program. Each week all the chaplains in our CPE class got together for one and a half hours to openly discuss our difficulties. Those difficulties could be personal issues, professional struggles, spiritual difficulties working in a pluralistic setting, ethics, or a trauma that upset us. Sometimes, there was silence for ten minutes or so before anyone broke the ice and began sharing his/her thoughts. We became vulnerable with each other and gained much insight, encour-agement, and support from the peer group. I have found this lacking in the pastorate. Pastors learn all about solving everyone else's problems but their own. They lack the peer group that is much needed. I would highly recommend a unit or two of CPE for pastors. It will help pastors be healthier and well-rounded in ministry. It emphasizes handling the stress of ministry in a heathy way. It does this by identifying one's own history of trauma, background, and experiences, and challenges them to use those experiences to integrate and reframe their thoughts to see things more clearly and objectively.

Chaplains can tend to be lone rangers. People think everything is okay in their lives, so they leave them alone, and they go unnoticed. Working outside of the church walls, they don't have the spiritual support a staff pastor has. So, like the polar bear analogy, they drift off into oblivion, doing their own thing. Chaplains sometimes have no supervisors or authority looking over their shoulders and doing what they want. Therefore, chaplains, in particular, must be intentional about accountability. We need to be involved in our own denominations and develop friendships with pastors who know us personally and come alongside of us in prayer and support.

BE GOOD TO YOURSELF; YOU DESERVE IT, TOO

Be kind to yourself. Don't be so hard on yourself. Allow for forgiveness, and mistakes. Treat yourself to something special. I hear women call it "retail therapy." I love to fish, myself. Take time to relax. The word *recreation* means to re-create, relax, rejuvenate, and have fun. We are a new creation in Christ Jesus, to spend time in His presence, so He can re-create us, rejuvenate us, relax us, and even restore us to wholeness. Take time for spiritual renewal.

Sometimes we chaplains need to remember we are not immune to compassion fatigue. I often teach compassion fatigue to caregivers, but I have to remember to put these practices into place myself because everyone is susceptible to this, especially those of us in ministry. In order for us to help others maintain a healthy lifestyle, we have to be doing it ourselves.

Do things you enjoy. Enjoyment produces endorphins that give us pleasure. When Dorothy and I had our third miscarriage, I was depressed. It affected me more than the first two because I knew we would never conceive. We needed time alone to take our minds off the pain. We went to Hershey Park for a day. We enjoyed shopping, eating out, and spending time together. It made a world of difference. We both felt so much better. That experience reminded me of how healthy self-care is.

Make sure you are taking a break from work and enjoy life before it passes you by. One of the saddest songs is written by Harry Chapin: "Cats in the Cradle." It's a song about a Dad who spends too much time at work and giving his family a lot of material things but neglecting the one thing they needed the most—him. Then when the Dad wanted to spend time with his son, his son was too busy at work. He realized, "He grew up to be just like me." Invest in yourself for the long haul. We all have twenty-four hours in a day: One third work; one third sleep; one third personal life. If you enjoy your job, if you enjoy your family, then you will enjoy your life! Maintain a balanced life. Keep a cheerful heart; it is good medicine!

Keep a compassionate heart especially toward yourself, so you can love others. When we are spiritually healthy, we minister in a healthy way.

SIMPLIFY MINISTRY

We have complicated chaplaincy with all its fancy outcomes, scales, theorems, and intellectualisms. Unfortunately, in some CPE programs, the education is the spirituality. Intellectualism, system theories, and philosophy of ministry become the dominate, competitive, and arrogant attitude rather than simply ministering God's grace to people. Ministry can become overly intellectual to the point of stupidity. It seems the more we learn, the dumber we get and the further away from God some CPE programs go. After thirty years of ministry, I have narrowed my style of ministry down to three things. First, leave them in a better attitude than when you arrived. Second, listen to their concerns and validate their feelings. And third, bring peace to the situation. In Proverbs 15:30b (NLT), it says "...good news gives health to their bones." This is my method for pastoral care, plain and simple. Whether they are Christian or not, I listen, show empathy, validate, and bring God's presence into the room. We interact and converse regarding their thoughts, fears, anxieties, and worries as they share their deepest concerns. We explore possibilities and how to resolve their fears. They are hurting and NEED to hear something uplifting and hopeful from a chaplain who hears a word from God. When they are done discussing their thoughts and need answers, I then share appropriate scripture, an inspirational story, and sometimes a condensed version of one of my sermons. They are looking to the chaplain to ease the pain. The chaplain delivers when God is invited into the situation. After we are done talking, I ask them to close their eyes as I sing a quiet and peaceful hymn. Then I pray. We allow time for the Holy Spirit to fill the atmosphere with His presence. When we open our eyes, we don't even want to speak. There are no words to say that can express what we just experienced. My ministry as an anointed man of God and a Spirit-filled chaplain is to bring God's presence into the situation so others can experience Him themselves and have faith to believe that He will care for them after our visit. The chaplaincy needs men and women of God who will abandon all they are and all they have to follow Jesus Christ and introduce Him to spiritually dying people.

Despite all of CPE's short-comings, I am thankful for the pluralistic education it provided to me in developing my character into being a much better chaplain than I would have been had I not taken CPE. When taking CPE, never forget that Jesus must be the foundation of your Clinical Pastoral Education.

CPE is designed to teach general principles of pastoral education to all students regardless of their faith. There are CPE programs that are Christian-oriented and offer credentials to certify chaplains.

BOUNDARIES

Establish clear, professional boundaries. Say "No" when you honestly cannot do it. Saying "No" is just as important as saying "Yes." Ask for help when feeling overwhelmed and overworked. When I first arrived after transferring to South Carolina, I was the only chaplain. The company grew, and I began working six and sometimes seven days a week. The overtime money was great, but after a few months, I noticed it started taking a toll on me. I went to my boss and explained the situation. My boss fully understood, and we both decided it was time to hire another chaplain.

Befriend healthy people. Some people take energy; others give energy. Find people who genuinely love and care for you and want the best for you. Establish real relationships of transparency, non-judgmental, and a safe environment to share thoughts, feelings, and life struggles. The actor Christopher Walken wisely said, "Unhealthy people gravitate toward healthy people. Be careful or they will drain you." When that happens, put those boundaries in place.

There are four ways to handle situations. Three are negative ways, but one is the best way. We can get aggressive and angry but that drives a wedge in relationships. Then there is the passive way to allow people to walk all over you. There is a passive/aggressive way when you let others walk on you, and then you explode, making a real mess. The best way is to be assertive. State your case calmly and don't worry about other's reactions. Protect yourself and manage your mental health.

Along this way of thinking is to protect yourself from abuse. Identify abusive people. Abusive people can be defined as one who harms people verbally, emotionally, physically, sexually, or spiritually. They manipulate through coercion, false guilt, and fear. Their primary interest is not relating with you but rather controlling you and getting what they want. Set boundaries and refuse to be treated poorly. Highlight unhealthy relationships from your past. Normal may have been abusive. Abused people often marry abusive people because that is their normal. This is where the chaplain can change the trajectory of a person's life by discipling him/her with healthy biblical lifetstyles. God's way is the best way! Teach others to re-examine their lives and relearn what healthy relationships are.

Probably the most important discipline is to know when to stop and when to continue. As I mentioned before, I will say again. Jesus withdrew to a solitary place. We have to remember we need to withdraw from intense situations and let our minds relax again. But then again there are times when we all have to just keep going. Even though Jesus' cousin (John the Baptist) had been beheaded, and He wanted to withdraw to a solitary place to grieve, He looked up and saw the multitudes and had compassion on them. He put aside His own needs, and out of His tiredness, His fatigue, and His grief, He began ministering to them. There are times we need to put our own needs aside, and gather ourselves together and minster even when we are emotionally exhausted.

Chaplains have demanding ministries that require long term commitments. To last in ministry, it is imperative we take care of ourselves first, so we can care for others. If we are going to last, we have to learn to process high levels of stress professionally and personally in healthy ways. Be intentional, set goals, and make plans. Healthy living takes work and planning. Balance our lives with home, work, and recreation. If you don't do these three things, we will be shooting stars that last but a moment. Do these three things, and we will last in ministry for the long haul.

CHAPTER THIRTY-THREE

Conclusion

I am not sure how much longer I have to live. I was exposed to toxic chemicals in the military, and my health is getting worse each year. Many of my health issues are directly related to the exposure. I am not angry or bitter. God used it in my life to make me a better man and chaplain. In fact, I am grateful for all that God has blessed me with in this life. When my time here is over, I am ready to meet Him. Until then I will continue to serve Him.

Therefore, I wanted to write this book as an older-seasoned chaplain to his younger colleagues. I want to let you know that you will make mistakes. I wish I could turn back the clock and have some do-overs, but I can't. We only get one offer at this life, and we need to make every moment count. "So, teach us to number our days, that we may apply our hearts unto wisdom" (Psalm 90:12, KJV).

This book was not designed to give you all of life's answers, but hopefully, it will make for some round table discussion. I hope it has provoked deep thought in a good way, as you wrestle with your calling and navigating through life, marriage, family, and chaplaincy. I want younger chaplains to understand your unique calling to Holy Spirit-filled chaplaincy. I want to emphasize the importance of leaning on the Holy Spirit in your ministry. Let Him guide you into all truth and give you the wisdom to know what to do in every situation. I thank God for each one of you and your response to saying, "Yes," to your calling. I pray that more and more young men and women receive a calling to go outside the church walls in specialized ministries and para-church organizations to build the Kingdom of God. I am encouraged by the Assemblies of God to include the chaplain department under the umbrella of home missionaries along with Chi-Alpha and other parachurch ministries. I feel chaplain ministry is the wave of the future, answering the Great Commission to go out into all the world "making disciples of all nations!"

Accept the Call to Chaplaincy

I f this book has inspired you, and God has been speaking to you about entering into the chaplaincy, answer the call. If you have the courage to stand alone, apart from the status quo; if you are willing to be misunderstood by the church and the world; if you want to be used by God to make a real difference in the lives of people outside of the church walls, then this ministry is for you. Answer the call! You will be in one of the most exciting ministries the Holy Spirit is doing in the world today.

I cannot improve on God's Word, so I will leave you with one last scripture verse: "But you Timothy, are a man of God; so, run from all these evil things. Pursue righteousness and a godly life, along with faith, love, perseverance, and gentleness. Fight the good fight of faith. Hold tightly to the eternal life to which God has called you, which you have declared so well before many witnesses. And I charge you before God, who gives life to all, and before Christ Jesus, who gave a good testimony before Pontius Pilate, that you obey his command without wavering. Then no one can find fault with you from now until our Lord Jesus Christ comes again" (1 Timothy 6:11-14, NLT).

Blessings to You All!
From the Boyce Family

Quotes and Resources

Adsit, Chris. *The Combat Trauma Healing Manual: Christ-centered Solutions for Combat Trauma.* BookSurge Publishing; 1st Edition. 2007.

American Psychological Association. "ADHD." Washington: 2024.

Arroyo, John Captain Jr. JR U.S. Army (RET) with Corvin, Stan Corvin, Jr. JR U.S. Army (RET). *Attacked at Home! a Green Beret's Survival Story of the Fort Hood Shooting.* Southwestern Legacy Press: Gallatin, TN 37066.

Bacharach, Burt and David, Hal. "What the World Needs Now Is Love." I 1965.
> A 1965 popular song that was first recorded and made famous by Jackie DeShannon. (Lyrics.com.)

Barnes, Albert notes.
> Isaiah wrote this to the Jews leaving Babylon. After seventy years of captivity, some had gotten comfortable in Babylon. Some rose to positions of power and prominence and did not want to give up their positions of authority to start all over again in Jerusalem. Most people by this time were born and raised in Babylon. They buried family members there and felt that it was their home.

Beliles, Mark A. and McDowell, Stephen K. *America's Providential History.* The Providence Foundation: Charlottesville, VA. 1989.

Benchley, Peter. *Jaws.* Steven Spielberg, Director. 1975.

Bible Hub. Chapter 15.
> Paul goes on to address adulterers and perverts. Literally sexually immoral and homosexuals.

Chapin, Harry. "Cats in the Cradle." Cherry Lane Music: 1987.

Clay, Doug. CEO and General Superintendent of General Council of the Assemblies of God.

Delgado, Brother Anebal. YCIBI Instructor.

Dunstan, Richard. *A Poor Priest for the Poor—the Life of Father Rick Thomas*. Lord's Ranch Press: 2018.

Dunlop, Aaron. *Thinkgospel*. "The Juke-Edwards Story: A Contrast in Family Legacy."

Facebook@Swizz.

Foxe, John. *Christian Martyrs of the World.* Barbour and Company, Inc. 1989.

Harbaugh, Gary. L. *Pastor as Person*. Augsburg Publishing House: Minneapolis, MN. 1984.

Hunt, Angela. *The Risen*. Bethany House Publishing: MN. 2015. (271-272).
> When Peter was asked why he followed Jesus, he said, "I saw Him hug a leper. The leper said he hadn't been hugged in a long time.... Jesus then kissed his hands. As the man walked away, he became healed.... That is why I follow Jesus."

Influence Magazine. Summer 2023.
> The future is Pentecostal.

Keller, Tim and Kathy Keller. *The Meaning of Marriage: God's Plan for Sexual Intimacy. 4 Principles for Married Couples.* Tacoma Christian Counselor.

> "Indeed, sex is perhaps the most powerful God-created way to Help you give your entire self to another human being. Sex is God's appointed way for two people to reciprocally say to one another, 'I belong completely, permanently, and exclusively to you.' Sex...is your covenant renewal service."

Kenzy, John Dr. "Leadership Class, YCIBI." Chapter 13.

> "The model of corporate leadership looks like a triangle with the leader as the person on top while those underneath serve him."

Kiefer, James E. *Biographical Sketches of Memorable Christians of the Past.*

Knuth, Elizabeth. "Chapter 5: The Gift of Tears in Teresa of Avila." *Mystics Quarterly* (Vol. 20, No. 4). Penn State University Press. December 1994. pp. 131-142.

Matsakis, Aphrodite, Ph.D. *I Can't Get Over It: A Handbook for Trauma Survivors.* Second edition. New Harbinger Publications, Inc. 1996.

Maxwell, John. *The Leadership Handbook: 26 Critical Lessons Every Leader Needs.* Harper Collins: 59.

> John Maxwell destroyed this philosophy by saying, "If you try to do what you are not gifted in, then someone who excels in that area will far more exceed you because you are not gifted for that position. Find what you are good at and excel in that."

Ministers Life Insurance Company. "Stress and Burnout."

> "The stress that the average minister bears would bring most people to their knees." Chapter 20.

National Association of Veterans Affairs Chaplains. "Code of Ethics." 2024.

New Living Translation Bible Commentary. Tyndale Publishing. NAVACBCC@gmail.com.

New York Times. Colson, Charles W.: Watergate Felon Who Became Evangelical Leader Dies.

Record, Sister Carol. Sermon: "Throw Another Log on the Fire."

Rolle, Richard and Clifton Wolters, Trans. *The Fire of Love and the Mending of Life*. Penguin Classics: 1972.

Shaw, Steve. *Arnold Schwarzenegger Volume Workout Routines*. Chapter 11, Internet.

> Arnold Schwarzenegger didn't get all those muscles by eating Junk food and sitting on his name-brand recliner watching the Flintstones Cartoons. He went to the gym daily. His lifestyle consisted of five to six feedings a day. He ate 5000 calories per day compared to most normal people eating between 1500 and 1800 calories per day. On day one, he worked on his chest and back muscles. On day two, he worked on his shoulders and arms. On day three, he worked on his legs and lower back. On day four, he worked on his chest and back. On day five, he worked on his shoulders and arms again. And on day six, he worked on his legs and lower back. Finally, on day seven, he rested from his labors. This meant dedication, commitment,and hard work to accomplish and win the title of Mr. Olympia seven times.

Story, Dan. *The Christian Combat Manual*. AMG Publishers: 2007. Stress and Burnout.

Tennyson, Alfred Lord. "In Memoriam." England: 1850.

"The Voice of the Martyrs." Internet.

> Saint Telemachus, a fourth-century monk, was so appalled by the gladiator fighting that he ran out into the colosseum and tried to stop the two men from killing one another. The crowd was so angry at the monk, they stoned him to death. The Christian emperor Honorius was so moved by the monk's martyrdom that he issued a ban on gladiator fighting.

Unity Klan. "Enemy's Camp." Amazon Music Unlimited.

Veterans Affairs Chaplaincy. *NAVAC Code of Ethics*. National Association of Veterans Affairs. Chaplains. Whitaker House. 1982.

Warner, Michael Pastor. "Bloom Where You Are Planted." Sermon The practice of the presence Of God by Brother Lawrence.

Webb, Gary. *2020 Assemblies of God Chaplain's Conference.* "Compassion Fatigue Seminar."

Winship, A. E. *Jukes-Edwards: A Study in Education and Heredity*. 1900.

Zurlo, Gina Dr. *Global Christianity*. Zondervan Academic: 2022.

Author Bio

CHAPLAIN JOHN P. BOYCE is an ordained minister and endorsed chaplain with the Assemblies of God Theological Seminary of Springfield, Missouri. He earned a diploma from Youth Challenge International Bible Institute (YCIBI) of Sunbury, Pennsylvania; a B.A. in Biblical Studies from Central Bible College of Springfield, Missouri; a Master of Divinity from the Assemblies of God Theological Seminary of Springfield, Missouri; and has Six Units of Clinical Pastoral Education from The Williamsport Hospital, Williamsport, PA.

Chaplain Boyce has served as a hospital chaplain, veteran's administration chaplain, pastor, and for the last nineteen years, he has served as a hospice chaplain, which is most near and dear to his heart. Chaplain Boyce's passion is to minister God's grace, love, compassion, and salvation message to the sick and dying. His personal mission statement is "To minister the compassionate love of Jesus Christ through Pastoral Care."

Pastor John resides in Myrtle Beach, South Carolina, where he enjoys fishing and walks on the beach. He and his wife, Dorothy, have three children and one granddaughter.

www.ingramcontent.com/pod-product-compliance
Lightning Source LLC
Chambersburg PA
CBHW070908120626
46546CB00001B/178